Ken Hom | Complete Chinese Cookbook

KEN HOM

Complete Chinese Cookbook

FIREFLY BOOKS

To the memory of my mother, who taught me food as a cultural expression

A FIREFLY BOOK

Published by Firefly Books Ltd. 2011

First printing

Publisher Cataloging-in-Publication Data (U.S.)
Hom, Ken.
    Complete Chinese cookbook / Ken Hom.
[352] p. : col. photos. ; cm.
Includes index.
Summary: Chinese recipes and their related ingredients and techniques.
ISBN-13: 978-1-55407-943-8
1. Cooking -- China. I. Lindsay, James. II. Title.
641.5951 dc22   TX724.5.C5H65   2011

Library and Archives Canada Cataloguing in Publication
Hom, Ken
    Complete Chinese cookbook / Ken Hom.
Includes index.
ISBN 978-1-55407-943-8
    1. Cooking, Chinese. 2. Cookbooks. I. Title.
TX724.5.C5H653 2011   641.5951   C2011-901609-5

Published in the United States by
Firefly Books (U.S.) Inc.
P.O. Box 1338, Ellicott Station
Buffalo, New York 14205

Published in Canada by
Firefly Books Ltd.
66 Leek Crescent
Richmond Hill, Ontario L4B 1H1

Portrait photography by Noel Murphy © Woodlands Books 2011
Food photography by Jean Cazals © Woodlands Books 2011
Jacket design by Two Associates

Printed in China

CONTENTS

FOREWORD

When I first began teaching Chinese cooking over forty years ago,
I never imagined it would become as popular worldwide as it is today.
Nor would I have dreamed in a million years that China would arise from
its turbulent past of social and political turmoil to take its rightful place
in the world. Today, you cannot read a newspaper or magazine without
seeing several articles every day on China. Its vast international trade has
had a major impact on Chinese food and created a rush to export their
ingredients, making them available at an affordable price as well. There
is no better time to cook Chinese than now. I have seen Chinese food go
from a culinary and exotic niche to being part of the global table. Its quick
cooking methods hold enormous appeal for those who are rushed but
want to eat well and in a healthy way.

I remember when traveling in China in the early 1980s how disappointed
I was at the general level of cooking and how I lamented the lack of
attention to quality. Now, I am just astonished how quickly the Chinese
have reclaimed their cuisine, as a rising middle class has clamored for
excellence and quality. All this in a short period of thirty years.

I am proud to have witnessed in my lifetime this transformation of the
country of my ancestors and I revel in its future, which appears brighter
than ever. This book contains memories of recipes from my family home,
my mother, my village in China, the Chinese restaurant I worked in and
the countless Chinese meals I have had. I am only too delighted to share
all of this with you.

I wish you happy eating and good health!

Ken Hom

INTRODUCTION

Chinese cookery has taken an amazing journey since I first began to teach it forty years ago. Perhaps the best metaphor is reflected in contemporary China today. Awareness of China, its culture, history and cuisine, in the 1970s was limited mostly to academics, a few travelers who had been to the Far East and small geographical pockets where there were Chinese restaurants. China had been, for the most part, closed to the world as it went through a century of political and social turmoil before transforming itself in the 1980s to emerge on the world scene as a strong economic dynamo, taking up one-third of the world's economic growth. This transformation has had a deep impact on China itself, as it modernizes its infrastructure, education and society. Foreigners began opening restaurants in China to take advantage of the boom, five-star hotels popped up to meet the demand of travelers from all over the world and with this came a reemergence of Chinese cuisine. As the ever-growing middle class demanded higher standards of cooking, this was met by enterprising restaurant owners and food companies. Free markets inspired chefs and home cooks alike, as they revisited old recipes and started inventing new ones. Chinese food has never been better than in China today.

But what of the awareness of Chinese cuisine in the West? In many countries, it has become one of the most popular cuisines. In the UK, to "eat Chinese" is almost as normal as eating fish and chips, whether it be a takeout or restaurant dining. Ready-made Chinese meals are a favorite in many homes. Top Chinese restaurants have been awarded the coveted Michelin stars in Asia, the US and the UK, while travel magazines vie to promote the hottest new Chinese restaurants for the traveling public.

I have often been asked why Chinese food is such a global phenomenon. I think it is perceived as healthy; it is quick (even more so with a wok), which is perfect for today's fast-paced lifestyle; it has a wide variety of flavors and combinations, with something for everyone, from vegetarians to those who love spicy food, and it is so wonderfully tasty and colorful.

However, to discover the deep roots of this ancient cuisine, it is helpful to explore the various regional styles that make it so eclectic.

I begin, naturally, in the south, which is where my ancestors and family come from.

THE SOUTHERN SCHOOL

History
This is the region of Guangdong (Cantonese) cuisine, which is probably the best known in the West because in the nineteenth century many Chinese families emigrated from this area of China to Europe, Australia and America. Cantonese cooking is popular throughout the world, and is regarded by many as the haute cuisine of China. Some people attribute this to the influence of the brilliant chefs of the Imperial court, who fled to Guangzhou (Canton) when the Ming dynasty was overthrown in 1644.

Style
The Cantonese prefer their food slightly undercooked, so that the natural flavors and colors are preserved. For this reason stir-frying and steaming are two of the most popular methods of cooking. They also avoid overuse of chilies, spices and heavy oils, and concentrate instead on achieving a subtle, yet harmonious, blend of colors, textures, aromas and flavors. Rice is the staple of the Cantonese diet and forms the basis of many meals — the area is known as one of the "rice-bowls" of China.

Delicacies
The Cantonese are especially interested in exotic delicacies, such as dog, snake, frogs' legs and turtle. The area is also famous for its sweet and sour dishes, such as Sweet and Sour Pork (page 99), as well as for its dim sum — a range of delicious snacks that are served as a late breakfast or light lunch — and for its widespread use of flavorsome soy, hoisin and oyster sauces.

THE NORTHERN SCHOOL

History
This area stretches from the Yangzi (Yangtze) River to the Great Wall of China and embraces the culinary styles of Shandong (Shantung), Henan and Beijing (Peking). The Imperial court of China was based in Beijing (Peking), and its influence on the culinary style of the area is still reflected in some of its more complicated and spectacular dishes.

Style
A distinguishing feature of northern cuisine is the use of grains, rather than rice, as the staple food, particularly wheat, corn and millet, which are eaten in the form of bread, noodles, dumplings and pancakes. Because of the harshness of the climate, fresh vegetables are available only at certain times of the year. To compensate for this, northerners have learned how to preserve foods to see them through their long winters. Vegetables that store well, like sweet potatoes, turnips, onions and cabbages, are widely used, and the region specializes in a range of preserved ingredients, such as dried mushrooms, dried and smoked meats and pickled fruits and vegetables. Meat is in much shorter supply than in the other regions of China, although beef, mutton and goat are available, as well as pork. This area contains many of China's four million Muslims, who shun pork, and their presence has greatly affected its cuisine.

Delicacies
Of all the elaborate banquet dishes in Chinese cuisine, the celebrated Beijing (Peking) duck is the most glorious. Its subtlety and sophistication are a distinct contrast to other

more strongly flavored dishes that characterize northern cooking, depending heavily on garlic, green onions, leeks, sesame seeds and oil, and sweet bean sauce.

THE EASTERN SCHOOL

History
This region stretches from the eastern coast to central China. It contains the cooking styles of Fujian (Fukien), Jiangxi, Zhejiang and, most important of all, Shanghai, which is the biggest city in China and its greatest port. The region has traditionally contained some of the most fertile land in all China, which provides a rich variety of fresh fruit and vegetables, and the area is noted for its vegetarian cuisine. The countryside is dominated by the magnificent Yangzi (Yangtze) River, and the coastline is very long. Consequently, fresh fish and shellfish are also found in abundance.

Style
Eastern cooks prefer light and delicate seasonings to maximize the natural flavors of their fresh ingredients. The preferred cooking techniques are stir-frying, steaming, red-cooking (slow simmering in a dark soy sauce) and blanching.

Delicacies
The eastern region is famous for some special ingredients, such as Shaoxing rice wine and notably, black vinegar, which is used both for cooking and as a dipping sauce, Zhejiang ham, which is rather like raw lean smoked bacon, and rice wine. Sugar is widely used in the cooking of meat and vegetables, as is a great deal of oil, earning this area a reputation for rich food. Soy sauce from this area is said to be the best in China.

THE WESTERN SCHOOL

History
This area is entirely inland and includes the provinces of Sichuan (Szechuan) and Hunan, the birthplace of the late Chairman Mao. This "land of abundance," as it is sometimes called, is virtually surrounded by mountains and was almost cut off from the rest of China until the 1900s.

Style
Nowadays Sichuan cuisine in particular is popular in the West. In this area, summers are hot and sultry and the winters mild. Fruit and vegetables are plentiful, as are pork, poultry and river fish. Dishes from this area are usually artful combinations of many flavors, and can be hot, sour, sweet and salty all at once.

Delicacies
The distinguishing aspect of the western culinary style is its reliance on very strong flavorings and hot spices, particularly red chilies, Sichuan peppercorns, ginger, onions and garlic. Outsiders used to suggest that such ingredients were used to mask the taste of the food, which had deteriorated in the area's muggy heat. However, regional chefs stand by their cuisine and their command of the art of seasoning.

MODERN CHINESE CUISINE
The Revolution in China in 1949 and its aftermath had consequences for cooking as well as profound political and social effects. Within China, the great cookery

tradition became for quite some time almost moribund. Revolutionaries deemed the art of cooking an elitist and reactionary enterprise, a reminder of Imperial days, and therefore best repressed. However, in the 1980s mainland Chinese leaders decided to allow and encourage the reemergence of the grand cuisine, an essential part of the booming tourism business. Since then, there have been dramatic transformations in regard to culinary matters. The material results of economic reforms, especially in agriculture and transportation, and the changed political atmosphere have led to the reopening of traditional cookery schools and of privately owned restaurants and food stalls.

Ingredients that used to be exported or otherwise not available are once again in good supply at affordable prices. People once again began to celebrate the seasons, special events and anniversaries with the customary feasts and banquets. In its attempt to create a new Chinese socialist nationalism, the Communist regime had banned many traditional and all regional food specialities; today, all these favorites have reemerged.

I myself have witnessed and experienced these transformations during the last decade. From being a country in which it was next to impossible to find a decent restaurant or obtain a delectable meal, China has made enormous strides toward regaining the glories of its wonderful cuisine. There are now excellent private restaurants in the major cities as well as in small villages, wonderful street stall offerings throughout the country, and marvelous home-cooked meals everywhere. Much remains to be done, and there are still disappointing culinary experiences to be had, but the Chinese

people are truly well advanced in the drive to reclaim their glorious cooking heritage.

The grand tradition of Chinese cookery has not only survived but has also been developed to a high degree of excellence in Taiwan and Hong Kong. Many international food critics and gourmets now consider Hong Kong to be the greatest center of Chinese cookery in the world. In this bustling, energetic place there are over 40,000 restaurants and food stalls, all competing for the custom of the inhabitants, many of whom eat most of their meals out, and the many tourists. Perhaps no other people in the world are so food-conscious.

Indeed, I have observed the emergence or crystallization of what I call the "new Hong Kong cuisine." This is a new culinary style of lighter, modern, imaginative Chinese cuisine that combines the best of the ancient Chinese canon with the most compatible influences from the best of the world's cuisines. It is a type of Chinese food that has become the favorite of restaurant-goers throughout the world.

YIN AND YANG: THE CHINESE DIET

The Chinese diet is a very healthy one, since it depends on cooking methods that preserve vitamins and use small quantities of meat and no dairy products. Underlying all Chinese cooking is the ancient yin yang theory of food science, which is closely related to Chinese beliefs about health. In China, all foods are divided into one of three groups: yin, for cooling foods; yang, for heating foods; and yin yang for neutral foods. To the foreigner there is little obvious logic in the way the foodstuffs are assigned to these categories. Yin foods include items as diverse as beer, crab, duck and soda water. Yang foods include brandy, beef, coffee and smoked fish. Neutral foods include bread, steamed rice, carrots, pigeons and peaches. Not only are all foods subdivided in this way but people are too. A yin person is quiet and introverted, while a yang person is a more active, outgoing type. The effect of different foods on an individual will depend on the way they conflict with or complement his or her personality type. The idea is to construct a meal and one's whole diet to achieve the right balance or harmony. Most Chinese have some knowledge of yin yang food science, as the idea is instilled into them from a very young age.

Apart from a sensible mixture of yin and yang foods, the art of Chinese cookery also lies in achieving a harmonious blend of color, texture, aroma and flavor. A typical Chinese meal consists of two parts — the fan, which is the staple grain, such as rice, noodles or dumplings, and the cai, which covers the rest of the dishes: meat, poultry, fish and vegetables. The average meal comprises three to four cai dishes, one fan dish and a soup. The cai dishes should each have a different main ingredient; for example, one meat, one fish and one vegetable. A variety of techniques will be used to cook these dishes. A fish may be steamed, a meat braised, while the vegetables may be stir-fried. The meal will also be designed so that each dish varies and yet complements the others in terms of appearance, texture and flavor. One dish will be spicy and another mild; one may be chewy and another crisp. The total effect should appeal to all the senses. All these dishes will be placed in the center of the table and shared between the diners, who help themselves and each other to a little of this, then a little of that. Eating for the Chinese is a communal experience, and a shared meal is regarded as the visible manifestation of the harmony that should exist between family and friends.

The subtle and distinctive taste of Chinese food depends in part on the use of some special Chinese ingredients. Of the recipes I have given in this book, some use ingredients that are more complicated than others. Where possible I have suggested suitable Western alternatives, but I'm afraid that if you want to cook authentic Chinese food there is ultimately no alternative but to track down a reliable source for the key ingredients. Fortunately, it is becoming easier to find some of these in supermarkets, and Chinese grocers are proliferating. The section on ingredients that follows this introduction (pages 14–37) lists all of the potentially confusing special ingredients that I have used in the recipes, and it will help you to know what to look and ask for without any trouble. You may find it useful to refer to this before embarking on a shopping trip to your nearest Chinese grocer.

CHINESE COOKING AT HOME

If you are new to Chinese cooking, there are a few golden rules that will help you get to grips with the basics:

Do not feel you have to prepare a meal that consists entirely of dishes from one particular region. Instead, select dishes that will provide a variety of colors, textures and tastes.

On pages 46–47 I have given some advice on how to put together a Chinese meal, and have suggested menus of varying complexity. I suggest that you start with the simple ones, which will give you experience in the basic cooking methods.

At first try just one or two Chinese dishes at a time, perhaps incorporating them into a Western meal. Chinese snacks, for example, make wonderful starters for any meal, and there are many Chinese dishes that can be successfully combined with Western-style meats and salads.

When you prepare your first entirely Chinese meal, select just two or three dishes and serve them simply, with some plain steamed rice.

Never select dishes that are all stir-fried, or you will have a traumatic time in the kitchen trying to get everything ready at the same time and will arrive at the table hot and flustered. Choose instead to do one braised dish, a cold dish, or something that can be prepared ahead of time when warmed through, and limit your stir-frying to just one dish. You will find the time spent cooking far more enjoyable if you stick to such a plan.

Many of the recipes in this book come not only from my family restaurant but also from my extensive travels and eating experiences during the last forty years in every far corner of China, as well as Hong Kong, Taiwan and Chinatowns worldwide. It is a great pleasure to share them with you, but do feel free, as I have, to change and experiment. After all, this is one of the great attributes of Chinese cookery: you can make any recipe your own.

There is an old Chinese proverb that says: "To the ruler, the people are heaven; to the people, food is heaven." Once you have embarked on the exciting road to discovering the mysteries and pleasures of Chinese cooking, you will soon discover just how sublime Chinese food can be. The time and the conditions are both propitious for the universal enjoyment of Chinese cookery. It can be done, and should be, as a part of our daily lives, both in the East and in the West.

INGREDIENTS

THE TASTES AND FLAVORS OF CHINA

Fresh ingredients, spices and sauces are all part of good cooking. Chinese cookery, with its long, ancient culinary history, is no different. You will discover a whole new world of tastes, smells and flavors, with ingredients that give Chinese food its addictive deliciousness.

Over a quarter of a century ago, when filming my first cookery TV series, I was worried about compromising the integrity of the programs by constantly referring to substitutes for authentic ingredients that were not then widely available. Of course, the last three decades have seen a lot of change, as the popularity of Chinese food and cooking has grown, it has opened up a new world of ingredients to the home chef. Many supermarkets now carry a wide variety of fresh ingredients, such as ginger and Chinese cabbage, as well as sauces, such as hoisin and oyster, and all kinds of noodles. Vast Chinese emporiums have popped up all over the country, even selling fresh water chestnuts and the more esoteric Chinese ingredients, such as fermented beancurd and dried lily buds. Whether you want to do a simple stir-fry or a more complicated dish, such as crispy duck, authentic ingredients are no longer the roadblock to a successful meal. You can easily re-create your favorite Chinese dishes at home now.

The success of Chinese cooking depends on layers of flavor, which are achieved not only by cooking techniques but also by using authentic ingredients. Now, hopefully, you will not have to scour the earth to find them. Once you master the taste and usage of these ingredients, you can experiment — for example, by adding a touch of sesame oil to your salad dressing. You will be doing what Chinese cooks have been doing for millennia: adapting ingredients to new uses and tastes!

The following is a list of the authentic ingredients that I have used in this book.

Meat

CAUL FAT

Caul fat is the lacy membrane that surrounds the organs in the abdominal cavity of the pig. The membrane is used by French and Chinese cooks to encase stuffings and to keep food moist while cooking. The fat itself melts entirely away during cooking, and because it both keeps foods moist and adds to their flavor, it is especially useful as a wrapping for delicate chicken, fish and seafood.

Caul fat is highly perishable, so buy it in small quantities and use it quickly. For longer storage, wrap it carefully and freeze. I find that soaking caul fat in cold water helps to separate the fat without tearing its lacy and fragile webs.

CHINESE SAUSAGES

Chinese sausages look exactly like thin salami and are about 6 in (15cm) long. They are made from duck liver, pork liver or pork meat, and are cured. They are dark red in color, with white flecks of fat, and their tasty flavor varies according to type, but they are sweet rather than spicy. Most commonly used to season chicken and rice dishes, they must be cooked before they can be eaten, and are available from Chinese grocers.

HAM (YUNNAN AND JINHUA)

Chinese hams are "cured," i.e., salted, seasoned, dried and smoked in regionally distinct ways. They can remain edible and flavorful for up to three years.

The most famous and highly valued Chinese hams are those from southwestern Yunnan and eastern Jinhua provinces.

Specialists in both regions breed particular types of pig; they follow their own secret and elaborate curing processes, and they insist that a special diet must be provided for those pigs that are destined to provide hams.

The Jinhua version has a succulence and a natural sweet flavor and aroma that, it is claimed, the curing process does not create but only captures. And those virtues are ascribed to the carefully controlled diet that these favored pigs enjoy before their destiny unfolds. The hams have a rich red color — in Chinese, the word for "hams" is "fire legs" — and are justly popular everywhere.

Hams of all regions are available at speciality shops in China (and in Chinatowns in the West). They may be seen hanging in the windows of such shops, which happily serve them by the slice. Unfortunately, cured Yunnan and Jinhua hams are not very easily available in the West. However, on rare occasion, Yunnan ham can be found in cans. I find Italian prosciutto (Parma ham) or lean smoked bacon (with any rind or fat cut away) perfectly acceptable substitutes for the wonderfully rich, smoky-flavored Chinese hams.

Fish and seafood

DRIED SEAFOOD

Fish are the most prevalent dried seafood in China. All types and sizes are dried, often to a semi-moist state that is a great favorite with the southern Chinese. The dried fish are cut up, then fried or steamed, sometimes alone but more often in combination with other foods. Today, we have fresh fish available to us, but the dried versions still retain their place in the cuisine as providers of a special taste and aroma.

There are many varieties of dried fish and seafood, including abalone, oysters, squid, scallops, jellyfish and shrimp. The quality is simply based on price, the more exotic and desirable varieties costing more than the lesser exotic and more widely available ones.

Dried fish will keep indefinitely, both dried and in oil. Store in a cool, dry place, away from light.

Useful hints *Soak dried fish or seafood in warm water for 30 minutes before use. When it has softened, remove any bones and chop. Some dried seafood, like abalone and squid, needs to be soaked for up to 24 hours before it can be used.*

Dried oysters

Dried oysters are a standard item in the coastal regions of southern China. Like many dried seafood preparations in China, these oysters are frequently used in finely minced form to enhance dishes. They are naturally sun-dried, usually without salting. They give a strong, distinctive, seaflavor to braised dishes and soups.

Useful hints *Use dried oysters carefully because they can overwhelm a dish with their assertive flavors. Soak them in a bowl of warm water until soft before using, for at least 1 hour, or even as long as overnight.*

Dried shrimp

Dried shrimp is used as a seasoning to perk up fried rice and other dishes. It gives an added dimension to soups and stuffings. Essentially made from small peeled shrimp that are dehydrated by the sun or air-dried. When cooked, they add a delicate taste to sauces; cooking moderates the shrimp's strong odor.

Dried shrimp will keep indefinitely if sealed in a glass container and kept cool in the fridge. Or, if you plan to use them within 1 month, they can also be stored in a cool, dry place until being used.

Useful hints *Soak the dried shrimp in warm water or Shaoxing rice wine, or steam them to soften them before using. The liquid they have been soaked in can be used in a recipe to give an added depth of flavor.*

FISH SAUCE

A fish sauce is usually a clear, brownish, salty liquid that is rich in protein. The sauces, in fact, were originally concocted as a means of preserving fish protein. Also known as fish gravy, *nước mâm* in Vietnam and *nam pla* in Thailand, fish sauce has a strong odor and a taste to match. Cooking or mixing it with other ingredients, however, diminishes the "fishy" flavor, and the sauce is so tamed that it adds a special richness, fragrance and quality to dishes. It is also used as a dipping sauce and is used like soy sauce in much of southeast Asia.

Fruits and vegetables

BAMBOO SHOOTS

Bamboo shoots generally fall into two broad categories: spring shoots and winter shoots. The winter ones are smaller and more tender than the spring ones, which tend to be quite large. Fresh bamboo shoots are sweet and crunchy, with a distinctive and unforgettable taste, but can be very expensive. They are too fragile to export, and I have only occasionally seen them in Chinese markets in the West.

We have to be satisfied with the canned varieties, which are at least more reasonably priced. Canned bamboo shoots tend to be pale yellow, with a crunchy texture and, in some cases, a slightly sweet flavor. In some Chinese markets, bamboo shoots preserved in brine are available, and these tend to have much more flavor than the canned variety.

Rinse canned bamboo shoots thoroughly and blanch them for 2 minutes in boiling water before use. Transfer any leftover shoots to a jar, cover them with fresh water and refrigerate them. If the water is changed daily they will keep for 2 or 3 days.

Useful hints *Buy whole bamboo shoots, rather than sliced, as they tend to hold their flavors a little better.*

Fresh bamboo shoots, if you should ever come across them, are prepared by first stripping off all the leaves and then trimming the hard base. Only the center core is edible, and this should be cut and blanched for at least 5 minutes to remove its bitterness. Then prepare the core according to the recipe and continue cooking.

BEANCURD

Beancurd, which is also known by its Chinese name, doufu, or by its Japanese name, tofu, has played an important part in Chinese cookery since it was discovered during the Han dynasty (206 BC–AD 220). It became known as "meat without bones" because it is highly nutritious, rich in protein and works well with other foods.

Beancurd is low in saturated fats and cholesterol, easy to digest, inexpensive and extremely versatile — it lends itself to all types of cooking. It is made from yellow soy beans that are soaked, ground, mixed with water and then cooked briefly before being solidified. Usually sold in two forms, as firm, small blocks or in a soft custard-like variety, beancurd is also available in several dried forms and in a fermented version.

Fresh beancurd, once opened, may be kept in this state in the fridge for up to 5 days, provided the covering water is changed daily. It is best to use the beancurd within 2 or 3 days of purchase.

Useful hints *To use solid beancurd, gently cut the amount required into cubes or shreds using a sharp knife. Do this with care, as it is fragile. It also needs to be cooked gently, as too much stirring can cause it to disintegrate. This does not, however, affect its nutritional value.*

Deep-frying beancurd transforms its texture to a sponge-like web, allowing the beancurd to absorb sauces when it is cooked again the second time.

Fermented beancurd (red and regular)

This is a cheese-like form of beancurd preserved in rice wine, in brine with rice wine or with chilies and condiments. It is very popular in China, where it is eaten by itself with rice or rice porridge, or used as an ingredient in cooking, or featured as a seasoning. It is often used as a flavoring agent, especially with braised meat dishes or vegetables.

It comes in several forms: red fermented beancurd has been cured in a brine with fermented red rice (a reddish flavoring made by adding annatto seeds to rice wine lees left after brewing rice wine), Shaoxing rice wine and crushed dried chili peppers; the regular variety is made with just rice wine. You can find this only at Chinese markets or grocers.

Once the jar has been opened, fermented beancurd will keep indefinitely if resealed and refrigerated.

Pressed seasoned beancurd

When water is extracted from fresh beancurd cakes, by pressing them with a weight, the beancurd becomes firm and compact. Simmered in water with soy sauce, star anise and sugar, the pressed beancurd acquires a smooth, resilient texture that is quite unusual. When cut into small pieces it can be stir-fried with meat or vegetables; when cut into larger pieces it can be simmered.

This beancurd is often vacuum-packed and should keep in the fridge for at least 1 week. Once opened it should be used within 2 or 3 days.

Useful hints *For vegetarian dishes, simply brush the beancurd cakes with oil and broil them. Or add them to vegetables instead of meat for a tasty main course.*

BITTER MELON

This unusual vegetable is very much an acquired taste. It has as many detractors as it has fans, even among the Chinese, but those who love it insist it is worth the effort needed to appreciate its taste. Bitter melon has a bumpy, dark to pale green skin, and a slightly bitter quinine flavor that has a cooling effect in the mouth. Not surprisingly, it was originally prized for its supposed medicinal qualities: something so bitter had to be good medicine. The greener the melon, the more bitter its taste.

Canned bitter melon is less appealing and should be avoided, as it tends to be overcooked and without flavor.

Store in the bottom of the fridge in a loose plastic or paper bag. It can keep there for about 3–5 days.

To use, cut in half, remove the seeds, and discard the interior membrane. Then, to lessen its bitter taste, either blanch or salt it, according to the instructions in the recipe.

BLACK BEANS
(FERMENTED BLACK BEANS, SALTED BEANS, PRESERVED BEANS)

These small black soy beans, also known as salted black beans or fermented black beans, are preserved by being cooked and fermented with salt and spices, making them pungent and soft. They have a distinctive salty taste and a pleasantly rich aroma, and are often used as a seasoning, usually in conjunction with garlic, fresh ginger or chilies. Black beans are especially good in steamed, braised and stir-fried dishes, imparting a wonderfully rich flavor to every dish. They should not be confused with the dried black beans used in Western cooking.

Black beans are readily available in the West. You can find them in cans or jars labeled "Black Bean Sauce," and some are good, but I like to buy the ones that come packed in plastic bags.

Depending on the recipe, the black beans should be lightly chopped or crushed to release their tangy aromas. The beans will keep indefinitely if stored in the fridge or in a cool place.

Useful hints *I recommend rinsing the black beans before use, as the salty flavor can be overpowering, but this is a matter of taste and you may find that for you the salt adds to the flavor of the dish.*

CABBAGE, BROCCOLI AND OTHER GREENS
(SEE ALSO PRESERVED VEGETABLES)

Beijing (Peking) cabbage (Chinese leaves)
The cabbages cultivated in China are more nutritious than the common Western varieties. They all have a mild taste, but Peking cabbages are particularly mild-tasting. In this regard they are more like broccoli than our cabbages. Peking cabbages have delightfully crisp, fibrous leaves, leading to their name of "celery cabbages." The Western vegetable they most closely resemble is our romaine lettuce.

This versatile green is used in soups and in stir-fried meat dishes. Its leaves, which readily absorb aromas and tastes, and its sweet, pleasant taste make it a favorite as a match for foods that have rich flavors. It is also enjoyed pickled with salt and chili.

Look for fresh cabbage that is not wilted. It should have a crisp appearance, with no yellow or brown spots.

Wrapped loosely in paper towels in the lower part of your fridge, it should last up to 1 week without any problems.

Useful hints *This cabbage can be used as a salad green. Do not boil it, as it is rather delicate and fragile. Light cooking is best. Every part of the cabbage can be used.*

Chinese broccoli
This very nutritious green leafy plant with smooth, round stems and small, white flowers is sometimes called Chinese kale and resembles Swiss chard in flavor.

Chinese broccoli is usually blanched in salted water and served with oyster sauce — it has character enough to go well with that distinctively flavored condiment. It also works well in stir-fries with meat, to be served with noodles and soups.

Store in a plastic bag in the salad drawer of the fridge, where it will keep quite happily for several days.

Useful hints *Use Chinese broccoli the way you would use regular broccoli, kale, Swiss chard or canola greens. It is one of the world's most nutritious vegetables, with one of the highest calcium contents of any food. It is also rich in iron, vitamin A and vitamin C.*

Chinese flowering cabbage
It would be tedious to list all the types of Chinese cabbage that are cultivated and consumed in enormous quantities every day in China. It is safe to say, however, that Chinese flowering cabbage is among the most popular. A relative of another favorite green, bok choy, this cabbage is slimmer, with yellow flowers that are eaten along with the leaves and stems. Its attributes make it more desirable and more expensive than bok choy.

Stir-frying is the preferred cooking method, the leaves require little cooking to bring out their delicate mustard flavor.

Store in the salad drawer of the fridge. Like bok choy, it should keep for around 1 week or so.

Useful hints *This vegetable is also delicious stir-fried with olive oil and garlic. Use it in fillings and with pasta. It makes a mustardy salad green; however, it needs to be washed well. The best way to prepare it is to trim and cut the leaves and then wash them in several rinses of cold water.*

Chinese white cabbage (bok choy)

Chinese white cabbage, popularly known as bok choy, is a nutritious and versatile vegetable. It has been grown in China since ancient times. Although there are many varieties — in Hong Kong alone, twenty kinds are available — the most common, best-known and most popular is the one with long, smooth, milky-white stems and large, crinkly, dark green leaves found in many supermarkets today. Bok choy has a light, fresh, slightly mustardy taste and requires little cooking. In China, it is used in soups, stir-fried with meat or simply blanched. When cooked, the leaves have a robust, almost spinach-like flavor, while the stalks are sweet and mild with a refreshing taste. Bok choy is often said to resemble Swiss chard in taste; however, it is not only milder but also juicier than chard.

Store bok choy wrapped tightly in paper towels in the salad drawer of your fridge, where it will keep for up to 1 week.

Useful hints *The best way to clean bok choy is to cut it according to the recipe, then rinse it in at least two or three changes of cold water. Drain thoroughly before cooking. Boy choy is delicious cooked in olive oil and garlic. Use it as you would spinach or cabbage.*

Other cabbage varieties from the bok choy family include choi sum (Chinese flowering cabbage, page 19) and Shanghai bok choy, often called baby bok choy. Use them in the same way as bok choy.

Red-in-snow cabbage (amaranth)

There are two varieties of this leafy vegetable. The green one is most similar to spinach, with a watercress-like, mild and slightly tart flavor. The other variety has red stems, and red coloration is prominent throughout the leaves too. It is a hardy vegetable and arrives in early spring, when it peeks through the snow that is still on the ground; hence its name, because of the way its crimson red leaves contrast with the snowy field. It is salt-pickled as well as eaten fresh. The pickled variety adds a pungent, slightly sour but not unpleasant taste to dishes when used as a flavoring. It can also be used as an interestingly textured vegetable ingredient in stir-fried and braised dishes. The fresh variety has a wonderful green pungent earthy taste.

The canned variety will last indefinitely in the fridge. The fresh version should be consumed within 2 days of purchase.

CHILIES

Fresh chilies

In Chinese cuisine, fresh chilies are stuffed or eaten whole. They are used to make sauces or pastes and are pickled and preserved for use in stir-fried and braised dishes. In China, fresh chilies are small and generally red, but there are also green varieties. Their taste is mildly spicy and pungent. Smaller varieties can be found, but the larger, longer ones are the ones most widely available.

Dried red chilies

Dried red chilies are used extensively in some regions of China. Drying is done for practical purposes so that chilies are always available. In the southwest region of Sichuan province and in Hunan, long strings of dried red chilies can be seen hanging in the kitchens of homes and restaurants. The drying process concentrates the power of the chili and adds vigor and complexity to spicy dishes.

Dried chilies will keep indefinitely in an airtight jar in a cool place.

Chili bean sauce or paste

There are many varieties of chili sauce and paste, but the basic ones include ground chilies, oil, salt and garlic fermented into a rich paste that ranges in taste from mild to very hot. Chinese cooks will also mix into the basic version such ingredients as ground soy beans, black beans, ginger, preserved vegetables and other condiments. In the so-called "hot bean pastes," soy beans predominate. Every chef in every region of China has his or her own special recipe for chili paste.

Be sure to store in the fridge, where it will keep indefinitely if kept in a tightly sealed jar.
Useful hints *There is a type of chili sauce that is used mainly as a dipping sauce. It is a hot, reddish, thin sauce made without any added beans and should not be confused with this thicker chili bean paste or sauce.*

Chili oil/chili dipping sauce

Chilli oil is used extensively in Chinese cooking. It is sometimes used as a dipping condiment as well as a seasoning. It is used to impart a sharp, hot flavor to cooked dishes. It is made from crushed dried chilies or small whole chilies, depending on the flavor you are seeking.

Commercial products are quite acceptable, but it is better to make your own version. Once made, pour the chilli oil into a tightly sealed glass jar and store in a cool, dark place, where it will keep for months.

To make chili oil/chili dipping sauce

Remember that chili oil is too dramatic to be used directly as the sole cooking oil; it is best used as part of a dipping sauce or as a condiment, or combined with other mild oils. I include the spices (pepper and black beans) for additional flavors, because then I can also use it as a dipping sauce.

1 cup (250ml) peanut or vegetable oil
4 oz (100g) coarsely chopped dried red chilies
4 tbsp (60ml) whole unroasted Sichuan peppercorns
3 tbsp (45ml) whole black beans, rinsed and chopped

Heat a wok over a high heat and add the oil. When the oil is very hot, add the rest of the ingredients and stir for 1 minute over low heat. Turn off the heat and allow to cool undisturbed. Leave it to stand overnight, then transfer to an airtight jar and keep in a cool, dry, dark place.

CHINESE LONG BEANS

Quite unrelated to our familiar green beans, these beans are neither crisp nor sweet. They do have a crunchy texture, but they have a mild, subtle taste and are best when combined with more strongly flavored foods. There are two varieties: pale green ones and dark green, thinner types. Both cook rapidly, and this makes them very suitable for stir-fry recipes.

Buy beans that are fresh and either a bright light green or deep dark green, with no dark marks. Although they are not crisp like Western green beans, they nevertheless should not be soft.

Store the fresh beans in a plastic bag in the fridge and use within 4 days.
Useful hints *Paired with assertive seasonings, these beans are very tasty when simply stir-fried, with or without meat. The Cantonese*

often cook them with black beans or fermented beancurd.

CHINESE WHITE RADISH (MOOLI)

Chinese white radish is also known as Chinese icicle radish or mooli, or by its Japanese name, daikon. It is long and white, rather like a carrot in shape but usually much larger. It is a winter radish or root and can withstand long cooking without disintegrating. It thus absorbs the flavors of the food it is cooked with and yet retains its distinctive radish taste and texture.

In China, these radishes are usually found in homemade dishes, treated as Western cooks use potatoes or carrots. They are never used unpeeled. They are not only cooked but are also pickled or salted and dried to preserve them. Crisp-textured and tender when cooked, they vary in flavor from sweet and mild to fairly hot and pungent. The stronger-flavored variety is used for pickles, the milder for cooking. Most of the hot flavor is in the skin, and when peeled the radish is mild-tasting. Like turnips, these radishes are most often stir-fried, braised, boiled or steamed and then combined with pork or beef. The milder radishes are even made into a savory pudding for dim sum in southern China. Unlike most root vegetables, these radishes are light and refreshing, not heavy and starchy.

You can find them in some supermarkets and almost always at Chinese markets.

CITRUS PEEL

Citrus peel is often used in braised or simmered dishes, its fruity essence suffusing the entire dish. Occasionally the peels are used in "master sauces," providing them with a contrasting flavor dimension. More rarely, they are used in stir-fry dishes.

Dried citrus peel is sold in Chinese stores or can be easily made at home. Stored in an airtight jar, the dried peel will last for months or years. When you are ready to use the peel, rehydrate it in a bowl of warm water for 20 minutes or until it is soft.

Useful hints *The peel can also be rehydrated in Shaoxing rice wine, then used along with the wine in the recipe.*

To make citrus peel at home

Wash and rinse the fruit well. Use a good vegetable peeler to carefully peel the skin off the fruit. Then, using a sharp knife, carefully separate the white pith from the peel. Dry the peel on a baking sheet in a warm place until it is firm, or place on a tray in direct sunlight. When the peel is dried, store in an airtight jar. It will improve with age.

EGGPLANTS

The most common type of eggplant, the large purple variety, is easily available; the Chinese prefer the more delicate flavor of the smaller, thinner eggplants, and these too are becoming more readily available in the West. Try to find the long, thin, light purple variety known as Chinese or Japanese eggplants. These look like young zucchinis and tend to be sweet and tender, with very few seeds. They should be eaten within a few days of purchase.

GARLIC

The Chinese have been cultivating garlic since at least 3000 BC, and Chinese cuisine is inconceivable without its distinct, sweet, pungent, aromatic contribution. Cooks often smash a clove of garlic into hot cooking oil; this "sweetens" the oil and gives it a bracing aroma. Once its essence has been captured by the oil, the garlic husk is removed and discarded. Garlic, whether whole, chopped, minced, crushed, pickled, boiled, smoked, in flavored oils and spicy sauces, by itself or with other robust ingredients, such as black beans, curry, shrimp paste, green onions or ginger, is an essential and revered element in the Chinese diet.

Peeling garlic cloves is laborious. However, the skin can come off quite easily by using the Chinese technique of quickly boiling the garlic cloves with the skin on for 2 minutes and then leaving them in the hot water for 5 minutes — be warned, though, as the boiling does mute the intensity of the garlic. The other trick is to bruise the cloves with the side of a Chinese cleaver or heavy kitchen knife; the skin then tends to break away.

Select garlic that is firm and preferably pinkish in color. It should be stored in a cool, dry place, but not in the fridge, where it can easily become mildewy or even begin to sprout.

GINGER

Ginger has a "clean" taste that adds subtlety to delicate dishes, such as fried seafood, and that counterbalances the stronger flavors of more robust dishes, such as beef and pork. Locals claim that the most aromatic and most potent ginger is to be found in Guangzhou (Canton), but throughout China ginger is used in all sorts of recipes, including soups, sauces and flavored beverages. Small wonder it is as ubiquitous in Chinese cuisine as garlic.

Young stem ginger often makes a seasonal appearance in the markets of China, but is occasionally now also found in the West, especially at Chinese grocers or supermarkets. It is knobby-looking and a kind of moist pink, looking rather naked. This is the newest spring growth of ginger and is usually stir-fried and eaten in various dishes. It is also commonly pickled in China. Because it is so tender, it does not need peeling and can be eaten as a vegetable.

To make ginger juice

Ginger juice is made from fresh ginger and is used in marinades to give a subtle ginger taste without the bite of the fresh chopped pieces. Here is a simple method of extracting ginger juice: cut unpeeled fresh ginger into 1 in (2.5cm) chunks and drop them into a running food processor. When the ginger is finely chopped, squeeze out the juice by hand through a cotton or linen cloth. Alternatively, mash the ginger with a kitchen mallet or the side of a cleaver or knife until most of the fibers are exposed, then simply squeeze out the juice by hand through a cloth. You can also put a piece of fresh ginger into a blender with 2 tbsp (30ml) of water, liquidize, then strain the juice.

LEEKS

The Western leek is larger and more fibrous than the Chinese leek. The Chinese leek is smaller and thinner and has a finer texture; its pungent and slightly acidic flavor sweetens with cooking.

Baby leeks, available in season at organic food stores and in some Chinese markets, are a good substitute for Chinese leeks, which are currently not available outside China. If you decide to try this alternative, try to look for firm stalks with no yellow or brown spots.

MUSHROOMS

Chinese dried black mushrooms

These "black" mushrooms actually range from light brown to dark brown in color. The most popular are the larger, light brown ones with a highly cracked surface. These are, predictably, the most expensive. But all versions and grades of this mushroom add a most desirable flavor and aroma to Chinese recipes. It is interesting to note that these mushrooms grow on fallen, decaying trees; the Chinese have been gathering them for over 1,000 years. The Japanese cultivate them by growing them on the shii tree, hence the familiar fresh shiitake mushrooms.

However, the Chinese rarely eat mushrooms fresh. They prefer the dried version because this process concentrates the smoky flavors and robust taste of the mushrooms and allows them to absorb sauces and spices, acquiring an even more succulent texture.

In Chinese markets that specialize in dried foods, you will find all grades and types of mushroom heaped in large mounds, with the most expensive elaborately boxed or wrapped in plastic. Depending on your budget, the lighter and more expensive grade is the best to buy.

Stored in an airtight container, dried mushrooms will keep indefinitely in a cool, dry place. Store them in the freezer if they will not be used frequently.

To use Chinese dried mushrooms

Soak the mushrooms in a bowl of warm water for about 20 minutes, or until they are soft and pliable. Squeeze out the excess water and cut off and discard the woody stems. The soaking water can be saved for use in soups and as rice water, as a base for a vegetarian stock, or for adding to sauces or braised dishes. Strain it through a fine sieve before using to filter out any sand or residue.

Chinese tree fungus (cloud ears)

These tiny, black, dried leaves are also known as cloud ears; when soaked, they puff up to look like little clouds. Soak the dried fungus in hot water for 20–30 minutes, until soft. Rinse well, cutting away any hard portions.

Chinese wood ear fungus

This is the larger variety of the Chinese tree fungus described above. Prepare, soak and trim in the same manner. During soaking, these mushrooms will swell up to four or five times their size.

Straw mushrooms

These are among the tastiest mushrooms found in China. When fresh, they have deep brown caps that are molded around the stem. In North America they are available only in cans. Drain them and rinse in cold water before use.

PRESERVED VEGETABLES (SEE ALSO CABBAGE, BROCCOLI AND OTHER GREENS)

Preserved mustard greens or cabbage
Mustard greens are known in Chinese as "greens heart" because only the heart of the plant is eaten; that is, the stem, buds and young leaf. They are unrelated to and quite unlike the mustard greens of the American South. The leaves are pickled with salt, water, vinegar and sugar, making a true sweet and sour food that is used as a vegetable or as a flavoring ingredient, especially in soups. A similar process is carried out with Chinese cabbage to produce Tianjin preserved vegetable.

The best form of these preserved mustard greens can be found in large crocks in Chinese markets, which usually means they are locally made. The next best alternative is the ones available in small crocks or cans, labeled "preserved vegetable" — these come from Hong Kong, Taiwan or China.

Remove from the crock or can and store the greens in a glass jar. They will keep indefinitely in the fridge.

Sichuan preserved vegetable
Also known as Sichuan preserved mustard stem or Sichuan preserved radish, one of the most popular of the large variety of pickled and preserved cabbages in China is Sichuan preserved vegetable, a speciality of Sichuan province. This is the root of the mustard green, pickled with salt, hot chilies and garlic. It is fermented in large pottery tubs, and the result is a strikingly piquant pickled vegetable. It is used to give a pleasantly crunchy texture and spicy, strong taste to stir-fried, braised or simmered dishes and soups. It is also used in stuffings, or thinly sliced and served as a cold appetizer.

Sichuan preserved vegetable is sold in cans or pottery crocks in Chinese grocery stores or in supermarkets.
Useful hints *Any unused vegetable should be transferred to a tightly covered glass jar and stored in the fridge, where it will keep indefinitely. Before using, rinse in cold water and then slice or chop as required.*

Tianjin preserved vegetable (see Preserved mustard greens)

SILK SQUASH (CHINESE OKRA)
A popular vegetable frequently found in markets throughout China, this is a long, thin, cylindrical squash (or melon), tapering at one end, with deep, narrow ridges. It is eaten when young, as it grows bitter with age. It is very similar to a zucchini in texture, with a wonderful earthy flavor. Some people find a similarity in taste and texture to okra, and it has hence been called Chinese okra. However, you must peel away the tough ridges. The inside flesh turns soft and tender as it cooks, finally tasting like a cross between a cucumber and a zucchini. Absorbent, it readily picks up the flavors of the sauce or food it is cooked with.

Good, firm silk squash should be stored at the bottom of the fridge and will keep for at least 1 week.

WATER CHESTNUTS

Fresh water chestnuts
Water chestnuts have been eaten in China for centuries. They need only light cooking

and are often added, chopped or sliced, to cooked dishes. They are also the source of water chestnut flour or powder, which is used to thicken sauces or to coat food.

In the West, fresh water chestnuts can be obtained from Chinese markets or some supermarkets. Fortunately, they arrive from Asia in vacuum packs that keep them quite fresh. When buying fresh ones, look for a firm, hard texture. The skin should be tight and taut. If you peel them in advance, cover them with cold water to prevent browning and store them in the fridge. They will keep, unpeeled, in a paper bag in the fridge for up to 2 weeks.

Canned water chestnuts

Canned water chestnuts are sold in many supermarkets and Chinese markets. A pale version of the fresh ones, they have a good texture but little taste because the flavor is lost in the canning process. Rinse them well in cold water before you use them.

Herbs and spices

CHINESE CHIVES

Chives are mild, small versions of the onion. Having no bulb, only the green shoots are eaten. There are several variations. Yellow chives are distinctly, if mildly, onion-flavored. Flowering chives have hollow stems topped by a flower bud. The tough ends are chopped off and the remainder is consumed as a vegetable. Green chives have a distinctive pungency that adds richness to stir-fried dishes.

They are highly perishable — most will remain fresh for 2 days, but yellow chives are extremely fragile and will keep for only 1 day. To prepare, select the freshest leaves possible, trim any decaying parts and proceed with your recipe.

CINNAMON BARK

In Chinese cuisine, cinnamon bark's aromatic virtues are exploited particularly well in braised dishes. Cinnamon sticks — curled, paper-thin strips — have a more concentrated and, therefore, more assertive spiciness and are preferred in recipes that involve robust flavors. The famous five-spice powder would be terribly lacking without cinnamon.

Look for thin, rolled cinnamon sticks or bark in Chinese markets or grocers. They are usually found in plastic bags and are inexpensive and very fresh. If you find cinnamon bark, look for firm aromatic-smelling specimens.

Useful hints *Ground cinnamon is not a satisfactory substitute for cinnamon bark.*

SICHUAN PEPPERCORNS

Not actually related to black pepper at all, Sichuan peppercorns are the dried berries of a shrub known as fagara, which is a member of the prickly ash tree family. Their smell reminds me of lavender, while their taste is sharp and slightly numbing to the tongue, with a clean lemon-like wood spiciness and fragrance. It is not these peppercorns that make traditional Sichuan cooking so hot; it is the chili peppers that create that sensation.

These peppercorns are one of the components of five-spice powder. They can be ground in a conventional pepper mill but should be roasted (see above, right) before grinding to bring out their full flavor.

To roast Sichuan peppercorns

Heat a wok or a heavy skillet to a medium heat. Add the peppercorns (you can roast up to about 4 oz [100g] at a time) and stir-fry them for about 5 minutes, until they begin to brown slightly and start to smoke. Remove the skillet from the heat and let them cool. Grind the peppercorns in a pepper mill, a clean coffee grinder, or with a mortar and pestle. Sift the ground pepper through a fine mesh and discard any hard hulls. Seal the mixture tightly in a screwtop jar to store. Alternatively, keep the whole roasted peppercorns in a well-sealed container and grind them when required.

To make seasoned salt and pepper

Roast Sichuan peppercorns with sea salt and grind coarsely together. Keep in a screwtop jar.

STAR ANISE

Star anise, also known as Chinese anise or whole anise, is the hard, star-shaped seedpod of a small tree that grows in southwestern China. It is similar in flavor and fragrance to common anise seed but is more robust and liquorice-like. It is an essential ingredient of five-spice powder and, like cinnamon bark, is widely used in braised dishes, to which it imparts a rich taste and fragrance.

Flour, noodles and rice

FLOUR

Cornstarch

In China and throughout Asia there are many flours and types of starch. Cornstarch is among the most commonly used in Chinese cooking, although many traditional cooks prefer a bean flour because it thickens faster and holds longer. In China, sauces are light and must barely coat the food, which never "swims" in thick sauces. As part of a marinade, cornstarch helps to coat food properly and to give dishes a velvety texture. **Useful hints** *Mix 2 parts liquid to 1 part cornstarch before adding to a sauce.*

Glutinous rice flour

Also known as sweet rice flour or sweet rice powder, this flour is made from raw short-grain rice that becomes moist, firm and sticky when cooked.

Rice flour

Rice flour, sometimes called rice powder, is made from finely milled raw white rice and is used to make fresh rice noodles, pastry and sweets. Rice flour is a staple food item throughout China and southeast Asia.

NOODLES

Egg noodles and wheat noodles

The egg noodle, made from wheat flour and egg, is a little like Italian pasta. The most common of these are the thin, round strands that are commonly available both fresh and dried. Egg noodles tend to be yellowish in color, and are used in stir-fried dishes, as well as in soups.

Wheat noodles contain no eggs; they are made from wheat flour, water and salt, and are whiter-looking. They too are available fresh and dried, and like egg noodles, they are used in soups as well as stir-fried. Although many types of fresh noodles are now available in supermarkets, they tend to be more starchy than Chinese-made noodles.

Useful hints *Dried noodles should be cooked in simmering salted water for 3–5 minutes, while fresh noodles need slightly less time. It is best to give fresh noodles a quick rinse after cooking before stir-frying them or putting them in soups.*

To cook wheat and egg noodles
Noodles are very good blanched and served with main dishes instead of plain rice. I think dried wheat or fresh egg noodles are best for this. If you are using fresh noodles, put them into a sauce pan of boiling water and cook them for 3–5 minutes, or until you find their texture done to your taste. If you are using dried noodles, either follow the instructions on the packet, or cook them in boiling water for around 4–5 minutes. Drain and serve.

Rice noodles
Fresh rice, or fen, noodles are made from a mixture of rice flour, wheat starch (not flour) and water. This mixture is steamed into large sheets and then, when cooked, is cut into noodles to be eaten immediately.

Dried rice noodles are made from a dough of finely ground rice flour and water. This is then extruded into opaque white noodles of varying thickness and size. One of the most common types is rice stick noodles, which are flat and about the length of a chopstick. Deep-fried, they puff up instantly and become delicately crisp and light. Because they are absorbent and have little flavor of their own, they readily take on the taste and fragrance of the foods with which they are cooked.

All types of dried rice noodles are widely available. I especially like the ones from China and Thailand, which come attractively wrapped in paper or cellophane and often tied with red ribbon. Fresh rice noodles can be found only in Chinese markets or grocers.

Useful hints *Rice noodles are very easy to use. Simply soak them in warm water for around 20 minutes, until they are soft. Drain them in a colander or sieve and they are ready to use in soups and stir-fries.*

Transparent (cellophane) or bean thread noodles
These noodles are not made from a grain flour but from ground mung beans, which are also the source of the more familiar bean sprouts. Freshly made bean thread noodles can sometimes be seen in China fluttering in the breeze on lines like long threads of fabric. They are available dried, and are very fine and white. They are never served on their own, but are added to soups or braised dishes, or deep-fried and used as a garnish. Once they are soaked they become soft and slippery, springy and translucent. When fried, they puff up immediately and become very white and crisp.

Useful hints *Bean thread noodles should be soaked in hot water for about 5 minutes before use, rather than boiled. As they are rather long, you may find it easier to cut them into shorter lengths after soaking. If you are frying them, omit the soaking but make sure you separate them first.*

RICE

Glutinous rice
There are some 2,500 different varieties of rice, but for cooking purposes only one distinction is crucial. Glutinous rice has proteins that do not dissolve in water, and they absorb twice their weight in water when cooked.

Round and pearly white, glutinous rice cooks into a sticky mass that makes it suitable for use in stuffings, puddings and pastries. After being ground into flour, it is used for pastries, sweet dumplings and cakes. **Useful hints** *Glutinous rice must be soaked for at least 8 hours or overnight for best results. It should then be rinsed and drained before cooking. Line the bottom of a steamer with damp cheesecloth and steam the rice gently for 1–1½ hours. Alternatively, you can cook it on the stove with water.*

Long-grain rice
This is the most popular rice for cooking in China, where there are many different varieties. Although the Chinese go through the ritual of washing it, rice purchased at supermarkets doesn't require this step.

Short-grain rice
Short-grain rice is most frequently found in northern China and is used for making rice porridge, a popular morning meal.

SPRING ROLL WRAPPERS
These are the paper-thin skins that are filled with bean sprouts and other vegetables to make spring rolls. They are about 6 in (15cm) square, white, and are made from a soft flour and water dough. Since they are very thin and probably too tricky to make at home, I suggest you buy them frozen in packets of 20 from Chinese grocers. They keep well in the freezer, wrapped in plastic wrap.

WONTON SKINS
In China, wonton skins and other such doughs were traditionally made painstakingly by hand, the entire extended family engaging in the process while sitting around the main table of the house. Today, fortunately, there is no need to summon the family from the four corners of the earth! There are very good commercially made wonton skins that are made from egg and flour and can be bought fresh or frozen, not only at Chinese markets but, increasingly, at ordinary supermarkets as well. They range from very thin to medium pastry-like wrappings, stretched like freshly made noodles. They can be stuffed with ground meat, then fried, steamed or used in soups. They are sold in little piles of 3 in (7.5cm) squares (or sometimes a bit larger), wrapped in plastic. Wonton skins freeze very well; however, they should be well wrapped before freezing. Fresh wonton skins will keep for about 5 days if stored in plastic wrap or a plastic bag in the fridge. If you are using frozen wonton skins, thaw them before use.

Nuts, seeds and oils

OILS AND FATS

Corn oil
Corn oil is a light, healthful, mostly polyunsaturated oil that is good for cooking and also has a high burning temperature. Being thus similar to peanut oil, I find it an adequate substitute and ideal in Chinese cookery for stir-frying or deep-frying. It has a heavier, distinct flavor and is an easily acquired taste.

Other vegetable oils
Some of the cheaper vegetable oils are available in China: these include canola, cottonseed, soy bean, safflower and sunflower

oils. They are quite edible and serviceable but not as good or as effective as peanut oil.

Peanut (groundnut) oil

Peanut oil is the most popular cooking oil because of its mild, unobtrusive taste and because it heats to a high temperature without burning. It is thus perfect for stir-frying and deep-frying. The semi-refined peanut oils in China are cold-pressed, retain the fragrance of fresh peanuts and possess a distinctive flavor preferred by many cooks. Look for semi-refined oil.

Useful hints *In most cases peanut oil can be reused at least once. Simply cool the oil after use and filter it through cheesecloth or a fine strainer into a jar. Cover it tightly and keep it in a cool, dry place. If kept in the fridge it will become cloudy, but it will clarify again at room temperature. For clarity of flavor, I use oils only once. The best Chinese cooking requires that only fresh oil be used.*

Sesame oil

Chinese cooks prefer lighter, more subtly flavored oils for cooking, and so sesame oil is used only as a flavoring oil in marinades or as a final seasoning.

Useful hints *Sesame oil is a wonderfully aromatic addition to marinades, whether Chinese or otherwise. Use it like walnut oil, adding a few drops to your salad dressing.*

PEANUTS

Peanuts are valued as a versatile and congenial element in many recipes. They are usually stir-fried or boiled before being added. They are also eaten as salted snacks or ground into a peanut sauce condiment.

SESAME SEEDS

These seeds are usually pressed into oils or made into pastes to serve as flavoring agents or in sauces. Some seeds may be toasted and used as a garnish for foods, sweets and breads.

To make toasted sesame seeds

Heat a skillet until hot. Add the sesame seeds and stir occasionally. Watch them closely, and when they begin to lightly brown, after about 3–5 minutes, stir them again and pour them onto a plate. When they are thoroughly cool, store them in a screwtop glass jar in a cool, dark place. Alternatively, preheat the oven to 325°F (160°C) and spread the sesame seeds out evenly on a baking sheet. Roast them in the oven for about 10–15 minutes, until they are nicely toasted and lightly browned. Allow them to cool and store them in a screwtop glass jar until you are ready to use them.

Sauces, pastes, vinegars and wine

Chinese cookery involves a number of thick and tasty sauces and pastes. They are essential to the taste of Chinese cooking, and it is worth making the effort to obtain them.

BEAN SAUCE, YELLOW BEAN SAUCE, BROWN BEAN SAUCE, BEAN PASTE, SOY BEAN CONDIMENT

This thick, spicy, aromatic sauce is made with yellow beans, flour and salt, fermented together. Correctly blended, it is quite salty but provides a distinctive taste to sauces.

Seasonings made from germinated soy

beans are one of the oldest forms of food flavoring in China. Before 200 BC the ancient Chinese used a form of salted and fermented soy beans, which forms the basis of bean sauce. Modern bean sauce follows the ancient recipe for pickled yellow soy beans in a salty liquid.

There are two forms: whole beans in a thick sauce, and mashed or puréed beans (sold as crushed or yellow bean sauce). Which one is used will depend on the recipe. **Useful hints** *Bean sauce is a good foundation for making a unique sauce: combine it with hoisin sauce and chili bean sauce.*

CHILI SAUCE

Chili sauce is a bright red, hot sauce made from chilies, vinegar, sugar and salt. It is sometimes used for cooking, but it is mainly used as a dipping sauce. If you find it too strong, dilute it with hot water. Do not confuse this sauce with chili bean sauce, which is a much thicker, darker sauce used for cooking.

HOISIN SAUCE

Hoisin sauce is part of the bean sauce family. It is a rich, thick, dark, brownish red sauce made from soy bean paste, garlic, vinegar, sugar, spices and other flavorings. It is at once sweet and spicy. The texture ranges from creamy thick to thin. It is used in China as a condiment and as a glaze for roasted meats. In the West, it is often used as a sauce (mixed with sesame oil) for Beijing (Peking) duck instead of the traditional bean sauce. **Useful hints** *Chee hou sauce is a slightly stronger version of hoisin sauce and can be used as a substitute.*

OYSTER SAUCE

This very popular and versatile southern Chinese sauce is thick, brown and richly flavored. To make it, fresh oysters are boiled in large vats and seasoned with soy sauce, salt and a selection of spices and seasonings. The original version of oyster sauce contained pieces of dried fermented oysters, but these are no longer included. **Useful hints** *Oyster sauce is delicious as a dipping sauce. Dilute it with a little water or oil. It can also be used directly from the bottle over blanched vegetables.*

PLUM SAUCE

Plums have been grown in China since ancient times. The fresh fruits spoil quickly, and in order to capture their juicy richness the Chinese hit upon the idea of preserving them with ginger, chili, spices, vinegar and sugar. It is a popular item in Chinese restaurants, where it is sometimes used wrongly with Beijing (Peking) duck.

RICE VINEGAR

Vinegars are widely used in Chinese cooking. Unlike Western vinegars, they are usually made from rice and grains. There are many varieties, ranging in flavor from the spicy and slightly tart to the sweet and pungent. They should not be confused with Western wine vinegars, which are quite different and much more acidic.

Black rice vinegar

Black rice vinegar is dark in color, with a rich but mild taste and a depth of flavor similar to Italian balsamic vinegar. It is popular in northern China, where it is used for braised dishes, noodles and sauces.

Red rice vinegar

Red rice vinegar is a clear, pale red vinegar. It has a delicate, tart, slightly sweet and salty taste and is usually used as a dipping sauce for seafood or dumplings.

Sweet rice vinegar

This vinegar is a brownish-black color and thicker than plain rice vinegar. It is processed with sugar and star anise, and the result is an aromatic, caramel taste. Unlike other vinegars, it has very little tartness. It is used in large quantities for braised pork dishes.

White rice vinegar

White rice vinegar is clear and mild in flavor. It has a faint taste of glutinous rice and is used for sweet and sour dishes. Western cider vinegar can be substituted.

SESAME PASTE

Chinese sesame paste is quite different from the Mediterranean tahini, which is made from seeds that are still raw when ground, producing a much lighter color and taste. The Chinese use sesame paste either in sauces or as an integral ingredient in both hot and cold dishes.

Useful hints *If the paste has separated in the jar, empty the contents into a blender or food processor and blend or process well. Always stir well before using.*

If you can't find any sesame paste, use a smooth peanut butter instead.

SHAOXING RICE WINE

Shaoxing rice wine is China's most famous wine and has been so for over 2,000 years. It is kept in cellars until it matures, usually for ten years, although some have been aged for as long as 100 years. With its amber color, bouquet and alcohol content, it more resembles sherry than grape wine. The wine is drunk warm or at room temperature. And it is always consumed in the context of a meal.

Useful hints *Do not confuse Shaoxing rice wine with Japanese sake, which is a Japanese version of rice wine and quite different.*

A good-quality, dry, pale sherry can be substituted but cannot equal its rich, mellow taste. Western grape wines are not an adequate substitute.

SHRIMP PASTE (SHRIMP SAUCE)

This is made from pulverized salted shrimps, which are then allowed to ferment. It is available as shrimp paste, the mixture having been dried in the sun and cut into cakes, or as shrimp sauce, which is packed directly into jars in its thick, moist state. Once packed, the light pink shrimp sauce slowly turns a greyish shade, acquiring a pungent taste as it matures. Popular in southern Chinese cooking, this ingredient adds a distinctive flavor and fragrance to dishes.

SOY SAUCE

An ancient seasoning, soy sauce was first used in China more than 3,000 years ago, when it consisted of a thin, salty liquid in which fragments of fermented soy bean floated. It is made from a mixture of soy beans, flour and water, which is then naturally fermented and aged for some months. The distilled liquid becomes soy sauce. There are two main types, light and dark.

Light soy sauce

As the name implies, this is light in color, but it is full of flavor and is the best one to use for cooking. It is known in Chinese markets as Superior Soy and is saltier than dark soy sauce.

Dark soy sauce

This sauce is aged for much longer than light soy sauce, hence its darker, almost black color. It is slightly thicker and stronger than light soy sauce and is more suitable for stews. I prefer it to light soy as a dipping sauce. It is known in Chinese markets as Soy Superior Sauce, and, although used less than light soy, it is important to have some at hand.

Delicacies

BIRD'S NEST

A truly exotic food, bird's nest is one of the most sought-after delicacies of China. It literally is a bird's nest, made from the regurgitated spittle of a certain breed of swallow, the Collocalia from the east Asian tropics: Thailand, Vietnam, Java and the Philippines. It is sold dried and must be soaked before using. The result is a flavorless, soft, crunchy jelly that relies for flavor on a rich sauce or broth and may be served either savory or sweet. Bird's nest is also used in extravagant stuffings.

Useful hints *Soak the bird's nest overnight in cold water. Then simmer it for 20 minutes in plain water. Finally, rinse again in cold water and squeeze dry before proceeding with the recipe.*

DRIED LILY BUDS

Also known as tiger lily buds, golden needles or lily stems, dried lily buds are the unopened flowers of a type of day lily. About 2 in (5cm) in length, they have a slightly furry texture and an earthy fragrance and serve well as an ingredient in muxi (mu shu) dishes, a stir-fried pork dish with cloud ears and hot and sour soup, providing texture as well as additional dimension to dishes.

Before using, soak the buds in hot water for about 20 minutes, or until soft. Cut off the hard ends and shred or cut the buds in half according to the recipe directions.

SHARK'S FIN

I no longer eat or cook shark's fin — sharks are being killed and endangered for their fins and therefore it is no longer a viable part of my Chinese diet. In fact, I have encouraged my Chinese friends not to order or eat it.

Although shark meat has been eaten for a long time, it is the shark fin that is a delicacy in China. Like bird's nest, it is an exotic food and is thus one of the most expensive ingredients in Chinese cooking. It is served as a soup or braised in a rich stock, or even stir-fried. Chinese restaurants sometimes offer a long list of shark's fin dishes. Perhaps more than anything else, it is a symbol of extravagance.

Other sauces

SWEET AND SOUR SAUCE

Unlike some poorly made sweet and sour sauces found in careless and mediocre Chinese restaurants, this one, inspired by several I've had in China, has just the right balance of flavors. You can even use it as a barbecue sauce, as well as for dipping homemade Fried Wontons (page 66) or Spring Rolls (page 67).

½ cup (120ml) Chinese white rice vinegar
salt and white pepper
5 tbsp (75ml) sugar
3½ tbsp (50ml) tomato paste or ketchup
1 tbsp (15ml) light soy sauce
1 tsp (5ml) cornstarch, mixed with 1 tsp (5ml) water

Combine all the ingredients in a small saucepan and simmer for about 5 minutes. Cool the sauce and use.

VINEGAR AND SHREDDED GINGER SAUCE

A delicious and refreshing sauce that is wonderful served with rich meat dumplings such as Shanghai-style Wontons (page 54). The fresh ginger should be shredded as finely as possible for the best results. The bite of the fresh ginger is a wonderful counterpoint to the meat. This sauce can be made up to an hour before you need it.

3½ tbsp (50ml) Chinese black or red rice vinegar
4 tbsp (60ml) finely shredded fresh ginger

Put the vinegar into a small, deep dish and pile the ginger shreds on top. Allow to sit for 5 minutes before serving.

GINGER SAUCE

This simple sauce can be served with Drunken Chicken (page 148) or any other cold meats. If you are a real lover of ginger, it can be used as a dip for anything you wish. It is so easy to make and can be prepared hours in advance.

3 tbsp (45ml) finely chopped fresh ginger
salt
1½ tbsp (22ml) peanut or vegetable oil

Combine the finely chopped fresh ginger and 2 tsp (10ml) of salt in a small dish. Heat the peanut or vegetable oil in a small skillet or wok until it is smoking and pour this over the ginger and salt mixture. Allow to sit for at least 5 minutes before serving.

GINGER AND GREEN ONION SAUCE

This is a childhood favorite of mine that brings back many memories. It's wonderful with Steeped Chicken (page 170) as an alternative to the Cantonese-style sauce suggested on that page.

2 tsp (10ml) finely chopped fresh ginger
3 tbsp (45ml) finely chopped green onions
2 tsp (10ml) light soy sauce
salt and white pepper
1½ tbsp (22ml) peanut or vegetable oil

Combine the finely chopped fresh ginger, finely chopped green onions and soy sauce in a small dipping sauce dish. Season with ½ tsp (2ml) of salt and a little white pepper to taste. Heat the oil in a small skillet or wok until it is smoking, then pour it over the mixture. Serve the sauce at once to make the most of the fresh flavors.

CHILI BEAN SAUCE

This is a perfect sauce for lovers of chili who want to add an extra spicy note to foods such as dumplings, or to any meat or vegetable dish.

2 tbsp (30ml) chili bean sauce
2 tbsp (30ml) finely chopped green onions
1 tbsp (15ml) peanut or vegetable oil
1 tsp (5ml) sesame oil

Mix the chili bean sauce and green onions in a small dish. Heat the peanut oil and sesame oil together in a small saucepan until almost smoking. Pour the hot oil over the chili mixture. Allow to sit for 5 minutes before serving.

ENGLISH MUSTARD SAUCE

A very English mustard sauce, this has nevertheless become quite popular in southern China and especially in Hong Kong, having been brought there by the British over 100 years ago. It is easy to make. Using hot water makes the sauce hotter. The thin film of oil prevents it from crusting and helps to keep it smooth. Use it with Spring Rolls (page 67) or as a delightfully different dipping sauce to add a fiery note to any dumpling recipe.

2 tbsp (30ml) dry yellow English mustard powder
2 tbsp (30ml) hot water
2 tsp (10ml) peanut or vegetable oil

Put the mustard into a small mixing bowl and gradually stir in the hot water until it is thoroughly mixed, without any lumps. Allow the sauce to sit for around 2 minutes, then pour the oil over the surface to cover. The sauce is now ready to serve.

SOY, GREEN ONION AND FRESH CHILI DIPPING SAUCE

You will frequently find this very popular sauce served with seafood.

1 fresh mild red chili, seeded and finely shredded
3 tbsp (45ml) finely shredded green onions
2 tbsp (30ml) light soy sauce
1 tbsp (15ml) dark soy sauce
1½ tbsp (22ml) peanut oil

Combine the chili, green onions and soy sauce in a dish. Heat the oil in a small saucepan until it is almost smoking and pour this over the chili mixture. Allow the sauce to sit for 10 minutes before serving.

GARLIC AND VINEGAR DIPPING SAUCE

The zesty bite of the raw garlic is mellowed by the vinegar in this dipping sauce.

1 tbsp (15ml) finely chopped garlic
3 tbsp (45ml) Chinese white rice vinegar

Combine the garlic and vinegar in a small dish and allow to sit for at least 10 minutes before using.

SALT AND PEPPER DIP

This dip is a favorite condiment found often on Chinese tables.

2 tbsp (30ml) roasted Sichuan peppercorns, finely ground and sieved (page 29)
3 tbsp (45ml) salt

Heat a wok or large skillet until it is hot and add the peppercorns and salt. Stir-fry for 1 minute, then remove and allow to cool. Put it into a blender for 1 minute.

EQUIPMENT

Traditional Chinese cooking equipment is not essential for the preparation of Chinese food, but there are some tools that will make it very much easier. Moreover, there is an advantage in using classic implements that have been tried and tested over many centuries.

WOK

All your faith in Chinese cookery and your own skills will come to nothing without a good wok. A most useful and versatile piece of equipment, the wok may be used for stir-frying, blanching, deep-frying and steaming foods. Its shape, with deep sides and either a tapered or a slightly flattened but still round bottom, allows for fuel-efficient, quick and even heating and cooking. In the stir-frying technique, the deep sides prevent the food and oils from spilling over; in deep-frying, much less oil is required because of the shaped concentration of the heat and ingredients at the wok's base.

There are two basic wok types: the traditional Cantonese version, with short rounded handles on either side of the edge or lip of the wok, and the pau wok, which has one long handle between 12–14 in (30–35cm) long. The two-handled model is easier to move when it is full of liquid. It is thus best for steaming and deep-frying because it is easier to hold over the heat with one hand while your free hand is stirring the foods with a long spoon or spatula. The long handle also keeps you more safely distanced from the possibility of splashing hot oils or water.

The round-bottomed wok may be used only on a gas stove. However, woks are now available with flatter bottoms, designed especially for electric stoves. Although this shape really defeats the purpose of the traditional design, which is to concentrate intense heat at the center, it does have the advantage over the ordinary skillet in that it has deeper sides.

CHOOSING A WOK

Choose a large wok — preferably one that's around 12–14 in (30–35cm) in diameter, with deep sides. A heavier wok, preferably made of carbon steel, is superior to the lighter stainless steel or aluminium type, which cannot take very high heat and tend to scorch both themselves and the food. However, there are also excellent non-stick woks on the market now that perform perfectly well.

Seasoning a wok

All woks (except non-stick ones) need to be seasoned. Many also need to be scrubbed first. This is the only time you will ever scrub your wok. Scrub it with a cream cleanser and water to remove as much of the machine oil as possible. Then rinse it, dry it and put it on the stove on low heat. Add 2 tbsp (30ml) of cooking oil and, using paper towels, rub it over the inside of the wok. Heat the wok slowly for about 10–15 minutes, then wipe it thoroughly with more kitchen paper. The paper will become blackened. Repeat this process of coating, heating and wiping until the paper towels remain clean. Your wok will darken and become well seasoned with use, which is a good sign.

Cleaning a wok

Once your wok has been seasoned, it should never be scrubbed with soap and water. Plain clear water is all that is needed. The wok should be thoroughly dried after each use. If it does rust a bit, it must be scrubbed with a cream cleanser and reseasoned.

WOK ACCESSORIES

Wok stand

This is a metal ring or frame designed to keep a conventionally shaped wok steady on the stove, and it is essential if you want to use your wok for steaming, deep-frying or braising. Stands come in two designs. One is a solid metal ring punched with about six ventilation holes. The other is like a circular, thin, wire frame. If you have a gas stove, use only the latter type, as the more solid design does not allow for sufficient ventilation and may lead to a buildup of gas.

Rack

When steaming foods in your wok, you will need a wooden or metal rack or trivet to raise the food above the water level. Wok sets usually include a rack, but any rack that keeps the food above the water so that it is steamed and not boiled will suffice.

DEEP-FAT FRYER

This is very useful, and you may find it safer and easier to use for deep-frying than a wok. The quantities of oil given in the recipes are based on the amount required for deep-frying in a wok. If you are using a deep-fat fryer instead, you will need about double that amount, but never fill it more than half-full with oil.

CLEAVER

To Chinese cooks the cleaver is an all-purpose cutting instrument that makes all other knives unnecessary. Once you gain competence with a cleaver, you will see how it can be used on all types of food, to slice, dice, chop, fillet, shred, crush or whatever. Of course, you may use your own familiar kitchen knives, but if you decide to invest in a cleaver, choose a good-quality stainless steel model and keep it sharpened.

STEAMER

Steaming is a method well worth learning. In China, bamboo steamers have been in use for thousands of years. They come in several sizes, of which the 10 in (25cm) one is the most suitable for home use. The food is placed in the steamer, and that in turn is placed above boiling water in a wok or saucepan. To prevent the food sticking to the steamer as it cooks, clean, damp cheesecloth may be used underneath the food itself. A tight-fitting bamboo lid prevents the steam escaping.

CLAY OR SAND POTS

For braised dishes, soups and rice cooking, the Chinese rely on lightweight clay pots, whose design allows for the infusion of aromas and tastes into foods. Their unglazed exteriors have a sandy texture, hence their alternative name. They are to be used directly on the stove, but you should never put an empty sand pot onto a heated element or place a hot sand pot on a cold surface: the shock will crack it. Clay pots should always have at least some liquid in them, and when filled with food, they can take very high heat. If you have an electric stove, use a heatproof pad to insulate the pot from direct heat.

TECHNIQUES

Chinese cooks through the ages have relied not only on ingredients but also on cutting and cooking techniques to achieve the special taste and texture that are the hallmarks of good Chinese food. It is a multi-step process that may involve cutting meat or vegetables at a certain angle, in pieces or shreds, sometimes marinating, then heating the wok first, adding the oil, removing the food after the first few minutes of contact with the oil and allowing it to rest while completing the rest of the dish. It may sound complicated but it really isn't. It takes a bit of practice, but once mastered, these easy steps will be a part of the way you cook Chinese. These steps or techniques are a vital component of Chinese cookery. Think of them as a different way of preparing and cooking food that has been handed down to us over thousands of years. Don't be afraid to try these techniques: you will master them in no time at all!

CUTTING TECHNIQUES

Slicing

This is the conventional method of slicing food. Hold the food firmly on the chopping board with one hand and cut it straight downwards into very thin slices. Meat is always sliced across the grain to break up the fibers and make it more tender when it is cooked. If you use a cleaver rather than a knife for this, hold the cleaver with your index finger over the far side of the top of the cleaver and your thumb on the side nearest you to guide the cutting edge firmly. Hold the food with your other hand, turning your fingers under for safety. Your knuckles should act as a guide for the blade.

Horizontal or flat slicing

This is a technique for splitting food into two thinner pieces while retaining its overall shape, as in slicing kidneys. Hold the blade of the cleaver or knife parallel to the chopping board. Place your free hand on top of the piece of food to keep it steady. Using a gentle cutting motion, slice sideways into the food.

Depending on the recipe you may need to repeat this process, cutting the two halves into even thinner flat pieces.

Diagonal slicing

This technique is used for cutting vegetables such as asparagus, carrots or green onions. The purpose is to expose more of the surface of the vegetable for quicker cooking. Angle the knife or cleaver at a slant and cut evenly.

Roll cutting

This is rather like diagonal slicing but is used for larger vegetables such as zucchinis, large carrots and eggplants. As with diagonal slicing, this technique allows more of the surface of the vegetable to be exposed to the heat during cooking. Begin by making a diagonal slice at one end of the vegetable. Then turn it 180° and make the next diagonal slice. Continue in this way until you have chopped the entire vegetable into evenly sized, diamond-shaped chunks.

Shredding

This is a process like the French julienne technique, by which food is cut into thin, fine, matchstick-like shreds. First cut the food into slices and then pile several slices on top of each other and cut them lengthwise into fine strips. Some foods, particularly meat and chicken breasts, are easier to shred if they are first stiffened slightly in the freezer for about 20 minutes.

Dicing

This is a simple technique for cutting food into small cubes or dice. The food should first be cut into slices. Stack the slices and cut them again lengthwise into sticks. Then stack the strips or sticks and cut them crosswise into evenly sized cubes or dice.

Mincing

This is a fine-chopping technique. Chefs use two cleavers to mince, rapidly chopping with them in unison for fast results. One cleaver or knife is easier for the less experienced! First slice the food and then, using a sharp knife or cleaver, rapidly chop the food until it is rather spread out over the chopping board. Scrape it into a pile and chop again, and continue chopping until the food reaches the desired state. You may find it easier to hold the knife or cleaver by the top of the blade (rather than by the handle) with two hands. A food processor may also be used for this, but be careful not to overmince the food.

OTHER PREPARATION TECHNIQUES

Marinating

Steeping raw meat or poultry for a time in a liquid such as soy sauce, rice wine or sherry and cornstarch improves its flavor and tenderizes it. The marinating time is usually at least 20 minutes, in order to infuse the meat or poultry properly with the flavors of the marinade.

Thickening

Cornstarch blended with an equal quantity of water is frequently used in Chinese cookery to thicken sauces and glaze dishes. Always make sure the mixture is smooth and well blended before adding it.

Velveting

Velveting is used to prevent delicate foods like chicken breasts from overcooking. The food is coated with a mixture of unbeaten egg white, cornstarch and sometimes salt. It is then put into the fridge for about 20–30 minutes to ensure that the coating adheres to the food. The velvet cornstarch cloak protects the flavor and texture of the food when it is cooked in hot oil or water.

COOKING TECHNIQUES

Blanching

Putting food into hot water or into moderately hot oil for a few minutes will cook it briefly but not entirely. It is a sort of softening-up process to prepare the food for a final cooking. Chicken is often blanched in oil or water after being velveted. Meat is sometimes blanched to rid it of unwanted gristle and fat and in order to ensure a clean taste and appearance. Blanching in water is common with hard vegetables such as broccoli and carrots. The vegetable is plunged into boiling water for several minutes. It is then drained and plunged into cold water to arrest the cooking process. In such cases blanching usually precedes stir-frying to finish the cooking. You must always avoid overcooking your foods at the blanching stage.

Poaching

This is a method of simmering food gently until it is partially cooked. It is then put into soup or combined with a sauce and the cooking process is continued. Delicately flavored and textured foods such as eggs and chicken are often simmered.

Stir-frying

This is the most famous of all Chinese cooking techniques and it is possibly the trickiest to master, since success with it depends on having all the required ingredients prepared, measured out and immediately at hand, and on having a good source of fierce heat. Its advantage is that, properly executed, stir-fried foods can be cooked in minutes in very little oil, so they retain their natural flavors and textures. It is very important that stir-fried foods are not overcooked or made greasy.

Having prepared all the ingredients for stir-frying, here are the next steps:

Heat the wok or skillet until it is very hot before adding the oil. This prevents food sticking and will ensure an even heat. Peanut oil is my favorite precisely because it can take this heat without burning.

Add the oil and, using a metal spatula or long-handled spoon, distribute it evenly over the surface. It should be very hot indeed — almost smoking — before you add the next ingredient, unless you are going on to flavor the oil.

If you are flavoring the oil with garlic, green onions, ginger, dried red chilies or salt, do not wait for the oil to get so hot that it is almost smoking. If you do, these ingredients will very quickly burn and become bitter. Toss them in the oil for a few seconds. In some recipes these flavorings will be removed and discarded before cooking proceeds.

Now add the ingredients as described in the recipe and proceed to stir-fry by tossing them over the surface of the wok or skillet with the metal spatula or long-handled spoon. If you are stir-frying meat, let each side rest for just a few seconds before continuing to stir. Keep moving the food from the center of the wok to the sides.

Some stir-fried dishes are thickened with a mixture of cornstarch and cold water. To avoid getting a lumpy sauce when attempting this, be sure to remove the wok or skillet from the heat for a minute before you add the cornstarch mixture, which must be thoroughly blended before it is added. The sauce can then be returned to the heat and thickened.

Deep-frying

This is one of the most important techniques in Chinese cooking. The trick is to regulate the heat so that the surface of the food is sealed but does not brown so fast that the food is uncooked inside. Although deep-fried food must not be greasy, the process does require a lot of oil. The Chinese use a wok for deep-frying, which requires rather less oil than the more stable deep-fat fryer, but you should avoid using the wok unless you are very sure of it. If you do, be certain that it is fully secure on its stand and on no account leave the wok unsupervised.

Here are some points to bear in mind when deep-frying:

Wait for the oil to get hot enough before adding the food. The oil should give off a haze and almost produce little wisps of smoke when it is the right temperature, but you can test it by dropping in a small piece of food. If it bubbles all over, the oil is sufficiently hot. Adjust the heat as necessary to prevent the oil from actually smoking or overheating.

To prevent splattering, use paper towels to thoroughly dry the food that is going to be deep-fried. If the food is in a marinade, remove it with a slotted spoon and let it drain before putting it into the oil. If you are using batter, make sure all the excess batter drips off before adding the food to the hot oil.

Oil used for deep-frying can be reused. Cool it, then strain it into a jar through several layers of cheesecloth or through a fine mesh to remove any particles of food that might otherwise burn if reheated and give the oil a bitter taste. Label the jar according to what food you have cooked in the oil and reuse it only for the same thing. Oil can be used up to two times before it begins to lose its effectiveness.

Shallow-frying
This technique is similar to sautéing. It involves more oil than stir-frying but less than deep-frying. Food is fried first on one side and then on the other. Sometimes the excess oil is then drained off and a sauce is added to complete the dish. A skillet is ideal for shallow-frying.

Slow-simmering and steeping
These processes are similar. In slow-simmering, food is immersed in liquid that is brought almost to a boil, and then the temperature is reduced so that it simmers, cooking the food to the desired degree. This is the technique used for making stock. In steeping, food is similarly immersed in liquid (usually stock) and simmered for a time. The heat is then turned off and the remaining heat of the liquid finishes off the cooking processes.

Braising and red-braising
This technique is most often applied to tougher cuts of meat and certain vegetables. The food is usually browned and then put into stock that has been flavored with seasonings and spices. Red-braising is simply the technique by which food is braised in a dark liquid such as soy sauce. This gives food a reddish-brown color, hence the name of the method. This type of braising sauce can be saved and frozen for reuse. It can be reused many times and becomes richer in flavor each time.

Steaming
Steamed foods are cooked by a gentle, moist heat, which must circulate freely in order to cook the food. It is an excellent method for bringing out subtle flavors, and is therefore particularly appropriate for fish. The Chinese use bamboo steamers, but you could use any one of several utensils, as follows:

Using a bamboo steamer in a wok:
For this you need a large bamboo steamer about 10 in (25cm) wide. Put about 2 in (5cm) of water into the wok and bring it to a simmer. Put the bamboo steamer containing the food into the wok, where it should rest safely perched on the sloping sides. Cover the steamer with its lid and steam the food until it is cooked. Replenish the water as required.

Using a wok as a steamer:
Put about 2 in (5cm) of water into the wok, then put in a metal or wooden rack and bring the water to a simmer. Put the food to be steamed on a plate. Lower the plate onto the rack and cover the wok tightly with a wok lid. Replenish the water as necessary, though it should never make contact with the food.

Using a roasting pan or pot as a steamer:
Put a metal or wooden rack into the pan or pot, then pour in about 2 in (5cm) of water and bring it to a simmer. Put the food to be steamed on a plate. Lower the plate onto the rack and cover the pan or pot with a lid or with foil. Replenish the water as necessary during the cooking time.

Using a metal steamer:
If you have a metal steamer wide enough to take a plate of food, this will give you very satisfactory results. Make sure of the level of the water in the base: it must not all evaporate, nor should it be so high as to touch the food.

Roasting

In China roasting is done only in commercial establishments, since most homes do not have ovens. The Chinese roast food in large, metal, drum-shaped ovens that stand about 5 ft (1.5m) high and are fueled by charcoal. The food is hung on hooks inside the oven. The idea is to expose all the surface area of the food to the heat to give it a crisp outer coating and a moist interior. You can replicate the Chinese method by putting food on a rack in a roasting pan so that the hot air of the oven can circulate around it.

Barbecuing

This is a variation on roasting and is not very common in Chinese cookery. Marinated meat is placed over a charcoal fire and the meat is constantly basted to keep it moist. Today modern broilers and outdoor barbecues produce much the same result.

Twice-cooking

As the name implies, this is a two-step process involving two quite different techniques, such as simmering and stir-frying. It is used to change the texture of food, to infuse it with flavor and to render foods that are difficult to cook into a more manageable state.

Reheating foods

Steaming is one of the best methods of reheating food, since it warms it without cooking it further and without drying it out. To reheat soups and braised dishes, bring the liquid slowly to a simmer but do not boil. Remove it from the heat as soon as it is hot to prevent overcooking.

GARNISHES

The Chinese pay much attention to the presentation of their cuisine. We like to decorate dishes with various kinds of garnish, ranging from the simple green onion brush to the more elaborate tomato rose. Here are some instructions for making simple, attractive garnishes:

Green onion brushes

1. Cut off and discard the green part of the green onion and trim off the base of the bulb. You should be left with a 3 in (7.5cm) white segment.
2. Make a lengthwise cut about 1 in (2.5cm) long at one end of the green onion. Roll the spring onion 90° and cut again. Repeat this process at the other end.
3. Soak the green onions in iced water and they will curl into flower brushes. Spin or pat them dry before use.

Radish roses

1. Remove any leaves, then trim the top and the root end of the radish.
2. Make thick, rounded cuts to form petals.
3. Soak the radishes in iced water for about an hour.

Carrot flowers

1. Peel the carrots and cut them into 3 in (7.5cm) chunks.
2. Cut a V-shaped slice down the length of each chunk. Repeat, making 3–4 more lengthwise cuts around each.
3. Now slice the carrots crosswise to form thin flower shapes. Soak them in cold water until required.

Fresh chili flowers

1. Trim the tip of the chili but do not remove the stem.
2. Make 4 cuts lengthwise from the stem of the chili to the tip to form 4 sections. Remove and discard any seeds.
3. Soak the chilies in cold water. They will "flower" in the water.

Tomato roses

1. Select firm tomatoes and, using a very sharp knife, peel off the skin from the top in one piece, as though you were peeling an apple. Do not break the strip.
2. Roll the strip of tomato skin into a tight coil.
3. Turn the coil over and you should have a tomato rose.

Cucumber fans

1. Using a sharp knife, cut the rounded end off half a cucumber. Then cut in half lengthwise.
2. Turn each cucumber piece so that the skin side is uppermost. Make a horizontal slice to reduce the thickness of each cucumber piece so that you end up with a slice that is mainly skin with just a little flesh.
3. Now make parallel cuts down the length of the slice. The cuts will have to curve slightly so that you will be able to splay the slices out like a fan.
4. Starting with the second slice of the fan, bend every alternative slice back toward the base, tucking them in so that they stay securely folded in place.
5. Keep the cucumber fans in cold water until you are ready to use them.

MENUS AND HOW TO EAT CHINESE FOOD

Traditionally, Chinese meals consist of a soup; a rice, noodle or bread dish; a vegetable dish and at least two other dishes that may be mainly meat, fish or chicken. The meal may be preceded and concluded with tea, but during the meal itself soup — really a broth — will be the only beverage that is served. That is, soup is drunk not as a first course as in the West but throughout the meal. The exception to this is a banquet, when soup, if served at all, usually comes at the end of the meal or as a palate-cleanser during the dinner.

When you do devise an all-Chinese meal, try to have a good mix of textures, flavors, colours and shapes. Apart from a staple dish, such as steamed rice, you should opt for a variety of meat, poultry and fish. It's important to try to select one or two things that can be prepared in advance.

TABLE SETTING

You don't need special crockery or cutlery for serving Chinese food, although I think it tastes decidedly better when it is eaten with chopsticks. Each person will need a rice bowl, a soup bowl, a teacup and a small plate for any bones and such. A small dish or saucer each will also be needed to serve dipping sauces.

WHAT TO DRINK

If you want to be authentic, serve an appropriate soup with your Chinese meal. If you prefer, you could serve Chinese tea without milk and sugar. There are three different types of Chinese tea. Green or unfermented tea is made from green leaves that, when infused, result in a refreshing astringent taste. Black tea is made from fermented black leaves and is red when infused. It has a hearty, robust flavor. Oolong tea is made from partially fermented leaves and is strong and dark. I think green jasmine tea is the nicest with food.

Chinese wines are usually made from fermented rice, the most famous being Shaoxing, also used for cooking. It has a very different flavor from wine made from grapes and is rather an acquired taste. Many Western wines go very well with Chinese food, particularly dry whites and light reds.

MENUS AND SERVINGS

Although most Chinese meals consist of at least three dishes, plus rice and soup, I recommend that you concentrate on achieving success with relatively few dishes until you become more familiar with Chinese cooking techniques and with the recipes.

Chinese cooking can be very time-consuming. The recipes in this book are based on the expectation that you will cook two meat, chicken or fish dishes per meal. (This is in addition to a vegetable dish, rice or noodles and, probably, a soup.) Once you gain confidence you will be able to cope with preparing more dishes and be able to serve a more authentic Chinese meal.

Suggested menus

Here are some suggestions for a variety of well-balanced and delicious menus:

EVERYDAY FAMILY MEALS

SERVES 4
Tomato Eggflower Soup (page 92)
Steamed Fish Cantonese Style (page 220)
Stir-fried Beef with Orange (page 126)
Lettuce with Oyster Sauce (page 270)
Steamed Rice (page 288)

Kidney and Beancurd Soup (page 85)
Stir-fried Ground Pork (page 108)
Cold Marinated Bean Sprouts (page 280)
Stir-fried Ginger Broccoli (page 259)
Steamed Rice (page 288)

Fried Wontons (page 66)
Beef Soup with Cilantro (page 95)
Stir-fried Cucumbers with Hot Spices (page 260)
Peaches in Honey Syrup (page 339)

Curried Corn Soup with Chicken (page 76)
Five-spice Spareribs (page 103)
Fried Fish with Ginger (page 212)
Cold Spicy Noodles (page 313)
Stir-fried Chinese Greens (page 245)

SUMMER DINNER PARTIES

SERVES 6
Sesame Shrimp Toast (page 62)
Ban Doufu (page 60)
Stir-fried Pork with Green Onions (page 110)
Stir-fried Spinach with Garlic (page 247)
Steamed Rice (page 288)
Fruit Compote (page 339)

SERVES 4
Cold Spicy Noodles (page 313)
Chicken in Black Bean Sauce (page 162)
Stir-fried Scallops with Pig's Kidneys (page 236)
Cold Sweet and Sour Chinese Leaves (page 277)
Steamed Pears (page 340)

WINTER DINNER PARTIES

SERVES 4
Hot and Sour Soup (page 82)
Sichuan Shrimp in Chili Sauce (page 224)
Five-spice Red Braised Pigeons (page 186)
Braised Cauliflower with Oyster Sauce (page 251)
Steamed Rice (page 288)

SERVES 4–6
Wonton Soup (page 90)
Curried Chicken with Bell Peppers (page 149)
Beijing (Peking) Braised Lamb (page 134)
Braised Spicy Eggplants (page 263)
Steamed Rice (page 288)
Shrimp Crackers (page 63)
Mongolian Hot Pot (page 136)
Stir-fried Pork with Green Onions (page 110)

SPECIAL DINNER OR BANQUET

This menu should be attempted when you feel reasonably competent at Chinese cooking.

SERVES 6–8
Caramelized Walnuts (page 64)
Corn Soup with Crabmeat (page 91)
Rainbow Beef in Lettuce Cups (page 124) or Beijing (Peking) Duck (page 182) with Chinese Pancakes (page 324)
Eggplant with Sesame Sauce (page 272)
Braised Pork with Beancurd (page 118)
Toffee Apples and Bananas (page 342)

APPETIZERS

The popularity of Chinese appetizers has rocketed in recent years with the international growth of dim sum. It's not hard to see why — hot, sour, sweet or spicy, you can find here the perfect appetizer for any meal.

Beijing (Peking) Dumplings — Guotie and Jiaozi

This is a popular and rather substantial snack from northern China. The dumplings can be shallow-fried (guotie), boiled (jiaozi) or steamed, but I find shallow-frying to be the tastiest way of cooking them. They can be frozen, uncooked — you don't need to thaw before cooking, but you will need to cook them for a little longer.

MAKES ABOUT 18

FOR THE DOUGH

2¼ cups (560ml) all-purpose
 flour
1 cup (250ml) very hot water

FOR THE FILLING

8oz (225g) ground fatty pork
6oz (175g) Chinese leaves,
 finely chopped
2 tsp (10ml) finely chopped
 fresh ginger
1 tbsp (15ml) Shaoxing rice
 wine or dry sherry
1 tbsp (15ml) dark soy sauce
1 tsp (5ml) light soy sauce
3 tbsp (45ml) finely chopped
 green onions
2 tsp (10ml) sesame oil
1 tsp (5ml) sugar
2 tbsp (30ml) cold Chicken
 Stock (page 75) or water
salt and black pepper

FOR COOKING

1–2 tbsp (15–30ml) peanut oil
⅔ cup (150ml) water

TO SERVE

Chinese white rice vinegar
Chili Oil (page 23)
light soy sauce

First make the dough. Put the flour into a large bowl and stir in the hot water gradually, mixing with a fork or with chopsticks until most of the water is incorporated. Add more water if the mixture seems dry. Then remove the mixture from the bowl and knead for about 8 minutes until smooth, dusting the dough with a little flour if it is sticky. Put the dough back into the bowl, cover it with a damp towel and let it rest.

Meanwhile, combine the filling ingredients in a large bowl, add 1 tsp (5ml) of salt and ½ tsp (2ml) of pepper, and mix.

After around 20 minutes, take the dough out of the bowl and knead it again for about 5 minutes. Form it into a roll about 9 in (23cm) long and about 1 in (2.5cm) in diameter. Cut the roll into about 18 equal segments.

Roll each dough segment into a small ball. Then roll each ball into a small, round, flat "pancake" about 2½ in (6cm) in diameter. Arrange them on a lightly floured baking sheet and cover with a damp tea towel until you are ready to use them.

Put about 2 tsp (10ml) of filling into the center of each "pancake" and fold in half. Moisten the edges with water and pinch together with your fingers. Pleat around the edge, pinching to seal well. (The dumpling should look like a small turnover, with a flat base and a rounded top.) Transfer the finished dumpling to the floured sheet and keep it covered.

Heat a large skillet (preferably non-stick) until hot. Add 1 tbsp (15ml) of oil followed by the dumplings, flat side down. Turn down the heat and cook for about 2 minutes, until they are lightly browned. (You may need to cook in two batches.) Add the water (half at a time if you've got two batches), then cover and cook for about 12 minutes, or until most of the liquid is absorbed. Cook, uncovered, for a further 2 minutes, then remove. Serve with 3 bowls, containing the Chinese white rice vinegar, Chili Oil (page 23) and light soy sauce, to dip.

Steamed Open Dumplings

This is a favorite snack in many dim sum teahouses throughout southern China. It is a wonton or egg dough dumpling that is filled and steamed instead of being poached and deep-fried. Steamed dumplings have a character wholly different from pan-fried or boiled dumplings. The texture and taste of the steamed dumpling filling is more pronounced, yet delicate and subtle at the same time. The skin, once steamed, retains a slightly chewy texture. This dish can be made ahead of time and reheated by steaming when you are ready to serve it.

MAKES ABOUT 40

1 packet of wonton skins (about 40 skins)

FOR THE FILLING

4 oz (100g) water chestnuts, fresh or canned

4 oz (100g) uncooked shrimp, peeled

12 oz (350g) ground fatty pork

2 tbsp (30ml) finely chopped Parma ham or lean smoked bacon

1 tbsp (15ml) light soy sauce

1 tsp (5ml) dark soy sauce

1 tbsp (15ml) Shaoxing rice wine or dry sherry

3 tbsp (45ml) finely chopped green onions

2 tsp (10ml) finely chopped fresh ginger

2 tsp (10ml) sesame oil

1 egg white, beaten

2 tsp (10ml) sugar

salt and black pepper

Start by preparing the filling. If you are using fresh water chestnuts, peel and chop them finely. If you are using canned water chestnuts, first rinse them well in cold water. Drain in a colander and then chop them finely. If you are using large uncooked shrimp, cut them down the back and remove the fine digestive cord. Coarsely chop the shrimp. Put the water chestnuts and shrimp into a bowl with the rest of the filling ingredients. Add 1 tsp (5ml) of salt and a little black pepper to taste, and mix very well.

Place a portion of filling on each wonton skin. Bring up the sides and press them around the filling mixture. Tap the dumpling on the bottom to make a flat base. The top should be wide open, exposing the filling.

Set up a steamer or put a rack inside a wok or large, deep saucepan. Pour in about 2 in (5cm) of water and bring it to a boil. Put the dumplings on a plate and lower it into the steamer or onto the rack.

Cover the pan tightly, turn the heat to low and steam gently for about 20 minutes. (You may have to do this in several batches.) Serve the dumplings hot with your choice of dipping sauce (see pages 36–37). Keep the first batch warm by covering them with foil and placing them in a warm but switched-off oven until all the dumplings are ready to serve.

Sichuan Dumplings in Spicy Sauce

Sichuan's robust recipes are famous in terms of taste, texture, color and aroma. Here the dumplings are lighter because of the addition of egg whites, and the sharp spices have been partially replaced by less aggressive but still savory seasonings. You will find that these dumplings are a sparkling opener for any meal; alternatively, they make a light lunch in themselves.

Wonton skins can be bought fresh or frozen from Chinese grocers and supermarkets. Be sure to thaw them thoroughly if they are frozen.

MAKES ABOUT 25–30

8 oz (225g) wonton skins
FOR THE FILLING
1 oz (25g) Chinese dried black
  mushrooms
1 lb (450g) ground fatty pork
4 tbsp (60ml) chopped green
  onions or Chinese chives
1 egg white
1 tbsp (15ml) cornstarch
2 tsp (10ml) sesame oil
salt and black pepper
FOR THE SAUCE
1 tbsp (15ml) peanut oil
2 tsp (10ml) Chili Oil (page 23)
1 tbsp (15ml) finely chopped
  garlic
2 tbsp (30ml) finely chopped
  green onions
2 tsp (10ml) roasted and ground
  Sichuan peppercorns
  (page 29)
3 tbsp (45ml) sesame paste
2 tbsp (30ml) dark soy sauce
1 tbsp (15ml) sugar
2 tsp (10ml) chili bean purée
⅓ cup (75ml) Chicken Stock
  (page 75)

Soak the mushrooms in a bowl of warm water for about 20 minutes, or until they are soft and pliable. Squeeze out the excess water and cut off and discard the woody stems. Finely chop the mushrooms and combine them with the rest of the filling ingredients. Add 2 tsp (10ml) of salt and a little black pepper to taste, and mix well.

Place 1 rounded tsp (5ml) of filling in the center of the first wonton skin. Gather the 4 sides up over the filling, allowing it to fold in pleats naturally. Gently pinch the wonton skin together just at the top of the filling to seal. Continue until you have used up all the stuffing.

Heat a wok or large skillet until hot and add the peanut and chili oils. Add the garlic and green onions and stir-fry for 20 seconds, then add the rest of the sauce ingredients and simmer for 5 minutes. Remove to a bowl.

Bring a medium-sized saucepan of water to a boil and poach the dumplings for about 3 minutes, or until they float to the top. Remove, drain and serve with the spicy sauce.

Shanghai-style Wontons

This Shanghai-style wonton dish was inspired by a light, flavorful soup I enjoyed at the trendy Joyce Café in Hong Kong. The menu features a mixture of Eastern and Western influences and includes many vegetarian offerings. I found this one particularly delightful to the eye as well as to the palate. The wontons are filled with chopped fresh bok choy mixed with spicy preserved vegetables, and they are served floating in a fragrant soup.

Wonton skins can be obtained from Chinese grocers and supermarkets. They are yellowish in color, square, and are packaged in small stacks. They can be bought fresh or frozen, but be sure to thaw them thoroughly if they are frozen. Do not be intimidated by the stuffing process: you will soon be a master at it.

SERVES 4–6

8 oz (225g) wonton skins
5 cups (1.2L) Chicken Stock
   (page 75)
1 tbsp (15ml) light soy sauce
1 tsp (5ml) sesame oil
FOR THE FILLING
12 oz (350g) bok choy, coarsely
   chopped
2 oz (50g) Sichuan preserved
   vegetables, rinsed and finely
   chopped
2 tsp (10ml) light soy sauce
2 tbsp (30ml) finely chopped
   green onions
1 tbsp (15ml) Shaoxing rice
   wine or dry sherry
1 tsp (5ml) sugar
2 tsp (10ml) sesame oil
salt and white pepper
FOR THE GARNISH
chopped green onions

Blanch the bok choy in a saucepan of boiling water, then drain, squeezing out the excess liquid. Add all the other filling ingredients, add ½ tsp (2ml) of salt and some white pepper to taste, and mix well.

When you are ready to stuff the wontons, put 1 tbsp (15ml) of the filling in the center of the first wonton skin. Dampen the edges with a little water and bring up the sides of the skin around the filling. Pinch the edges together at the top so that the wonton is sealed; it should look like a small, filled bag. Continue until you have used up all the stuffing.

When the wontons are ready, bring the stock, soy sauce and sesame oil to a simmer in a large saucepan. In another large saucepan, bring salted water to a boil and poach the wontons for 1 minute, or until they float to the top. Remove them immediately and transfer them to the saucepan with the stock. (This procedure will result in a cleaner-tasting broth.) Continue to simmer them in the stock for 2 minutes.

Transfer the soup and wontons either to a large soup bowl or to individual bowls. Garnish with the green onions and serve immediately.

Vegetarian Dumplings

Dumplings in any form are universally popular in China. Dumplings in general may be shallow-fried, boiled, poached or steamed. One very popular way to make them is to simply poach them in hot water or broth and then dip them into a sauce that you concoct yourself, using Chili Oil, dark soy sauce and Chinese white rice vinegar.

MAKES 35–40

8 oz (225g) wonton skins

5 cups (1.2L) water

FOR THE FILLING

1 tbsp (15ml) peanut or
vegetable oil

2 tbsp (30ml) finely chopped
garlic

8 oz (225g) bok choy, finely
chopped

8 oz (225g) Chinese leaves,
finely chopped

4 oz (100g) fresh or frozen peas

1 oz (25g) Sichuan preserved
vegetables, rinsed and finely
chopped

2 tbsp (30ml) Shaoxing rice
wine or dry sherry

1 tbsp (15ml) dark soy sauce

2 tsp (10ml) sugar

1 tsp (5ml) sesame oil

salt and black pepper

2 tbsp (30ml) finely chopped
green onions

TO SERVE

Chinese white rice vinegar

Chili Oil (page 23)

dark soy sauce

chopped green onions

Heat a wok over high heat until it is hot, then add the oil. When it is hot and slightly smoking, add the garlic and stir-fry for 20 seconds. Then add the bok choy, Chinese leaves, peas and preserved vegetables and continue to stir-fry for 1 minute. Add the rice wine, soy sauce, sugar, sesame oil, 1 tsp (5ml) of salt and some pepper to taste, stir-fry for 3 minutes, then add the green onions. Cook for 3 more minutes, until most of the liquid has evaporated. Put the mixture into a bowl and allow it to cool thoroughly.

Put about 1 tbsp (15ml) of filling in the center of each wonton skin and fold in half. Moisten the edges with water and pinch together with your fingers. Pleat around the edge, pinching to seal well. Transfer the finished dumplings to a floured baking sheet and keep it covered with a damp tea towel until you have filled all the dumplings in this way.

Bring the water to a simmer in a large saucepan and poach the dumplings for 1 minute, or until they float to the top. Continue to simmer them for 2 more minutes, then transfer them to a platter. Set out bowls of white rice vinegar, chili oil and dark soy sauce. The idea is to let each person concoct their own dipping sauce by mixing these exactly to their taste.

Garnish the dumplings with chopped green onions and serve immediately.

Preserved Vegetable Dumplings

Preserved vegetables are a popular food found in China's colorful markets, where you will see them in stacks of different varieties. Traditionally, they were served to stretch or supplement the diet of the poorer classes, but today they are often used as a seasoning in stuffings, where their earthy, distinct flavors add a new dimension. Here they are combined in a pork-based filling, then encased in wontons and gently steamed. The flavors of the vegetables and other seasonings permeate the filling. If you prefer, you may substitute other finely chopped vegetables in place of the pork for an equally tasteful vegetarian dumpling. Either way, they will serve deliciously as an appetizer or a dim sum snack.

MAKES ABOUT 25

8 oz (225g) wonton skins
FOR THE FILLING
2 oz (50g) Chinese dried black
  mushrooms
1 oz (25g) Tianjin preserved
  vegetables, rinsed and finely
  chopped
8 oz (225g) ground fatty pork
3 tbsp (45ml) finely chopped
  green onions
2 tbsp (30ml) finely chopped
  cilantro
1 tbsp (15ml) finely chopped
  fresh ginger
2 tsp (10ml) light soy sauce
1 tsp (5ml) dark soy sauce
2 tsp (10ml) sugar
1 tbsp (15ml) Shaoxing rice
  wine or dry sherry
2 tsp (10ml) cornstarch
2 tsp (10ml) sesame oil
white pepper

Soak the mushrooms in a bowl of warm water for about 20 minutes, or until they are soft and pliable. Squeeze out the excess water, then cut off and discard the woody stems. Finely chop the mushroom caps. Rinse the preserved vegetables thoroughly and squeeze out the excess water.

Mix all the filling ingredients well in a medium-sized bowl. Put a generous tablespoon (15ml) of filling in the center of each wonton skin and fold over to form a triangle. Moisten the edges with water and pinch together with your fingers. Continue until you have used up all the filling. Place the dumplings in a bamboo steamer lined with damp cheesecloth.

Bring about 2 in (5cm) of water to a boil in a large deep saucepan. Place the steamer on top, cover tightly, and steam for around 15 minutes. Serve immediately.

Cold Cucumber Salad with Garlic

This delightful cold dish provided a refreshing starter on a humid summer night in Shanghai. A quick browning of the garlic in the wok gives off a wonderful aroma.

SERVES 4

1 lb (450g) cucumbers
salt
2 tsp (10ml) sugar
1 tbsp (15ml) Chinese white rice vinegar
1½ tbsp (22ml) peanut oil
1 tbsp (15ml) coarsely chopped garlic

Cut the cucumbers in half lengthwise and, using a spoon, remove the seeds. Cut the cucumber halves into 3 x ½ in (7.5 x 1cm) pieces.

Combine the cucumber pieces with 2 tsp (10ml) of salt, then put them into a colander set over a bowl and leave them for 10 minutes. Rinse them in cold water, blot them dry and toss with the sugar and vinegar.

Heat a wok or large skillet until it is hot and add the oil and garlic. Stir-fry for 15 seconds, until the garlic is lightly browned. Mix with the cucumbers and serve.

Pickled Young Ginger

Few foods are more refreshing to the palate than pickled young ginger. Once made, it can be eaten raw as a snack or appetizer or stir-fried with meat or vegetables. With it, you can turn simple Rice Congee (page 290) into a tasty treat. If necessary, you can use ordinary fresh ginger, but young ginger is preferable.

MAKES 1 Lb (450G)

1 lb (450g) young fresh ginger
salt
2⅓ cups (600ml) Chinese white rice vinegar
6 large garlic cloves, peeled and lightly crushed
2 cups (450ml) sugar

Wash the ginger well under cold running water, then trim, peel and cut into 3–4 in (7.5–10cm) chunks. Blanch in boiling water for 2 minutes, then drain. Rub the ginger with 2 tbsp (30ml) of salt and leave it to sit for 1 hour. Rinse well under cold running water, then dry thoroughly with paper towels and set aside.

Bring the vinegar, garlic, sugar and 1 tsp (5ml) of salt to a boil in a large enamel or stainless steel saucepan. Put the ginger into a heatproof bowl and pour the vinegar mixture over, making sure it is completely covered. When cool, pack the ginger and the liquid into a glass jar and refrigerate.

The ginger will turn slightly pink in about a week and be ready to use. It will keep for up to 3 months in the fridge.

Stuffed Bell Peppers

Red, green and yellow bell peppers are especially delicious when they are stuffed, and these snacks are featured on many dim sum menus in southern China. Easy to make, they also reheat well. The quick pan-frying before serving gives the snacks a crusty brownish top. They make an attractive dish for a light lunch or a perfect starter.

SERVES 6

1²⁄₃–2¼ lb (750g–1kg) red, green or yellow bell peppers, or a mixture, halved lengthwise and seeded
3 tbsp (45ml) cornstarch
1½ tbsp (22ml) peanut or vegetable oil

FOR THE FILLING

4 oz (100g) water chestnuts, fresh or canned
8 oz (225g) uncooked shrimp, peeled
8 oz (225g) ground fatty pork
1 egg white
2 tsp (10ml) cornstarch
1½ tbsp (22ml) light soy sauce
2 tsp (10ml) dark soy sauce
2 tsp (10ml) sesame oil
1 tbsp (15ml) Shaoxing rice wine or dry sherry
1 tsp (5ml) sugar
3 tbsp (45ml) finely chopped green onions
salt and black pepper

First prepare the filling. If you are using fresh water chestnuts, peel and chop them finely. If you are using canned water chestnuts, first rinse them well in cold water. Drain in a colander and then chop them finely. If you are using large uncooked shrimp, cut them down the back and remove the fine digestive cord. Coarsely chop the shrimp. Put the water chestnuts and shrimp into a bowl with the rest of the filling ingredients. Add 2 tsp (10ml) of salt and some black pepper to taste, and mix very well. Dust the bell pepper halves lightly with cornstarch and stuff them with the filling mixture. Now cut each stuffed bell pepper half into 2 or 4 chunks and arrange them on a heatproof plate.

Next, set up a steamer, or put a rack into a wok or deep saucepan, and fill it with 2 in (5cm) of water. Bring the water to a boil over high heat. Carefully lower the plate into the steamer or onto the rack. Turn the heat to low and cover the wok or saucepan tightly. Steam gently for 15 minutes. (You may have to do this in a couple of batches.) The snacks may be prepared in advance up to this point.

When you are ready to serve the bell peppers, heat a wok or a large skillet over high heat. Add the oil, and when it is very hot and slightly smoking, fry the peppers, stuffing side down, until they are lightly browned and heated through. Serve immediately.

Ban Doufu

In the middle of a Shanghai heatwave, my appetite was as languid as the weather, but I longed for some of the local specialities, especially something light and simple. A friend directed me to one of the many small private restaurants that now serve meals. The quality of the food was uneven, but one item was a delectable treat: a cold appetizer made from fresh beancurd. China is the place where soy beans were first cultivated, and the Chinese have been preparing all sorts of soy bean products for over 3,000 years. By the first millennium BC, the soy bean was already enshrined as one of the five sacred grains essential to Chinese civilization, the others being millet, glutinous millet, wheat and rice.

This recipe involves no cooking. The fresh, soft, silky-smooth beancurd — which is extremely nutritious but rather bland — needs only a touch of taste and texture, provided here by the dried shrimps (available from Chinese grocers and supermarkets) and preserved vegetables, to complete a truly delightful starter. This recipe requires very fresh beancurd — I use the soft version. Serve it cold.

SERVES 4

1 lb (450g) fresh, soft beancurd
2 tbsp (30ml) dried shrimps
2 tbsp (30ml) Sichuan
   preserved vegetables, rinsed
   and finely chopped
1 tbsp (15ml) chili bean sauce
1½ tbsp (22ml) sesame oil
FOR THE GARNISH
2 tbsp (30ml) finely chopped
   green onions (optional)

Gently drain the beancurd and soak it in several changes of cold water. Drain it again thoroughly, then cut it into 1 in (2.5cm) cubes. Place the beancurd on a serving platter and refrigerate.

Soak the dried shrimps in warm water for 20 minutes and drain thoroughly. Finely chop and place in a small bowl with the preserved vegetables and the chili bean sauce. Arrange this mixture evenly over the beancurd and drizzle with the sesame oil. Garnish with the green onions, if you wish, and serve at once.

Sesame Shrimp Toast

Sesame shrimp toast is a savory snack that is often served in dim sum restaurants outside China. Its origins are rather obscure, but I suspect it is a variation on the shrimp paste used widely in southern China for stuffings or for deep-frying into crispy balls. Whatever its origin, it is delicious and easy to make.

MAKES ABOUT 60

20 very thin slices of bread
3 tbsp (45ml) white sesame
   seeds
2 cups (450ml) peanut or
   vegetable oil

FOR THE SHRIMP PASTE

4 oz (100g) water chestnuts,
   fresh or canned
1 lb (450g) uncooked shrimp,
   peeled
salt and white pepper
4 oz (100g) ground fatty pork
1 egg white
2 tbsp (30ml) finely chopped
   green onions, white part only
1 tbsp (15ml) finely chopped
   fresh ginger
2 tsp (10ml) light soy sauce
2 tsp (10ml) sesame oil
2 tsp (10ml) sugar

If you are using fresh water chestnuts, peel and chop them finely. If you are using canned water chestnuts, first rinse them well in cold water. Drain in a colander and then chop them finely. Using a cleaver or a sharp knife, chop the shrimp coarsely and then mince them finely until they form a paste. Put the paste into a bowl, add 1 tsp (5ml) of salt and some white pepper, and mix in the rest of the shrimp paste ingredients. Alternatively, you could do this in a food processor. This step can be done hours in advance, but you should then wrap the paste well in plastic wrap and put it into the fridge until you need it.

Remove the crusts from the bread and cut each slice into rectangles about 3 x 1 in (7.5 x 2.5cm) — you should have about 3 pieces per slice. If the bread is fresh, place it in a warm oven to dry out. (Dried bread will absorb less oil.) Spread the shrimp paste thickly on each piece of bread. The paste should form a layer less than ¼ in (about 3mm) deep, although you can spread it more thinly if you prefer. Sprinkle the toasts with the sesame seeds.

Heat the oil to a moderate heat in a deep-fat fryer or wok and deep-fry several shrimp toasts at a time, paste side down, for 2–3 minutes. Then turn them over and deep-fry them for about 2 minutes more, or until they are golden brown. Repeat the process until they are all done. Remove with a slotted spoon, drain on paper towels and serve.

Cold Marinated Peanuts

Peanuts were introduced into China in the sixteenth century, and they quickly won an important place in Chinese agriculture. This dish may be made a day or two in advance and can be served cold or at room temperature.

SERVES 6–8

1 lb (450g) raw peanuts
3 tbsp (45ml) light soy sauce
3 tbsp (45ml) dark soy sauce
1 tbsp (15ml) finely chopped garlic
1 whole star anise
⅔ cups (150ml) Chinese white rice vinegar
⅓ cup (85ml) Shaoxing rice wine or dry sherry
salt and black pepper

First blanch the peanuts by immersing them in a saucepan of boiling water for about 2 minutes. Drain them and let them cool, and the skins should come off easily.

Put the blanched peanuts into a bowl and add all the other ingredients, along with 2 tsp (10ml) of salt and some black pepper to taste. Let the peanuts marinate in the mixture for at least 2 or 3 hours, stirring from time to time to ensure an even distribution of the marinade. Most of it will be absorbed by the peanuts. Serve with Pickled Young Ginger (page 58) as a snack or appetizer.

Shrimp Crackers

I have always had a fondness for crispy snacks, especially shrimp crackers. They are made from a combination of shrimp, starch, salt and (sometimes) sugar, pounded into a paste and then dried into hard, round chips. They are marvellous with drinks, and you may use them as a colorful and crispy garnish for Chinese dishes.

SERVES 4

2⅓ cups (600ml) peanut or vegetable oil
4 oz (100g) dried shrimp crackers

Heat a wok or a large skillet over high heat until it is hot. Add the oil, and when it is very hot and slightly smoking, test the temperature by dropping in one dried shrimp cracker. It should puff up and float to the top immediately. If it doesn't, wait until the oil is hot enough.

When the oil is ready, drop a handful of the crackers in and scoop them out immediately with a slotted spoon. Drain them on a baking sheet lined with paper towels. Repeat until all the crackers have been fried. The oil can be saved and used in fish or shrimp dishes.

Caramelized Walnuts

The first time I had this delicious snack was in Beijing, and I was determined to learn how to make them. As it turned out, they were surprisingly easy. The shelled walnuts must be blanched first to rid them of any bitterness. After that they are rolled in sugar, left to dry for several hours, then deep-fried to caramelize the sugar coating. Finally, they can be rolled in sesame seeds. The result is a classic contrast of tastes and textures. They can be served cold or warm and they are perfect with drinks.

SERVES 4

8 oz (225g) shelled walnuts
½ cup (120ml) sugar
2 cups (450ml) peanut or
    vegetable oil
3 tbsp (45ml) sesame seeds
    (optional)

Bring a saucepan of water to a boil. Add the walnuts and cook for about 10 minutes to blanch them. Drain the nuts in a colander or sieve, then pat dry with paper towels and spread them on a baking sheet. Sprinkle the sugar over the walnuts and roll them around to cover them completely. Place the sheet of sugared walnuts in a cool, draughty place for at least 2 hours, or preferably overnight, to allow the nuts to dry out.

Heat the oil in a deep-fat fryer or a wok to a moderate heat. Fry a batch of the walnuts for about 2 minutes, or until the sugar melts and the walnuts turn golden. (Watch the heat to prevent burning.) Remove the walnuts from the oil with a slotted spoon or strainer. For an added depth of flavor, you can sprinkle them with the sesame seeds at this point. Lay the walnuts on a non-stick baking sheet or a wire rack to cool. (Do not drain them on paper towels, as the sugar will stick when it dries.) Deep-fry and drain the rest of the walnuts in the same way. Serve the walnuts warm or, once cooled, they can be kept in a sealed glass jar for about 2 weeks.

Fried Wontons

Classic wontons become a savory treat when dipped into a sweet and sour sauce. They make a great snack or starter for any meal. The sauce can be made a day in advance, refrigerated, and brought to room temperature before serving.

SERVES 6

8 oz (225g) wonton skins
FOR THE FILLING
12 oz (350g) uncooked shrimp, peeled and minced coarsely
4 oz (100g) ground fatty pork
salt and black pepper
4 tbsp (60ml) finely chopped green onions
2 tsp (10ml) Shaoxing rice wine or dry sherry
1 tsp (5ml) sugar
2 tsp (10ml) sesame oil
1 egg white, lightly beaten
FOR THE SWEET AND SOUR DIPPING SAUCE
⅔ cups (150ml) water
2 tbsp (30ml) sugar
3 tbsp (45ml) Chinese white rice vinegar or cider vinegar
3 tbsp (45ml) tomato paste or ketchup
salt and white pepper
1 tsp (5ml) cornstarch, mixed with 2 tsp (10ml) water
FOR DEEP-FRYING
2⅓ (600ml) peanut or vegetable oil

Put the shrimp and pork into a large bowl, add 2 tsp (10ml) of salt and a little black pepper and mix well, either by kneading with your hand or by stirring with a wooden spoon. Then add the rest of the filling ingredients and stir well. Cover the bowl with plastic wrap and chill it for at least 20 minutes.

In a small saucepan, combine all the ingredients for the sweet and sour sauce, except the cornstarch mixture, then season with 1 tsp (5ml) of salt and ½ tsp (2ml) of white pepper. Bring to a boil, then stir in the cornstarch mixture and cook for 1 minute. Allow to cool and set aside.

When you are ready to stuff the wontons, put 1 tbsp (15ml) of the filling in the center of the first wonton skin. Dampen the edges with a little water and bring up the sides of the skin around the filling. Pinch the edges together at the top so that the wonton is sealed — it should look like a small, filled bag.

Heat a wok or a large skillet over high heat, until it is hot. Add the oil, and when it is very hot and slightly smoking, add a handful of wontons and deep-fry for 3 minutes, until golden and crispy. If the oil gets too hot, be sure to reduce the heat slightly.

Drain the wontons well on paper towels, and continue to fry until they are all cooked. Serve them immediately, with the sweet and sour sauce.

Spring Rolls

Spring rolls are among the best-known Chinese snacks. They should be crisp, light and delicate and go wonderfully with the Sweet and Sour Dipping Sauce on page 66.

MAKES ABOUT 15–18

1 packet of spring roll wrappers

FOR THE MARINADE

1 tsp (5ml) light soy sauce

1 tsp (5ml) Shaoxing rice wine
   or dry sherry

½ tsp cornstarch

½ tsp sesame oil

salt and black pepper

FOR THE FILLING

1 oz (25g) Chinese dried black
   mushrooms

4 oz (100g) uncooked shrimp,
   peeled and minced

4 oz (100g) ground pork

1½ tbsp (22ml) peanut oil

2 tbsp (30ml) finely chopped
   garlic

1 tbsp (15ml) finely chopped
   fresh ginger

1½ tbsp (22ml) light soy sauce

1 tbsp (15ml) Shaoxing rice
   wine or dry sherry

3 tbsp (45ml) finely chopped
   green onions

salt and black pepper

8 oz (225g) Chinese leaves,
   finely shredded

FOR THE EGG SEAL

1 egg, beaten

FOR DEEP-FRYING

5 cups (1.2L) peanut or
   vegetable oil

There are two types of wrappers: the Cantonese style, which is a smooth, heavier, noodle-type dough, and the Shanghai style, which is transparent, lighter and more like rice paper. I prefer the Shanghai type for this recipe.

Soak the mushrooms in warm water for 20 minutes. Then drain them and squeeze out the excess liquid. Remove and discard the stems and finely shred the caps into thin strips.

Combine the shrimp and meat with the marinade ingredients in a small bowl, along with ½ tsp (2ml) of salt and ¼ tsp (1ml) of black pepper.

Heat a wok or a large skillet over high heat until it is hot. Add the oil, and when it is very hot and slightly smoking, add the garlic and ginger and stir-fry for 20 seconds. Then add the rest of the filling ingredients, the shrimp/meat mixture, the mushrooms and 1 tsp (5ml) each of salt and black pepper, and stir-fry for 5 minutes. Place the mixture in a colander to drain and allow it to cool thoroughly.

Place 3–4 tbsp (45–60ml) of filling near the corner end of each spring roll wrapper, then fold in each side and roll up tightly. Use the beaten egg mixture to seal the open end by brushing a small amount along the edge. Then press the edge onto the roll. You should have a roll about 4 in (10cm) long, a little like an oversized cigar.

Wash the wok and reheat it over high heat until it is hot, then add the oil for deep-frying. When it is hot and slightly smoking, gently drop in as many spring rolls as will fit easily in one layer. Carefully fry them in batches until golden brown on the outside and cooked inside, about 4 minutes. Adjust the heat as necessary. Take the rolls out with a slotted spoon and drain on paper towels. Serve them at once, hot and crispy, with the Sweet and Sour Sauce on the side for dipping.

Curried Vegetarian Spring Rolls

Here I have taken the classic spring rolls and modified the recipe according to a version I enjoyed in Shanghai. Although they can be prepared ahead of time, it is best to deep-fry them at the last minute.

MAKES ABOUT 25

1 packet of rice paper wrappers
FOR THE DIPPING SAUCE
4 tbsp (60ml) light soy sauce
1 tsp (5ml) chili powder
1 tbsp (15ml) chopped garlic
1 tbsp (15ml) lime juice
1 tbsp (15ml) sugar
FOR THE FILLING
1 oz (25g) bean thread
    (transparent) noodles
½ oz (15g) dried Chinese wood
    ear mushrooms
1½ tbsp (22ml) peanut oil
6 oz (175g) onions, finely
    chopped
6 oz (175g) carrots, finely
    shredded
2 tbsp (30ml) chopped garlic
2 tbsp (30ml) finely chopped
    green onions
2 tbsp (30ml) finely chopped
    shallots
salt and black pepper
1½ tbsp (22ml) Madras curry
    powder
5 tbsp (75ml) all-purpose flour
FOR DEEP-FRYING
2 cups (450ml) peanut oil
TO SERVE
iceberg lettuce
sprigs of basil, mint or cilantro

Place all the ingredients for the dipping sauce in a blender, add 5 tbsp (75ml) of water and mix thoroughly.

Soak the noodles in a large bowl of warm water for about 15 minutes. When they are soft, drain them and discard the water. Cut them into 3 in (7.5cm) lengths, using scissors or a knife, and put them into a large bowl. Soak the wood ear mushrooms in warm water for about 20 minutes, until soft. Rinse well in cold water and squeeze out the excess liquid. Remove any hard stems and finely shred the mushrooms.

Heat a wok or a large skillet over high heat until it is hot. Add the oil, and when it is very hot add the wood ears, onions, carrots, garlic, green onions and shallots and stir-fry for 5 minutes. Then add 1½ tsp (7ml) of salt, ½ tsp (2ml) of black pepper and the curry powder and continue to stir-fry for 3 minutes. Allow the mixture to cool, then combine it with the noodles. In a small bowl, mix the flour with 5 tbsp (75ml) of water to form a paste.

When you are ready to make the spring rolls, fill a large bowl with warm water. Dip one of the rice paper wrappers into the water and let it soften, then remove and drain it on a towel. Put about 2 tbsp (30ml) of the filling on the softened wrapper, then fold in each side and roll it up tightly. Seal the ends with a little of the flour and paste mixture. You should have a roll about 3 in (7.5cm) long. Repeat the procedure until you have used up all the filling.

Heat the oil in a deep-fat fryer or a large wok until it is hot. Deep-fry the spring rolls, a few at a time, until they are golden brown. They have a tendency to stick to each other at the beginning of the frying, so fry just a few at a time. Do not attempt to break them apart should they stick together. You can separate them after they are removed from the oil.

Drain them on paper towels and serve at once, with lettuce leaves, herb sprigs and the dipping sauce.

Steamed Spareribs with Black Beans

This is a popular dim sum snack. The spareribs are steamed until the meat is so tender it melts in your mouth. The steaming process ensures that the meat is permeated by the pungent flavor and aroma of the black beans. It makes a nice appetizer for any meal, and can easily be reheated either in a steamer or a microwave.

SERVES 4

1⅔ lb (750g) pork spareribs
salt and black pepper
½ cup (120ml) Chicken Stock (page 75)
1½ tbsp (22ml) light soy sauce
2 tsp (10ml) dark soy sauce
2 tsp (10ml) sesame oil
1 tbsp (15ml) finely chopped fresh ginger
3 tbsp (45ml) coarsely chopped black beans
2 tbsp (30ml) finely chopped garlic
2 tbsp (30ml) seeded and coarsely chopped fresh red or green chilies
2 tsp (10ml) sugar
1½ tbsp (22ml) Shaoxing rice wine or dry sherry

If possible, ask your butcher to cut the spareribs into individual ribs and then into 2 in (5cm) segments. Otherwise you can do this yourself with a Chinese cleaver or a sharp, heavy knife.

Rub the spareribs with 2 tsp (10ml) of salt and let them sit in a bowl for about 20–25 minutes. Fill a large saucepan with water and bring to a boil. Turn the heat to low, add the spareribs and simmer them for 10 minutes. Drain them and discard the water.

Mix the rest of the ingredients together in a large bowl with 1 tsp (5ml) of salt and some black pepper. Add the spareribs, coating them well with the mixture. Transfer the mixture to a deep plate or dish.

Next, set up a steamer, or put a rack into a wok or deep saucepan, and fill it with 2 in (5cm) of water. Bring the water to a boil over high heat. Carefully lower the dish of spareribs into the steamer or onto the rack. Turn the heat to low and cover the wok or saucepan tightly. Steam gently for 1 hour, or until the spareribs are very tender. Remember to keep a careful watch on the water level and replenish it with hot water when necessary. Skim off any surface fat and serve.

You can make this dish ahead of time and reheat the ribs by steaming them for 20 minutes, or until they are hot, or by heating them through in a microwave.

Peanuts with Five-spice

This is a fragrant and savory way to raise nuts to new heights. Serve them as a snack with drinks, or as an easy starter to any meal.

SERVES 4

8 oz (225g) raw peanuts
1¼ cups (300ml) peanut oil
2 tbsp (30ml) finely chopped garlic
1 tbsp (15ml) finely chopped fresh ginger
1 tbsp (15ml) sugar
2 tsp (10ml) five-spice powder
salt
1 tsp (5ml) roasted and ground Sichuan peppercorns (page 29)
1 tsp (5ml) chili powder

Pick over the peanuts and remove any loose skins.

Heat a wok or a large skillet over high heat until it is hot, then add the oil. When it is hot and slightly smoking, fry the peanuts for 2 minutes, until they are lightly browned, then remove and drain well. Lay the peanuts on a baking sheet lined with paper towels.

Drain most of the oil from the wok (this oil can be saved for future use), leaving just 1½ tbsp (22ml). Reheat the wok and remaining oil, and when it is hot and smoking slightly, add the garlic and ginger and stir-fry for 1 minute. Then add the rest of the ingredients along with 2 tsp (10ml) of salt and return the peanuts to the wok. Continue to stir-fry for 2 minutes, stirring to mix well. Turn on to a baking sheet, allow to cool and serve.

Stir-fried Peanuts with Chilies

Peanuts are a legume and are therefore nutritious in various ways. As part of a vegetarian diet they perform a valuable function, not least because they are rather tastier than the usual legume. Viewed this way, one can only respect this humble food.

SERVES 4

8 oz (225g) raw peanuts
1½ tbsp (22ml) peanut oil
2 small fresh red chilies, finely chopped
2 tbsp (30ml) coarsely chopped garlic
2 tsp (10ml) sugar
salt

Pick over the peanuts and remove any loose skins.

Heat a wok over high heat until it is hot, then add the oil. When it is hot and slightly smoking, stir-fry the peanuts for 2 minutes, until they are lightly browned. Add the chilies and garlic and stir-fry for 2 minutes. Then sprinkle in the sugar and 1 tsp (5ml) of salt and continue to stir-fry for 2 minutes, stirring to mix well. Turn onto a serving dish and serve warm.

SOUPS

In everyday Chinese eating, soup is
something that is enjoyed throughout
the meal, alongside other dishes — so
you can understand why a delicious
soup recipe is an important part of
the culinary tradition.

The secrets of perfect stock

Chicken stock is an all-purpose base for soups and sauces. Its chief ingredient is inexpensive; it is light and delicious; and it marries well with other foods, enhancing and sustaining them. Small wonder that it is an almost universally present ingredient in Chinese cookery. Thus, from the Imperial kitchens to the most humble food stalls, good stock is the basic ingredient. The usual Chinese chicken stock is precisely that: the essence of chicken, with complements of ginger and green onions often added. Combined with the condiments that give Chinese food its distinctive flavor, good stock captures the essential taste of China. Many of the most famous recipes in the repertory require such stock. There are two basic types. One is a clear stock made from chicken bones and meat; the other is a richer stock that uses ham and pork bones. Different recipes call for different types of stock but both types make a solid base for soups and sauces. The simple recipes opposite reflect what I believe works best for any Chinese dish.

There are commercially prepared canned, cubed (dried) or fresh stocks, but many of them are of inferior quality, being either too salty or containing additives and colorings that adversely affect health as well as the natural taste of good foods. Stock does take time to prepare, but it is easy to make your own — and homemade really is the best. You can make a big batch and freeze it for your own use when needed.

Here are several important points to keep in mind when making stock:

- Good stock requires meat to give it richness and flavor. It is therefore necessary to use at least some chicken meat, if not a whole bird.
- The stock should never boil. If it does it will be undesirably cloudy and the fat will be incorporated into the liquid. Flavors and digestibility come with a clear stock.
- Use a tall, heavy saucepan so that the liquid covers all the solids and evaporation is slow.
- Simmer slowly and skim the stock regularly. Be patient — you will reap the rewards each time you prepare a Chinese dish.
- Strain the finished stock thoroughly through several layers of cheesecloth or a fine sieve.
- Let the stock cool thoroughly, refrigerate and remove any fat before freezing.

Remember to save all your uncooked chicken bones and carcasses for stock. They can be frozen until you are ready to make it.

Chicken Stock

**MAKES ABOUT 14 CUPS
   (3.5L)**

4½ lb (2kg) uncooked chicken
   bones, such as backs, feet,
   wings, etc.
1⅔ lb (750g) chicken pieces,
   such as wings, thighs,
   drumsticks, etc.
14 cups (3.5L) cold water
3 slices of fresh ginger
6 green onions, green tops
   removed
6 whole garlic cloves, unpeeled
   and lightly crushed
salt

Put the chicken bones and pieces into a very large saucepan.
(The bones can be put in either frozen or defrosted.) Cover
them with the cold water and bring it to a simmer.

Using a large, flat spoon, skim off the scum as it rises from
the bones. Watch the heat, as the stock should never boil.
Keep skimming until the stock looks clear. This can take
between 20–40 minutes. Do not stir or disturb the stock.
Now turn the heat down to a low simmer. Add the ginger,
green onions, garlic and 1 tsp (5ml) of salt. Simmer the stock
on very low heat for between 2–4 hours, skimming any fat
off the top at least twice during this time. The stock should
be rich and full-bodied, and simmering for such a long time
gives it (and any soup you make with it) plenty of taste.

Strain the stock through several layers of dampened
cheesecloth or through a very fine sieve, and then let it cool.
Remove any fat that has risen to the top. It can now be used
straightaway or transferred to containers and frozen.

Pork and Chicken Stock

Pork is used extensively in Chinese cookery, and pork bones, when added to chicken
stock, make for a richer, tastier and sweeter soup or broth. Use this stock as a light,
flavorful soup with your Chinese meals.

**MAKES ABOUT 9 CUPS
   (2.25L)**

1⅔ lb (750g) uncooked pork
   bones
9 cups (2.25L) Chicken Stock
   (see above)
2 slices of fresh ginger
3 green onions, green tops
   removed
salt

Put the pork bones into a heavy saucepan or ovenproof
casserole dish with the chicken stock. Bring the liquid to a
simmer and skim off any scum that rises to the surface. Then
add the ginger, green onions and ½ tsp (2ml) of salt and leave
to simmer on very low heat for 1½ hours.

Strain the stock through dampened cheesecloth or a fine
sieve, and leave it to cool. When the stock is cold, remove any
fat that has risen to the surface. It is now ready to be used as
soup or as a stock for other soups such as Ham and Marrow
Soup (page 81). You can also freeze it for future use.

Curried Corn Soup with Chicken

Curry is especially popular in southern and eastern China, where returning emigrants have brought its influence from southeast Asia. The Chinese favor curry powder or paste that comes from Madras, but, unlike Indians, Chinese cooks use curry only as a light addition to the usual Chinese seasonings, a subtle touch rather than a dominant tone.

This is not a traditional Chinese soup, but is my version of corn soup that has become popular in the West. It is easy to make and is delicious. If you use canned creamed corn, which is already quite thick, you could leave out the cornstarch mixture. The rich golden sheen of the curried soup makes it an appealing, bright starter for a dinner.

SERVES 4

1 lb (450g) fresh corn on the
   cob or 10 oz (275g) canned
   corn

8 oz (225g) boneless, skinless
   chicken breasts

1 egg white

salt

2 tsp (10ml) sesame oil

3 tsp (15ml) cornstarch

1 egg

5 cups (1.2L) Chicken Stock
   (page 75)

1 tbsp (15ml) Shaoxing rice
   wine or dry sherry

1 tbsp (15ml) Madras curry
   powder or paste

1 tsp (5ml) sugar

FOR THE GARNISH

2 tbsp (30ml) finely chopped
   green onions

If you are using fresh corn, wash the cobs and remove the kernels with a sharp knife or cleaver. You should end up with about 10 oz (275g). If you are using canned corn, empty the contents into a bowl and set it aside. Using a cleaver or a sharp knife, thinly slice the chicken breasts into fine shreds about 3 in (7.5cm) long. Mix the chicken shreds with the egg white, 1 tsp (5ml) of salt, half the sesame oil and 1 tsp (5ml) of cornstarch in a small bowl and refrigerate for 15 minutes. Beat the whole egg and the remaining 1 tsp (5ml) of sesame oil together in another small bowl and set it aside.

Bring a small saucepan of water to a boil. Turn off the heat and quickly blanch the chicken shreds until they just turn white. (This should take about 20 seconds.) Remove them from the water with a slotted spoon and drain them in a colander or sieve.

Bring the stock to a simmer in a large saucepan and add the corn. Simmer for 10 minutes, uncovered, then add the rice wine, curry powder, sugar and 1 tsp (5ml) of salt. If you want to thicken the soup, blend the remaining cornstarch with 2 tsp (10ml) of water and stir it in. Bring it back to a boil, then lower the heat and simmer for another 5 minutes. Add the blanched chicken shreds, then slowly pour in the egg and sesame oil mixture in a steady stream, stirring all the time, using a chopstick or fork to pull the egg slowly into strands. Transfer the soup to a tureen or individual bowls, garnish with the green onions and serve.

Chicken and Mushroom Soup

This soup combines two classic southern Chinese ingredients: chicken and dried mushrooms. Dark chicken meat from the legs and thighs is most often used for this soup to give it a rich, strong flavor and a good texture. Use Chinese dried mushrooms, as their smoky flavor enhances the total effect of the soup.

There are two techniques involved here. The chicken is first stir-fried to give it a rich flavor. Then all the other ingredients are simmered together with the cooked chicken. The result is a good, hearty soup. It also reheats nicely, tasting even better when made one day and eaten the next.

SERVES 4

8 oz (225g) boneless, skinless chicken thighs

2 tbsp (30ml) Shaoxing rice wine or dry sherry

2½ tbsp (37ml) light soy sauce

1 tsp (5ml) sesame oil

1 tsp (5ml) cornstarch

1 oz (25g) Chinese dried black mushrooms

5 cups (1.2L) Chicken Stock (page 75)

1 tbsp (15ml) finely chopped green onions

1 oz (25g) Parma ham or lean smoked bacon, shredded

salt and white pepper

2 tsp (10ml) peanut or vegetable oil

Cut the chicken into ½ in (1cm) cubes. Put into a bowl with 1 tbsp (15ml) of rice wine, 1½ tbsp (22ml) of soy sauce, the sesame oil and the cornstarch. Let the mixture stand for at least 20 minutes.

Soak the mushrooms in warm water for 20 minutes, then drain them and squeeze out the excess liquid. Remove and discard the stems and finely shred the caps.

Bring the stock to a simmer in a large saucepan. Drain the marinade from the chicken into the stock. Add the mushrooms, green onions, ham or bacon and the remaining 1 tbsp (15ml) each of soy sauce and rice wine. Add 1 tsp (5ml) of salt and ½ tsp (2ml) of white pepper.

Continue to simmer the soup, and meanwhile heat a wok or a large skillet over high heat. When it is very hot, add the oil, and when it is smoking, add the chicken. Stir-fry the chicken cubes over high heat until they are nicely browned. This should take about 5 minutes. Drain them in a colander and add them to the soup. Simmer for 5 minutes, and the soup is ready to serve.

Chicken and Spinach Soup

Spinach, with its distinctive taste and deep green color, is a particular favorite of the Chinese. This soup is a light one and is very attractive to look at. Its ingredients are blanched separately before they are finally combined with the stock just before serving. This way each ingredient retains its unique clean taste. It is an easy soup to make, and many of the steps can be done in advance.

SERVES 4

1 lb (450g) fresh spinach
6 oz (175g) chicken breasts
1 egg white
salt
1 tsp (5ml) cornstarch
5 cups (1.2L) Chicken Stock
    (page 75)
2 tbsp (30ml) light soy sauce
1 tbsp (15ml) Shaoxing rice
    wine or dry sherry
2 tsp (10ml) sesame oil
2 tsp (10ml) sugar
2 tbsp (30ml) finely chopped
    green onions

Remove the stems of the spinach and wash the leaves well. Blanch the leaves for a few seconds in a saucepan of boiling water, until they are just wilted. Then freshen them in cold water to prevent further cooking.

Cut the chicken into thin slices about 2 in (5cm) long and combine them with the egg white, cornstarch and ½ tsp (2ml) of salt. Set aside in the fridge for about 20 minutes.

Blanch the chicken slices in a separate saucepan of boiling water for 2 minutes, until they are slightly firm and white. Now drain both the spinach and the chicken slices. The soup can be prepared up to this point several hours ahead.

Just before you are ready to eat, bring the chicken stock to a simmer and add the soy sauce, rice wine, sesame oil and sugar. Add the blanched spinach and the chicken slices. Bring the soup back to simmering point and add the green onions. Serve at once.

Asparagus and Ground Chicken Soup

Although asparagus is relatively new in the repertory of Chinese vegetables, it has become quite popular in Hong Kong and southern China. In this light, flavorful soup, it is paired with chicken, which has been chopped and mixed with egg white. The result is a light soup of delicate flavors and contrasting colors: perfect as a starter.

SERVES 4

5 cups (1.2L) Chicken Stock
   (page 75)
8 oz (225g) fresh asparagus
8 oz (225g) boneless, skinless
   chicken breasts
1 egg white
1 tsp (5ml) sesame oil
salt and black pepper
2 tsp (10ml) Shaoxing rice wine
   or dry sherry
2 tsp (10ml) light soy sauce
FOR THE GARNISH
chopped green onions

Bring the chicken stock to a simmer in a medium-sized saucepan. Cut the asparagus on the diagonal into 1 in (2.5cm) pieces.

Cut the chicken breasts into small pieces. Put them into a food processor or blender with the egg white, sesame oil and ½ tsp (2ml) of salt, and blend until smooth. Put the mixture into a small bowl and cover with plastic wrap. Put it into the fridge for 5 minutes.

Add the asparagus, rice wine and soy sauce to the simmering stock and cook for 3 minutes, or until the asparagus is tender. Remove the saucepan from the heat and add the chicken mixture, stirring vigorously to break up any large lumps. Return the saucepan to the stove and simmer for another minute. Season with salt and pepper, garnish with green onions and serve at once.

Ham and Bean Sprout Soup

This is a simple soup that typifies the fresh, light cooking of the south.

SERVES 4

2 oz (50g) bean thread
  (transparent) noodles

3 oz (75g) fresh bean sprouts

5 cups (1.2L) Chicken Stock
  (page 75)

1 tbsp (15ml) light soy sauce

3 oz (75g) Parma ham or lean
  smoked bacon, shredded

2 tbsp (30ml) finely chopped
  cilantro

2 tbsp (30ml) finely chopped
  green onions

Soak the noodles in a bowl of warm water for 20 minutes, or until they are soft. Drain them thoroughly in a colander and cut them into 2 in (5cm) pieces. If you have the time, remove both ends of the bean sprouts. This will give the soup a cleaner look.

Bring the chicken stock to a simmer in a large saucepan. Add the drained noodles and soy sauce and simmer for 3 minutes. Then add the ham or bacon, cilantro and green onions and simmer for 30 seconds. Finally, add the bean sprouts and simmer for another 30 seconds, or until the bacon is cooked through. Serve at once.

Ham and Marrow Soup

This is an adaptation of a traditional recipe that calls for "hairy melon" or Chinese marrow, which is more appetizing than it sounds. Zucchinis will work here as well.

SERVES 4

8 oz (225g) marrow or zucchinis

5 cups (1.2L) Chicken Stock
  or Pork and Chicken Stock
  (page 75)

2 oz (50g) Parma ham or lean
  smoked bacon, shredded

1½ tsp (7ml) chili bean sauce

1½ tbsp (22ml) light soy sauce

2 tsp (10ml) dark soy sauce

1 tsp (5ml) Shaoxing rice wine
  or dry sherry

salt and white pepper

2 tsp (10ml) sesame oil

Trim the ends of the marrow or zucchinis and, if you are using marrow, remove the seeds. Cut into ½ in (1cm) cubes. Bring the stock to a boil in a large saucepan. Add the ham or bacon, marrow or zucchinis and the chili bean sauce, soy sauces and wine, plus a seasoning of ½ tsp (2ml) of salt and ¼ tsp (1ml) of white pepper. Simmer the soup, uncovered, for 15 minutes, then add the sesame oil and give it a good stir. Serve the soup immediately in individual bowls or a large soup tureen.

Hot and Sour Soup

This has become quite popular in the Western world because it is a heavy soup, suited to cold climates. It combines sour and spicy elements in a rich, tasty stock, and reheats very well. The list of ingredients may be daunting, but the recipe is, in fact, quite easy to make. It is a hearty soup that is almost a meal in itself and is perfect for a cold winter's night — especially if garnished with a fiery chili.

SERVES 4

4 oz (100g) lean boneless pork, finely shredded

1 oz (25g) dried Chinese mushrooms

½ oz (15g) dried Chinese wood ear mushrooms

2 eggs, beaten with a little salt

4 tsp (20ml) sesame oil

5 cups (1.2L) Chicken Stock (page 75)

salt and white pepper

8 oz (225g) fresh beancurd, drained and shredded

1½ tbsp (22ml) light soy sauce

1 tbsp (15ml) dark soy sauce

6 tbsp (90ml) Chinese white rice vinegar or cider vinegar

1 tbsp (15ml) Chili Oil (page 23)

2 tbsp (30ml) finely chopped fresh coriander

FOR THE MARINADE

1 tsp (5ml) light soy sauce

1 tsp (5ml) Shaoxing rice wine or dry sherry

½ tsp (2ml) sesame oil

½ tsp (2ml) cornstarch

a pinch each of salt and sugar

FOR THE GARNISH

dried chili (optional)

Combine the pork in a bowl with the marinade ingredients, mix well and set aside.

Soak the mushrooms in a bowl of warm water for about 20 minutes, or until they are soft and pliable. Squeeze out the excess water and cut off and discard the woody stems, then finely shred the mushrooms. In a small jug, combine the eggs with half the sesame oil and set aside.

Bring the stock to a simmer in a large saucepan and stir in 2 tsp (10ml) of salt. Stir in the pork with its marinade and simmer for 1 minute. Then add the shredded mushrooms and beancurd and continue to simmer for 2 minutes.

Now add the egg mixture in a very slow, thin and steady stream. Using a chopstick or a fork, pull the cooked egg slowly into strands.

Remove the soup from the heat and stir in the soy sauces, vinegar and 1 tsp (5ml) of white pepper. Give the soup a good stir, and finally add the remaining sesame oil, chili oil and cilantro and stir. Ladle into individual bowls or a large soup tureen and serve at once, garnished with dried chili, if you like.

Ham and Pigeon Steamed in Soup

The unusual technique used for making this soup is not difficult to master. It is called double-steaming, a process in which rich ingredients are steamed for hours in a covered casserole dish filled with soup. This extracts all the flavors from the ingredients, and is often used for making the classic Bird's Nest Soup as well as countless herbal medicinal broths. The result is a distinctive soup, clear and rich but also light. Other game birds, such as partridge, snipe, woodcock or quail, would work equally well.

This elegant, rich, clear consommé is particularly suitable for a dinner party. For easy planning, I would make it in advance and freeze it, as it reheats well.

SERVES 4

2 x 12oz–1lb (350–450g)
  pigeons
1oz (25g) Parma ham or lean
  smoked bacon, shredded
5 cups (1.2L) Chicken Stock
  (page 75)
4 green onions
4 slices of fresh ginger
2 tbsp (30ml) Shaoxing rice
  wine or dry sherry
salt

Using a sharp, heavy knife or cleaver, cut the pigeons into quarters. Bring a saucepan of water to a boil, then turn the heat down, add the pigeons and simmer them for 10 minutes. (This blanching rids the pigeons of some of their fat and impurities.) Remove them with a slotted spoon and discard the water.

Next, set up a steamer, or put a rack into a wok or deep saucepan, and fill it with 2 in (5cm) of water. Bring the water to a boil over a high heat.

Meanwhile, bring the stock to a boil in another large saucepan and pour it into an ovenproof glass or china casserole dish. Add the pigeons, ham, green onions, ginger, rice wine and ½ tsp (2ml) of salt and cover the casserole dish with a lid or foil. Place on the rack and cover the wok or deep saucepan tightly with a lid or foil. You now have a casserole dish within a steamer, hence the term "double-steaming." Turn the heat down and steam gently for 2–3 hours, or until the pigeon is tender. Replenish the hot water from time to time. An alternative method is simply to simmer the soup very slowly in a conventional saucepan, but the resulting taste will be quite different.

When the soup is cooked, remove all the ingredients with a slotted spoon and discard the green onions, ginger and ham. Serve the soup with the pigeon pieces. It can be served immediately or cooled and stored in the fridge or freezer to be reheated when required.

Kidney and Beancurd Soup

My mother often made kidney soup for our family dinner because it was tasty and inexpensive. Sometimes she added watercress or spinach to it. In this recipe the kidneys are cleaned in baking soda and quickly blanched before being added to the stock, which prevents the kidney juices from clouding the soup. This is a light and nutritious soup that reheats well.

SERVES 4–6

1 lb (450g) pig's kidneys
1 tsp (5ml) baking soda
2 tsp (10ml) Chinese white rice
  vinegar or cider vinegar
salt
14 oz (400g) fresh beancurd
5 cups (1.2L) Chicken Stock
  or Pork and Chicken Stock
  (page 75)
1 tbsp (15ml) finely chopped
  fresh ginger
2 tsp (10ml) finely chopped
  green onions
2 tbsp (30ml) light soy sauce
2 tsp (10ml) sugar

Using a sharp knife, remove the thin outer membrane of the kidneys. Then, with a sharp cleaver or knife, cut each kidney in half horizontally to keep the shape of the kidney. Now cut away the small knobs of fat and any tough membrane that surrounds them. Put the kidney halves flat on the cutting surface and score the top of each half, making light cuts in a crisscross pattern all over the surface. Then cut the halved kidneys into thin slices. Toss the kidney slices with the baking soda and let them sit for about 20 minutes. Then rinse them thoroughly with cold water and toss them with the vinegar and 1 tsp (5ml) of salt. Put them into a colander and let them drain for at least 30 minutes.

Bring a saucepan of water to a boil. Blot the kidney slices dry with paper towels and blanch them in the water for about 2 minutes. Drain them in a colander or sieve and set aside. Cut the beancurd into ½ in (1cm) cubes and place them in a colander to drain.

In a separate saucepan, bring the stock to a simmer and add the rest of the ingredients, together with the beancurd and 1 tsp (5ml) of salt. Simmer for about 5 minutes, then add the kidney slices. Give the soup several stirs and simmer for another 2 minutes. Serve at once, or allow to cool and reheat gently when required.

Cabbage and Pork Soup

Simple combinations of basic foods make tasty soups, and soups such as this one are typical fare in northern Chinese homes, especially in autumn and winter, when cabbage is abundant. This version is easy to make and very tasty, the sweetness of the cabbage blending nicely with the pork-flavored broth.

SERVES 4

5 cups (1.2L) Chicken Stock
  or Pork and Chicken Stock
  (page 75)
6 oz (175g) lean pork, shredded
4 tsp (20ml) light soy sauce
2 tsp (10ml) Shaoxing rice wine
  or dry sherry
½ tsp (2ml) sesame oil
½ tsp (2ml) cornstarch
1 tbsp (15ml) peanut or
  vegetable oil
12 oz (375g) Chinese leaves,
  shredded widthwise
1 tsp (5ml) dark soy sauce
salt and black pepper
FOR THE GARNISH
finely chopped green onions

Bring the chicken stock to a simmer in a medium-sized saucepan.

Combine the pork with half the light soy sauce, half the rice wine, the sesame oil and the cornstarch. Heat a wok until it is hot, then add the peanut oil. When the oil is hot and slightly smoking, add the pork and stir-fry for 1 minute. Remove from the heat and set aside.

Add the Chinese leaves, the dark soy sauce, the remaining light soy sauce and rice wine to the simmering stock and simmer for 5 minutes. Return the pork to the stock and simmer for another minute. Add salt and pepper to taste. Transfer to a large soup tureen or individual soup bowls, garnish with the green onions and serve at once.

Chinese Cabbage Soup

Classically simple clear soups such as this one are served in many Chinese homes. The soup is consumed as a beverage throughout the meal, and must therefore be light and refreshing. The Chinese leaves add a touch of sweetness, while the preserved vegetables add a nice bite. If you want the soup to be completely vegetarian, you can substitute water or vegetable stock for the chicken stock.

SERVES 4

5 cups (1.2L) Chicken Stock
   (page 75)
1 lb (450g) Chinese leaves,
   shredded width-wise
4 oz (100g) Sichuan preserved
   vegetables, rinsed and finely
   chopped
1 tbsp (15ml) light soy sauce
2 tsp (10ml) dark soy sauce
2 tbsp (30ml) Shaoxing rice
   wine or dry sherry
2 tsp (10ml) sugar
salt and black pepper
2 tsp (10ml) sesame oil
FOR THE GARNISH
chopped green onions

Bring the stock to a simmer in a medium-sized saucepan. Add the Chinese leaves and preserved vegetables and simmer for 3 minutes. Add the soy sauces, rice wine and sugar and simmer for 5 minutes. Season with salt and pepper to taste, and stir in the sesame oil. Transfer to a large soup tureen or individual soup bowls, garnish with green onions and serve straightaway.

Tianjin Cabbage with Chicken Consommé

A clear soup or consommé is a great southern Chinese speciality. The chicken stock is always superb, full of intense chicken flavor and taste, and only the best and most appropriate vegetable is added, in this case Tianjin preserved vegetable. It has just the right slightly sharp texture to accompany the light, distinctive taste of the broth. This is an elegant soup for a special dinner, and is easy to make if you have already prepared your stock. Leftover soup freezes extremely well.

SERVES 6–8

5 cups (1.2L) Chicken Stock
 (page 75)
1 x 4 lb (1.75kg) chicken, cut
 into pieces
4 green onions
3 slices of ginger
8 oz (225g) lean pork
8 oz (225g) Chinese leaves
3 tbsp (45ml) Tianjin preserved
 vegetable, rinsed and finely
 chopped
1 tbsp (15ml) peanut or
 vegetable oil
salt and white pepper

FOR THE MARINADE

2 tsp (10ml) dark soy sauce
1 tsp (5ml) Shaoxing rice wine
 or dry sherry
½ tsp (2ml) cornstarch

FOR THE GARNISH

1 tbsp (15ml) sesame oil

Bring the stock to a simmer in a large saucepan.

Bring a large saucepan of water to a boil and blanch the chicken pieces for 10 minutes. Cut the green onions into 2 in (5cm) pieces. Add the blanched chicken pieces to the stock, together with the ginger and green onions, and simmer for 30 minutes, skimming any scum and fat that may rise to the surface. Continue to simmer for 1 hour, then remove the chicken, ginger and green onions and discard. Skim off as much fat as possible from the stock.

Cut the pork first into slices and then into fine shreds. Put it into a large bowl with the marinade ingredients and refrigerate for 20 minutes.

Finely shred the Chinese leaves. Bring a saucepan of water to a boil and blanch the fresh leaves and preserved vegetable for 1 minute, then drain well and set aside.

Heat a wok or a large skillet until it is hot and add the oil. When it is hot, stir-fry the pork for 30 seconds, then remove with a slotted spoon and set aside.

Season the stock to taste and ladle it into a soup tureen. Add the stir-fried meat and vegetables, then stir in the sesame oil and serve at once.

Wonton Soup

This is one of the most popular soups on street food stalls throughout southern China, and it is equally popular in Chinese restaurants in the West. Ideally, soup wontons should be stuffed, savory dumplings poached in clear water and served in a rich broth. Unfortunately, in many restaurants the soup often arrives with wonton skins but very little filling. This recipe will enable you to make a simple but authentic wonton soup, perfect for any family meal.

SERVES 4–6

8 oz (225g) wonton skins
5 cups (1.2L) Chicken Stock
    (page 75)
1 tbsp (15ml) light soy sauce
1 tsp (5ml) sesame oil

FOR THE FILLING

8 oz (225g) peeled uncooked
    shrimp, deveined and
    coarsely chopped
8 oz (225g) ground pork
salt and white pepper
1½ tbsp (22ml) light soy sauce
2 tbsp (30ml) finely chopped
    green onions
1 tbsp (15ml) Shaoxing rice
    wine or dry sherry
1 tsp (5ml) sugar
2 tsp (10ml) sesame oil
1 egg white, beaten lightly

FOR THE GARNISH

2 tbsp (30ml) finely chopped
    green onions

To make the filling, put the shrimp and pork into a large bowl. Add 1 tsp (5ml) of salt and ½ tsp (2ml) of white pepper and mix well, either by kneading with your hand or by stirring with a wooden spoon. Then add all the other filling ingredients, and stir them well into the shrimp and pork mixture. Cover the bowl with plastic wrap and chill for at least 20 minutes.

When you are ready to stuff the wontons, put 1 tbsp (15ml) of the filling in the center of the first wonton skin. Dampen the edges with a little water and bring up the sides of the skin around the filling. Pinch the edges together at the top so that the wonton is sealed — it should look like a small, filled bag.

When the wontons are ready, bring the stock, soy sauce and sesame oil to a simmer in a large saucepan.

In another large saucepan, bring lightly salted water to a boil and poach the wontons for 1 minute, or until they float to the top. Remove them immediately and transfer them to the stock. This procedure will result in a cleaner-tasting broth. Continue to simmer them in the stock for 2 minutes, then transfer them either to a large serving bowl or to individual soup bowls. Garnish and serve immediately.

Corn Soup with Crabmeat

My mother often made this soup using fresh corn. For convenience, canned or frozen corn may be substituted, but I think my mother's recipe is quite superior because she cooked live crabs and picked the crabmeat herself. This soup reheats well and has a rich, thick texture.

SERVES 4

1 lb (450g) fresh corn on the
  cob or 10 oz (275g) canned or
  frozen sweetcorn
1 egg white
1 tsp (5ml) sesame oil
5 cups (1.2L) Chicken Stock
  (page 75)
1 tbsp (15ml) Shaoxing rice
  wine or dry sherry
1 tbsp (15ml) light soy sauce
2 tsp (10ml) finely chopped
  fresh ginger
1 tsp (5ml) sugar
2 tsp (10ml) cornstarch,
  blended with 2 tsp (10ml)
  water
salt and white pepper
8 oz (225g) freshly cooked or
  frozen crabmeat

FOR THE GARNISH

2 tbsp (30ml) finely chopped
  green onions

If you are using fresh corn, wash the cobs and remove the kernels with a sharp knife or cleaver. You should end up with about 10 oz (275g). Mix the egg white and sesame oil together in a small bowl and set it aside.

Bring the stock to a simmer in a large saucepan and add the corn. Simmer for 15 minutes, uncovered, then add the rice wine, soy sauce, ginger, sugar and cornstarch mixture, along with 1 tsp (5ml) of salt and ¼ tsp (1ml) of white pepper.

Bring back to a boil, then lower the heat to a simmer. Add the crabmeat, then slowly pour in the egg white mixture in a steady stream, stirring all the time. Transfer the soup to a tureen, garnish with the green onions and serve.

Tomato Eggflower Soup

Tomatoes were first introduced into China less than 200 years ago, probably brought by the Portuguese. They were gradually adopted into southern Chinese cuisine, and have become one of its most popular ingredients. Their intense, sweet flavor, brilliant color and versatility lend them perfectly to Chinese cookery. Here they are used to enhance my adaptation of lightly beaten eggs, which lie flat on the surface of the soup like lilies on a pond. This effect is created by gently guiding the eggs over the soup in strands instead of dropping the mixture in all at once, which would cause the egg to lump together. The egg mixture slightly thickens the soup, which nevertheless remains very light.

This is an impressive-looking soup but it is very easy to make. It is especially delightful in summer, when fresh tomatoes are at their most plentiful. Although canned tomatoes are acceptable, fresh ones are always preferable.

SERVES 4

5 cups (1.2L) Chicken Stock
   (page 75)
8 oz (225g) fresh or canned
   tomatoes
2 eggs
2 tsp (10ml) sesame oil
1 tsp (5ml) sugar
1 tbsp (15ml) light soy sauce
salt
3 tbsp (45ml) finely chopped
   green onions, white part only
FOR THE GARNISH
3 tbsp (45ml) finely chopped
   green tops of green onions

Put the chicken stock into a saucepan and bring it to a simmer.

If you are using fresh tomatoes, peel, seed and cut them into 1 in (2.5cm) cubes. If you are using canned tomatoes, chop them into small chunks. Lightly beat the eggs and combine them with the sesame oil in a small bowl.

Add the sugar, soy sauce and 1 tsp (5ml) of salt to the simmering stock, and stir to mix them in well. Then add the tomatoes and simmer for 2 minutes.

Stir in the green onions, then add the egg mixture in a very slow, thin stream. Using a chopstick or a fork, pull the egg slowly into strands. (I have found that stirring the egg in a figure of eight works quite well.)

Garnish the soup with the finely chopped green onion tops and serve.

Watercress Soup

Here is a soup from my childhood. My mother used to make it with pork pieces, and its delightful fragrance emanating from the kitchen signified good things to come.

SERVES 4

5 cups (1.2L) Chicken Stock
  or Pork and Chicken Stock
  (page 75)
2 tbsp (30ml) light soy sauce
1 tsp (5ml) sugar
salt and white pepper
5 oz (150g) watercress, stems
  removed
2 tsp (10ml) finely chopped
  fresh ginger
3 tbsp (45ml) finely chopped
  green onions

Bring the stock to a simmer in a large saucepan. Add the soy sauce and sugar, season with ½ tsp (2ml) of salt and ¼ tsp (1ml) of white pepper and simmer for 3 minutes. Then add the watercress leaves, ginger and green onions and continue to simmer the soup for another 4 minutes. Serve at once.

Beancurd Spinach Soup

A good homemade chicken stock is vital here, as the ingredients are subtly flavored.

SERVES 4

1 lb (450g) fresh spinach
1 lb (450g) fresh beancurd
5 cups (1.2L) Chicken Stock
  (page 75)
1 tbsp (15ml) Shaoxing rice
  wine or dry sherry
1 tbsp (15ml) light soy sauce
1 tsp (5ml) sugar
1 tsp (5ml) sesame oil
1 tsp (5ml) dark soy sauce
salt and black pepper
FOR THE GARNISH
chopped green onions

Remove the stems from the spinach and wash the leaves well. Leave them to drain in a colander. Gently cut the beancurd into ½ in (1cm) cubes and leave to drain on paper towels for 10 minutes.

Bring the chicken stock to a simmer in a medium-sized saucepan. Add the beancurd and simmer for 2 minutes. Then add the rest of the ingredients except the spinach, season with 1 tsp (5ml) of salt and some black pepper and simmer for another 10 minutes. The beancurd will swell, taking on the flavor of the soup.

Finally, add the spinach leaves and cook for 2 minutes. Garnish with the green onions and serve in individual bowls or a soup tureen.

Beef Soup with Cilantro

Beef is relatively unusual in classical Chinese cuisine, but it has become more common in modern China. However, you will note the small amount of beef that is being used here. This is a simple but satisfying and refreshing soup, rich and flavorful. As with all delicious soups, good stock is essential, and, although this is called beef soup, chicken stock is used as is normal in Chinese cookery. The soup is easily prepared and is perfect as a starter or, with the addition of some quickly blanched noodles, a light meal.

SERVES 4

8 oz (225g) ground beef

2 tsp (10ml) Shaoxing rice wine
   or dry sherry

3 tsp (15ml) cornstarch

1 tbsp (15ml) dark soy sauce,
   plus 2 tsp (10ml)

2 eggs, beaten

2 tsp (10ml) sesame oil

5 cups (1.2L) Chicken Stock
   (page 75)

3 tsp (15ml) sugar

2 tsp (10ml) light soy sauce

salt and white pepper

FOR THE GARNISH

3 tbsp (45ml) finely chopped
   green onions

3 tbsp (45ml) finely chopped
   cilantro

In a medium bowl combine the beef with the rice wine, 1 tsp (5ml) of cornstarch and 1 tbsp (15ml) of dark soy sauce. In a small bowl, combine the eggs with the sesame oil. In a second small bowl, mix the remaining 2 tsp (10ml) of cornstarch with 1 tbsp (15ml) of water.

Bring the chicken stock to a simmer in a large saucepan. Add the beef, 1 tsp (5ml) of sugar and the cornstarch mixture and stir for just 1 minute, breaking up any lumps of meat. Add the remaining 2 tsp (10ml) of dark soy sauce, the light soy sauce, the remaining sugar, 2 tsp (10ml) of salt and ½ tsp (2ml) of pepper and simmer for 2 minutes.

Next, add the egg mixture in a very slow, thin stream, using a chopstick or fork to pull the egg slowly into strands. Turn the mixture into a soup tureen or bowl, garnish with the green onions and cilantro and serve at once.

MEAT

Although the Chinese traditionally eat meat in fairly small quantities, they are very fond of it. Pork in particular is looked upon with great regard, but the versatility of regional cuisines means that every type of meat has a place on the Chinese table.

Honeyglazed Pork

This is my adaptation of a famous Chinese dish called Honey Ham with Lotus Seed. Chinese ham is braised in a sugar, Shaoxing rice wine and lotus seed mixture that has been reduced to a syrup, which glazes the ham like honey. This process usually takes about 4 hours, but I have found that the method can also be applied to thick pork chops, taking considerably less time while maintaining the excellent results. Serve with plain steamed rice and a simple green vegetable dish.

SERVES 4–6

1 lb (450g) boned pork chops, at least 1½ in (4cm) thick
salt
2 green onions
1½ tbsp (22ml) peanut or vegetable oil
2 slices of fresh ginger

FOR THE BRAISING SAUCE

2 cups (450ml) Shaoxing rice wine or dry sherry, or ¾ cup (175 ml) Shaoxing rice wine or dry sherry mixed with 1¼ cups (300ml) Chicken Stock (page 75)
2 tbsp (30ml) light soy sauce
½ cup (120ml) Chinese rock sugar or granulated sugar
3 tbsp (45ml) roasted Sichuan peppercorns (page 29)

Lightly salt the pork chops with ½ tsp (2ml) of salt and set them aside. Cut the green onions into 3 in (7.5cm) lengths.

Heat a wok or a large skillet over high heat. Add the oil, and when it is very hot and slightly smoking, reduce the heat and add the green onions and ginger. After a few seconds add the pork chops and cook until they are brown.

Bring the braising sauce ingredients to a boil in a heavy-based saucepan or ovenproof casserole dish, then turn the heat down to a simmer. Add the chops, green onions and ginger, turn the heat as low as possible, cover, and simmer for 15 minutes, or until the pork is tender.

When the chops are cooked, remove them from the liquid and let them cool slightly before you slice them, cutting them diagonally. Remove any surface fat from the braising liquid, then spoon some of the liquid over the pork slices. Serve the dish immediately.

The rest of the braising liquid can be cooled and frozen for future use. (Remove any surface fat before transferring it to the freezer.)

Sweet and Sour Pork

Properly prepared, sweet and sour Chinese dishes are so delicately balanced that one is hard pressed to describe them as either strictly sweet or sour.

SERVES 4

1 lb (450g) lean pork
1 tbsp (15ml) Shaoxing rice
   wine or dry sherry
1 tbsp (15ml) light soy sauce
2 tsp (10ml) sesame oil
salt
4 oz (100g) green bell pepper
   (about 1)
4 oz (100g) red bell pepper
   (about 1)
4 oz (100g) carrots
2 oz (50g) green onions
1 egg, beaten
2 tbsp (30ml) cornstarch, plus
   extra for dusting
2 cups (450ml) peanut or
   vegetable oil
3 oz (75g) canned lychees,
   drained, or fresh orange
   segments

FOR THE SAUCE

⅔ cups (150ml) Chicken Stock
   (page 75)
1 tbsp (15ml) light soy sauce
2 tsp (10ml) dark soy sauce
2 tsp (10ml) sesame oil
1½ tbsp (22ml) Chinese white
   rice vinegar or cider vinegar
1 tbsp (15ml) sugar
2 tbsp (30ml) tomato paste or
   ketchup
salt and white pepper
2 tsp (10ml) cornstarch

Cut the pork into 1 in (2.5cm) cubes. Put them into a bowl with the rice wine, light soy sauce, sesame oil and 1 tsp (5ml) of salt, and leave to marinate for 20 minutes.

Meanwhile, cut the green and red bell peppers into 1 in (2.5cm) squares. Peel the carrots and cut them into 1 in (2.5cm) pieces. Cut the green onions into 1 in (2.5cm) pieces. Bring a saucepan of water to a boil, add the carrots and blanch for around 4 minutes, then drain and set aside.

Mix the egg and cornstarch in a bowl until they are well blended into a batter. Lift the pork cubes out of the marinade, dust them with cornstarch, put them into the batter and coat each piece well. Heat the oil in a deep-fat fryer or a large wok until it is slightly smoking. Remove the pork pieces from the batter with a slotted spoon and deep-fry them. Drain the deep-fried pork on paper towels.

To make the sauce, combine the chicken stock, soy sauces, sesame oil, vinegar, sugar and tomato paste with ½ tsp (2ml) of salt and 1 tsp (5ml) of white pepper in a large saucepan and bring to the boil. Add all the vegetables and stir well.

In a small bowl, blend the cornstarch with 1 tbsp (15ml) of water. Stir this mixture into the sauce and bring it back to a boil, then turn the heat down to a simmer. Add the lychees or oranges and the pork. Mix well, then turn the mixture onto a deep platter and serve at once.

Chili Pork Spareribs

Here is a spicy and delicious way of preparing pork spareribs. Although the recipe involves a series of techniques, much of the work can be done ahead of time and the dish can be quickly completed at the last moment. The combination of spices and sauces is the hallmark of dishes from western China. It is worthwhile getting the chili bean sauce for an authentic taste. The spareribs can be finished in the oven, under a grill or on a barbecue.

SERVES 4

2⅓ cups (600ml) peanut or
   vegetable oil
1⅔ lb (750g) pork spareribs,
   separated into individual ribs

FOR THE BRAISING SAUCE

3⅔ cups (900ml) Chicken
   Stock (page 75)
2 tbsp (30ml) chili bean sauce
1 tbsp (15ml) Chinese rock
   sugar or granulated sugar
⅓ cup (85ml) Shaoxing rice
   wine or dry sherry
1½ tbsp (22ml) dark soy sauce
2 tbsp (30ml) light soy sauce
2 tbsp (30ml) finely chopped
   garlic
3 tbsp (45ml) finely chopped
   green onions
2 tbsp (30ml) whole yellow
   bean sauce
3 tbsp (45ml) hoisin sauce
2 tbsp (30ml) cornstarch, mixed
   with 3 tbsp (45ml) water

FOR THE GARNISH

chopped green onions

Heat the oil in a deep-fat fryer or a large wok, and deep-fry the spareribs until they are brown and crisp. Do this in several batches, draining each cooked batch well on paper towels.

Combine all the braising sauce ingredients in a large saucepan and bring to a boil. Add the deep-fried spareribs and simmer them, covered, for about 1 hour, or until they are tender. Drain off the sauce and remove any remaining fat. The sauce can now be frozen and reused next time you want to make this dish. The dish can be prepared up to this point the day before.

Preheat the oven to 350°F (180°C). Put the spareribs on a rack in a roasting pan and bake them in the oven for 15 to 20 minutes, until they are nice and brown. Baste them from time to time with the braising sauce, if you like. You can also cook the spareribs under a broiler or on a barbecue, until they are brown. Using a cleaver or a sharp, heavy knife, chop the spareribs into pieces 2½ in (6cm) long. Turn them onto a warm serving platter, garnish with green onions and serve at once.

Steamed Pork with Spicy Vegetables

Preserved vegetables are often used in meat dishes in China as a method of stretching and flavoring meats. This dish can be made with Sichuan preserved vegetables, which can be bought canned from Chinese grocers and have a pleasant crunchy texture. This recipe employs the technique of steaming, which keeps the dish moist and hot without any risk of overcooking the pork. It is a tasty family dish that reheats well.

SERVES 4

3 oz (75g) Sichuan preserved
    vegetables

1lb (450g) ground pork

1 egg white

1 tbsp (15ml) Shaoxing rice
    wine or dry sherry

1 tbsp (15ml) chili bean sauce

2 tsp (10ml) dark soy sauce

1 tsp (5ml) light soy sauce

2 tsp (10ml) sugar

3 tbsp (45ml) finely chopped
    green onions

1 tbsp (15ml) finely chopped
    fresh ginger

Rinse the preserved vegetables thoroughly under running water and drain in a sieve or colander. Then chop finely and put into a bowl. Add the pork and all the other ingredients and mix everything together very well. Put the mixture on a deep ovenproof plate, and make a well in the center where the juices can collect during cooking.

Next, set up a steamer, or put a rack into a wok or deep saucepan, and pour in 2 in (5cm) of water. Bring the water to a boil over a high heat. Carefully lower the plate of pork into the steamer or onto the rack. Turn the heat to low and cover the wok or saucepan tightly. Steam the pork gently for 40 minutes, or until it is cooked. Serve this dish on the plate on which it is steamed.

Five-spice Spareribs

This is a delightful meat dish that engages the palate with many contrasting tastes. The spareribs are first marinated, then deep-fried in oil, then slowly braised in an unusual, piquant sauce. They can be easily reheated, and the taste improves if they are cooked the day before they are eaten.

SERVES 4

1⅔ lb (750g) pork spareribs
2⅓ cups (600ml) peanut or
   vegetable oil

FOR THE MARINADE

1 tbsp (15ml) Shaoxing rice
   wine or dry sherry
1 tbsp (15ml) light soy sauce
1 tbsp (15ml) Chinese black rice
   vinegar or cider vinegar
2 tsp (10ml) sesame oil
1 tbsp (15ml) cornstarch

FOR THE SAUCE

2 tbsp (30ml) finely chopped
   garlic
2 tsp (10ml) five-spice powder
3 tbsp (45ml) finely chopped
   green onions
3 tbsp (45ml) Chinese rock
   sugar or granulated sugar
3 tbsp (45ml) Shaoxing rice
   wine or dry sherry
⅔ cup (150ml) Chicken Stock
   (page 75)
1½ tbsp (22ml) light soy sauce
2 tbsp (30ml) dried orange peel
   or fresh orange zest
⅓ cup (85ml) Chinese black
   rice vinegar or cider vinegar

Have your butcher separate the spareribs into individual ribs, and then into chunks approximately 3 in (7.5cm) long. Alternatively, do this yourself using a heavy, sharp cleaver that can cut through the bones. Mix the marinade ingredients together in a bowl and steep the spareribs in the marinade for about 25 minutes at room temperature. Remove the spareribs from the marinade with a slotted spoon.

Heat the oil in a deep-fat fryer or a large wok. When the oil is very hot and slightly steaming, slowly brown the marinated spareribs in several batches, until they are brown. Drain each cooked batch on paper towels. (Leave the cooking oil to cool. Strain it through a filter once it has cooled if you want to keep it for reuse when cooking pork.)

Put the sauce ingredients into a clean wok or large skillet. Bring the sauce to a boil, then reduce the heat. Add the spareribs and simmer them slowly, covered, for about 40 minutes, stirring occasionally. If necessary, add a little water to the sauce to prevent them drying up. Skim off any surface fat, turn onto a serving plate and serve at once.

Barbecued Roast Pork

Chinese homes do not usually have ovens, partly for reasons of space and partly because of the style of home cooking, which is usually done in one large wok. Instead we go to speciality shops that sell roast duck or pig and, in this case, barbecued pork. However, I've managed to make a good version of barbecued roast pork in a home oven. Remember, you don't have to eat all of it at once. It is wonderful in sandwiches or in wonton soups or fried rice. The cooked barbecued pork also freezes quite well.

MAKES 2¼ LB (1KG)

2¼ lb (1kg) boneless pork
   shoulder
3–5 tbsp (45–75ml) honey, for
   basting

FOR THE MARINADE

2 tbsp (30ml) light soy sauce
2 tbsp (30ml) Shaoxing rice
   wine or dry sherry
2 tbsp (30ml) sugar
1 tbsp (15ml) whole yellow bean
   sauce
2 tbsp (30ml) finely chopped
   garlic
2 tbsp (30ml) hoisin sauce
2 tbsp (30ml) fermented red
   beancurd
1 tbsp (15ml) five-spice powder
salt and black pepper

Cut the pork into 7 x 4 in (18 x 10cm) strips. Mix the marinade ingredients in a bowl, add the pork, and leave to marinate overnight in the fridge.

Preheat the oven to 350°F (180°C). While it is heating up, place the pork strips on a rack in a roasting pan, breast side up. Put ⅔ cup (150ml) of water into the roasting pan. (This will prevent the fat from splattering.) Put the pork into the oven and roast for 45 minutes, basting from time to time with the honey. Then turn the heat up to 400°F (200°C) and continue to roast for a further 15 minutes.

Remove the pork from the oven and leave until it is cool enough to handle. Then slice thinly and serve.

Cold Beijing (Peking) Pork

Cold platters are commonly served at banquets in the north of China. The flavor and texture of the meat in this dish reminds me of a European pâté, and it has a very rich flavor. It should be prepared a day in advance and served cold, making menu-planning easier. The pork is first blanched for a few minutes to rid it of any impurities, and is then slowly simmered in a rich liquid infused with Chinese spices. The cooked meat is removed and the braising liquid reduced. This is then poured over the pork, which is left to marinate overnight. This is ideal for summertime and would make a tasty cold dish for a picnic.

SERVES 4–6

1⅔ lb (750g) pork leg, fillet end or shoulder, in one piece

FOR THE BRAISING LIQUID

5 cups (1.2 L) Chicken Stock (page 75)

3 slices of fresh ginger

3 green onions

5 whole star anise

3 tbsp (45ml) Shaoxing rice wine or dry sherry

2 tbsp (30ml) five-spice powder

5 tbsp (75ml) Chinese rock sugar or granulated sugar

5 tbsp (75ml) dark soy sauce

1 tbsp (15ml) roasted Sichuan peppercorns (page 29)

salt

Bring a saucepan of water to a boil. Add the pork and blanch it for about 3–5 minutes. Remove it from the saucepan with a slotted spoon and discard the liquid, then remove the rind from the pork and chop it into small pieces. Rinse the saucepan clean and put back the pork. Add all the braising liquid ingredients and the pieces of rind and season with 1 tbsp (15ml) of salt. Bring the mixture to a boil, then turn the heat down to a very low simmer. Cover the saucepan and simmer for about 2 hours.

Remove the cooked pork from the saucepan with a slotted spoon and skim off as much fat from the liquid as possible. Turn the heat back to high and reduce the liquid to about half. Put the pork into a bowl or deep dish. Strain the reduced liquid and pour it over the meat. Allow it to cool and put it into the fridge. Let it sit in the fridge for at least 8 hours before serving, overnight if possible.

Just before serving, remove the pork and slice it as thinly as possible. If the juice has jelled, cut it into cubes and arrange it as a garnish around the sliced pork, otherwise simply pour some of the cooled liquid over the pork slices and serve.

Steamed Pork Loaf

This is typical of the type of Chinese home cooking I grew up with. It was nutritious and cheap, and my mother often served this variation of steamed pork loaf. The inexpensive salted fish extended the meat, while its briny spiciness added depth to the robust flavor of the pork. Because of the salted fish, the mixture stood up well even with our primitive refrigeration. To me, it tasted even better when it was served two days later.

Salted fish is available from Chinese grocers, both in dried form and in jars of oil. If you are using dried salted fish, be sure to soak it in warm water for 20 minutes before chopping, but salted fish in oil does not need soaking — simply drain it.

SERVES 4

6 oz (175g) water chestnuts, fresh or canned

1 lb (450g) ground fatty pork

3 tbsp (45ml) finely chopped green onions

3 tbsp (45ml) drained salted fish in oil or dried fish, soaked, finely chopped

1 tbsp (15ml) finely chopped fresh ginger

1 tbsp (15ml) light soy sauce

2 tsp (10ml) Shaoxing rice wine or dry sherry

1 tsp (5ml) sugar

2 tsp (10ml) cornstarch

2 tsp (10ml) sesame oil

4 tbsp (60ml) Chicken Stock (page 75)

salt and black pepper

If you are using fresh water chestnuts, peel and chop them finely. If you are using canned water chestnuts, first rinse them well in cold water. Drain in a colander and then chop them finely.

In a large bowl, mix the pork with the water chestnuts, then add the rest of the ingredients. Season with 1 tsp (5ml) of salt and ½ tsp (2ml) of black pepper and mix well with your hands. Transfer the mixture onto a deep heatproof plate and form into a flat loaf shape.

Set up a steamer, or put a rack into a wok or deep saucepan, and fill it with about 2 in (5cm) of water. Bring the water to a boil, then reduce the heat to a low simmer. Gently lower in the loaf, still on its plate, cover, and steam for 25 minutes or until the pork is cooked through. Serve immediately.

Stir-fried Ground Pork

The secret of this delicious, easy-to-prepare and inexpensive dish lies in the use of preserved vegetables, which are typical of northern Chinese cuisine. In the north, people must preserve vegetables by salting or pickling, since the winters are long and cold. If you like your dish a bit spicier, like me, use Sichuan preserved vegetables.

SERVES 4

4 oz (100g) Tianjin or Sichuan
    preserved vegetables
1½ tbsp (22ml) peanut or
    vegetable oil
1 lb (450g) ground pork
2 tbsp (30ml) dark soy sauce
1 tbsp (15ml) Shaoxing rice
    wine or dry sherry
2 tsp (10ml) sesame oil
2 tsp (10ml) sugar
TO SERVE
lettuce leaves or Chinese
    Pancakes (page 324)
FOR THE GARNISH
3 tbsp (45ml) finely chopped
    green onions
fresh chili (optional)

Rinse the preserved vegetables well in cold water. Drain them in a colander and blot them dry with paper towels. Chop them finely and set them aside.

Heat a wok or a large skillet until it is hot. Add the oil, and when it is very hot and slightly smoking, add the pork and stir-fry it for 2 minutes, stirring constantly to break up any lumps. Add the preserved vegetables and the rest of the ingredients and continue to stir-fry for another 5 minutes, or until the pork is cooked.

If you are serving the pork with Chinese pancakes or lettuce leaves, have each person pile a little of the meat mixture into a pancake or leaf, wrap it up well and eat it with his or her fingers.

Stir-fried Pork with Green Onions

This is a basic stir-fried dish in the southern Chinese tradition. The key to success in this recipe is not to overcook the pork.

SERVES 3–4

1 lb (450g) boneless pork fillet
1 tbsp (15ml) Shaoxing rice
   wine or dry sherry
1 tbsp (15ml) light soy sauce
2 tsp (10ml) sesame oil
1 tsp (5ml) cornstarch
8 green onions
1 tbsp (15ml) peanut or
   vegetable oil
1 tsp (5ml) sugar
salt and black pepper

Cut the pork into thick slices 2 in (5cm) long. Put into a bowl and mix in the rice wine, soy sauce, sesame oil and cornstarch. Let the mixture sit for 10–15 minutes so that the pork absorbs the flavors of the marinade. Cut the green onions on the diagonal into 2 in (5cm) lengths.

Heat a wok or large skillet until it is very hot. Add the oil, and when it is very hot and slightly smoking, add the pork slices and stir-fry them until they are brown. Add the green onions, sugar, 2 tsp (10ml) of salt and 1 tsp (5ml) of black pepper and continue to stir-fry until the pork is cooked and slightly firm. This should take 3–4 minutes. Remove the pork from the pan and arrange on a warm serving platter. Pour over any juices remaining in the wok and serve at once.

Roast Crispy Pork Belly

The secret of getting crispy skin here is to blanch the skin and to let it dry using a technique similar to the one used for Beijing (Peking) Duck (page 182).

SERVES 4–6

3 lb (1.5kg) boneless pork belly,
   with rind
FOR THE MARINADE
4 tbsp (60ml) coarse sea salt
2 tbsp (30ml) roasted and
   ground Sichuan peppercorns
   (page 29)
2 tbsp (30ml) five-spice powder
1 tbsp (15ml) sugar
white pepper

Pierce the rind side of the pork with a sharp fork or knife until the skin is covered with fine holes. Insert a meat hook into the meat to secure it. Bring a saucepan of water to a boil and ladle the hot water over the rind side of the pork several times.

Heat a wok or a large skillet, add the salt, peppercorns, five-spice, sugar and 2 tsp (10ml) of white pepper and stir-fry the mixture for 3 minutes, until it is hot. Allow the mixture to cool slightly and rub over the flesh side of the pork. Hang the meat to dry for 8 hours or overnight in a cool place.

Preheat the oven to 400°F (200°C). Place the pork on a rack, rind side up, over a baking sheet of water and roast for 20 minutes, then reduce the heat to 350°F (180°C) and roast for 2 hours. Finally, turn the heat up to 450°F (230°C) and roast for a further 15 minutes. Remove from the oven, allow to cool and serve carved into bite-sized pieces.

Chiu Chow–style Sweet and Sour Pork

This is a delicious and unusual version of sweet and sour pork, based on a recipe from a region of southern China. You can use either fresh or canned water chestnuts.

SERVES 4

6 oz (175g) water chestnuts
1 lb (450g) ground fatty pork
1 egg white
2 tbsp (30ml) light soy sauce
1 tbsp (15ml) dark soy sauce
2 tbsp (30ml) Shaoxing rice
   wine or dry sherry
1½ tbsp (22ml) sugar
salt and black pepper
8 oz (225g) caul fat, for
   wrapping
4 oz (100g) green bell pepper
   (about 1)
4 oz (100g) red bell pepper
   (about 1)
4 oz (100g) carrots
4 green onions
cornstarch or potato flour, for
   dusting
2 cups (450ml) peanut or
   vegetable oil
3 oz (75g) canned lychees

FOR THE SAUCE

⅔ cup (150ml) Chicken Stock
   (page 75)
1 tbsp (15ml) light soy sauce
2 tsp (10ml) dark soy sauce
2 tsp (10ml) sesame oil
1½ tbsp (22ml) Chinese white
   rice vinegar
1 tbsp (15ml) sugar
2 tbsp (30ml) tomato paste or
   ketchup
salt and white pepper

If you are using fresh water chestnuts, peel and chop them finely. If you are using canned water chestnuts, first rinse them well in cold water. Drain in a colander and then chop them finely.

Mix the pork with the egg white and 4 tbsp (60ml) of cold water by hand. The mixture should be light and fluffy. Do not use a blender, as it would make the mixture too dense. Then add the water chestnuts, soy sauces, rice wine, sugar, 2 tsp (10ml) of salt and ½ tsp (2ml) of black pepper and mix for another 30 seconds. Divide the pork into small rounds, each about the size of a golf ball. Cut the caul fat into 3 in (7.5cm) squares and wrap one around each pork round.

Meanwhile, cut the green and red bell peppers into 1 in (2.5cm) squares. Peel the carrots and cut them thinly on the diagonal. Cut the green onions into 1 in (2.5cm) pieces. (The uniform size of the meat and vegetables adds to the visual appeal of the dish.) Bring a saucepan of water to a boil and blanch the carrots and bell peppers until just tender, about 4 minutes, then drain and set aside.

Dust the pork rounds with cornstarch, shaking off any excess. Heat the oil in a deep-fat fryer or a large wok until it is slightly smoking. Turn the heat to moderate and deep-fry the rounds until they are crispy. Drain them on paper towels.

Combine the sauce ingredients along with ½ tsp (2ml) of salt and 1 tsp (5ml) of white pepper in a large saucepan and bring to a boil. Add all the vegetables and stir well. Bring back to a boil, then turn the heat down so that the mixture is simmering and cook for 2 minutes. Drain and add the lychees and the pork and mix well. Turn the mixture onto a deep platter and serve at once.

Pork with Black Bean Sauce

Pork goes particularly well with black beans, the salty and pungent flavor of which is so distinctively southern Chinese. This simple, homely, stir-fried dish is one I often ate as a child. Sometimes my mother would vary the taste by adding an extra spicy touch of chili bean sauce. It is very quick to cook and goes well with plain rice and any stir-fried vegetable.

SERVES 4

1 lb (450g) lean pork
1½ tbsp (22ml) peanut or
   vegetable oil
1½ tbsp (22ml) black beans,
   coarsely chopped
1 tbsp (15ml) finely chopped
   garlic
3 tbsp (45ml) finely chopped
   green onions
1 tbsp (15ml) chopped shallots
1½ tbsp (22ml) light soy sauce
1 tsp (5ml) sugar
1 tbsp (15ml) Chicken Stock
   (page 75) or water
1 tbsp (15ml) sesame oil

FOR THE MARINADE
1 tbsp (15ml) Shaoxing rice
   wine or dry sherry
1 tbsp (15ml) light soy sauce
2 tsp (10ml) sesame oil
1 tsp (5ml) cornstarch

FOR THE GARNISH
chopped green onions

Cut the pork into thin slices 2 in (5cm) long. Put the slices into a small bowl and mix them well with the marinade ingredients. Let them marinate for about 20 minutes.

Heat a wok or large skillet until it is hot. Add half the oil, and when it is very hot and almost smoking, lift the pork out of the marinade with a slotted spoon, put it into the wok and quickly stir-fry it for about 2–3 minutes. Transfer it to a bowl.

Wipe the wok clean, reheat it and add the rest of the oil. Then quickly add the black beans, garlic, green onions and shallots. A few seconds later add the soy sauce, sugar, chicken stock and sesame oil. Bring to a boil, then return the pork to the wok or skillet and stir-fry for another 5 minutes. Turn everything onto a platter and serve at once.

Mu Shu Pork with Chinese Pancakes

This popular northern Chinese dish has become fashionable in the West. It is not difficult to see why: the shredded ingredients have a delightful textural quality, and the combination, flavored by hoisin sauce (in Beijing a salty bean paste would be used) and enclosed by Chinese pancakes, works beautifully.

SERVES 4

1 lb (450g) boneless pork fillet
1 egg white
2 tsp (10ml) cornstarch
salt and black pepper
2 oz (50g) Chinese wood ear
   mushrooms
1 oz (25g) dried lily stems,
   soaked
1¼ cups (300ml) peanut or
   vegetable oil, plus
   1½ tbsp (22ml)
4 eggs, beaten
6 green onions, finely shredded
1 tsp (5ml) sugar
1 tbsp (15ml) Shaoxing rice
   wine or dry sherry
1½ tbsp (22ml) light soy sauce
2 tsp (10ml) sesame oil

TO SERVE

Chinese Pancakes (page 324)
hoisin sauce, for dipping

Cut the pork into thin strips about 3 in (7.5cm) long. Combine them with the egg white, cornstarch and ½ tsp (2ml) of salt in a small bowl, and place in the fridge for about 20 minutes.

Soak the mushrooms in warm water for 20 minutes, then drain them and squeeze out the excess liquid. Rinse them in several changes of water, then remove and discard the stems and finely shred.

Trim the hard ends of the lily stems and shred them by pulling them apart. Heat a wok or large skillet until it is very hot and add the 1¼ cups (300ml) of oil. When it is very hot, remove the wok from the heat and immediately add the pork strips, stirring vigorously to keep them from sticking. When the pork turns white, about 1 minute, quickly drain it in a stainless steel colander set over a bowl. Save 2 tbsp (30ml) of the oil and discard the rest.

Wipe the wok clean. Reheat it until it is hot, then add the reserved 2 tbsp (30ml) of oil. Immediately add the eggs and gently stir-fry them by lifting the mixture up and around until it is set. Remove it immediately and drain on paper towels, then cut it into strips.

Wipe the wok clean with paper towels and reheat. When it is very hot, add the remaining 1½ tbsp (22ml) of oil. Add the shredded lily stems, wood ears and green onions and stir-fry for 1 minute, then add the rest of the ingredients along with 1 tsp (5ml) each of salt and black pepper, and stir-fry for another 2 minutes. Return the cooked pork and egg to the wok or skillet and stir-fry the mixture for another 2 minutes, mixing thoroughly. Serve at once with Chinese pancakes and hoisin sauce.

Twice-cooked Pork

This recipe captures many of the elements of authentic, ancient Chinese cuisine. Most of the flavor of pork is concentrated in the fat, but the problem with fatty meat is its chewy, greasy texture. Twice-cooking is the age-old Chinese solution to this problem. First the meat is simmered slowly to make it tender and to render some of the fat; then it is stir-fried to rid it of most of the remaining fat. Despite the loss of so much of the fat, the meat retains its authentic pork flavor. Here the pork is finished off in a spicy mixture that makes it delicious and mouthwatering. This dish goes well with plain rice and reheats well.

SERVES 4

2¼ lb (1kg) pork belly, with rind

4 slices of fresh ginger

6 green onions

2 tbsp (30ml) peanut or vegetable oil

3 tbsp (45ml) finely chopped garlic

1 small onion, thinly sliced

1 red bell pepper, seeded and thinly sliced

1 green bell pepper, seeded and thinly sliced

8 oz (225g) leeks, white part only, shredded

3 tbsp (45ml) Chicken Stock (page 75)

3 tbsp (45ml) hoisin sauce

1½ tbsp (22ml) chili bean sauce

2 tbsp (30ml) Shaoxing rice wine or dry sherry

1 tbsp (15ml) dark soy sauce

1 tsp (5ml) sugar

Bring a saucepan of salted water to a boil. Add the pork belly and simmer for 10 minutes, skimming all the while. Add the ginger and green onions, turn the heat to low, cover tightly and simmer for 1½ hours. Drain the meat thoroughly in a colander. Discard the liquid and the aromatics. When the meat is cool enough to handle, cut it into 2 x ½ in (5 x 1cm), bite-sized pieces.

Heat a wok over high heat until it is hot. Add the oil, and when it is very hot and slightly smoking, add the meat and use the wok cover to keep the fat from splattering. Stir-fry for 20 minutes, until the meat is brown and the fat is rendered. Drain carefully in a colander, keeping 1 tbsp (15ml) of oil in the wok. Reheat the wok, and when it is hot, add the garlic, onion, bell peppers and leeks and stir-fry for 4 minutes, or until the vegetables are tender. Then add the rest of the ingredients, season with 1 tsp (5ml) of salt and return the pork to the mixture. Turn the heat down, cover, and braise for 15 minutes, until tender. Turn onto a platter and serve at once.

Lionhead Pork Meatball Casserole

This dish has a fanciful name and is very popular in eastern as well as other parts of China. The meatballs are said to resemble a lion's head and the leaves its mane. It is a hearty and delicious dish. The secret of its distinctive texture may be found in the combination of cold water and egg white with fatty ground pork, the result being a light and fluffy meatball. In China the mixing is done by hand, with the cook throwing the meat against the side of a bowl to tenderize and fluff the meat. This dish can be prepared ahead of time and reheated.

SERVES 3–4

1 lb (450g) Chinese leaves
6 oz (175g) water chestnuts, fresh or canned
1 lb (450g) ground fatty pork
1 egg white
4 tbsp (60ml) cold water
2 tbsp (30ml) light soy sauce
1 tbsp (15ml) dark soy sauce
2 tbsp (30ml) Shaoxing rice wine or dry sherry
1½ tbsp (22ml) sugar
salt and black pepper
cornstarch, for dusting
3–5 tbsp (45–75ml) peanut or vegetable oil
4 garlic cloves, peeled and crushed
2 cups (450ml) Chicken Stock (page 75)

Separate the stalks from the Chinese leaves and cut them into 2 in (5cm) strips. If you are using fresh water chestnuts, peel and chop them finely. If you are using canned water chestnuts, first rinse them well in cold water. Drain in a colander and then chop them finely.

Mix together the pork, egg white and cold water by hand. The mixture should be light and fluffy. Do not use a blender, as it would make the mixture too dense. Add the water chestnuts, soy sauces, rice wine, sugar, 2 tsp (10ml) of salt and ½ tsp (2ml) of black pepper and mix for another 30 seconds.

Divide the mixture into 6 equal parts and roll each one into a large meatball. Dust each meatball with cornstarch. Heat a wok over a high heat until it is hot. Add 3–4 tbsp (45–60ml) of oil, and when it is very hot and slightly smoking, add the meatballs, turn the heat down and brown them slowly. Remove the meatballs from the wok and drain on paper towels.

Wipe the wok clean with paper towels and reheat it over high heat until it is hot. Add 2 more tsp (10ml) of oil, and when it is very hot and slightly smoking, add the garlic and stir-fry for 10 seconds. Then add the Chinese leaves and stir-fry for 20 seconds. Add the chicken stock and continue to cook for 2 minutes, until the leaves are soft. Transfer the mixture to an ovenproof casserole dish. Lay the meatballs on top of the leaves, bring the mixture to a boil, then turn the heat to very low, cover and simmer for 1½ hours.

Arrange the Chinese leaves on a platter or in individual bowls, lay the meatballs on top, pour the sauce over the dish and serve at once.

Braised Pork with Beancurd

This is one of the most famous family dishes in China. It is sometimes known as "Ma Po's" beancurd. My mother used to make a wonderful version of this simple peasant dish, using a range of spices to transform fresh but rather bland beancurd into truly delicious fare. This recipe is typical of the Chinese flair for stretching scarce meat, and it makes an economical, tasty and very nutritious dish.

SERVES 4

1 lb (450g) fresh, soft, silky
   beancurd
1½ tbsp (22ml) peanut or
   vegetable oil
2 tbsp (30ml) finely chopped
   garlic
1 tbsp (15ml) finely chopped
   fresh ginger
12 oz (350g) ground pork or
   ground beef
3 tbsp (45ml) finely chopped
   green onions
2 tbsp (30ml) chili bean sauce
1 tsp (5ml) sugar
1½ tbsp (22ml) Shaoxing rice
   wine or dry sherry
1 tbsp (15ml) dark soy sauce
1 tbsp (15ml) light soy sauce
1½ tbsp (22ml) whole yellow
   bean sauce
5 tbsp (75ml) Chicken Stock
   (page 75)

FOR THE GARNISH

1 tsp (5ml) roasted and ground
   Sichuan peppercorns
   (page 29)
2 tbsp (30ml) finely chopped
   green onions

Gently cut the beancurd into ½ in (1cm) cubes and put them into a sieve to drain. Then lay them on paper towels to drain for another 10 minutes.

Heat a wok or a large skillet over high heat until it is hot. Add the oil, and when it is very hot and slightly smoking, add the garlic and ginger. A few seconds later, add the ground pork or beef and stir-fry for 2 minutes. Then add all the other ingredients except the beancurd. Bring the mixture to a boil, then turn the heat down to low. Add the beancurd and mix it in well but gently, taking care not to break up the chunks. Let the mixture simmer slowly, uncovered, for about 15 minutes. If necessary add a little more chicken stock during this time. Garnish with the ground Sichuan peppercorns and chopped green onions.

Braised Pork Belly Shanghai Style

Pork belly is an inexpensive cut of pork that is very popular in Chinese cuisine, and it has always been a favorite of mine. At first glance it might look rather fatty and unappetizing, but its gelatinous texture is highly prized by the Chinese, and when it is properly cooked the taste is unbeatable. In this recipe the long simmering process renders down most of the fat, leaving a juicy, delicious dish that goes very well with plain steamed rice.

SERVES 6

3 lb (1.5kg) pork belly,
   including the bones
salt
3 tbsp (45ml) peanut oil
FOR THE BRAISING LIQUID
6 slices of fresh ginger
5 cups (1.2L) Chicken Stock
   (page 75)
2⅓ cups (600ml) Shaoxing rice
   wine or dry sherry
⅔ cup (150ml) light soy sauce
⅔ cup (150ml) dark soy sauce
⅔ cup (150ml) Chinese rock
   sugar or granulated sugar
2 tsp (10ml) five-spice powder
3 tbsp (45ml) whole yellow
   bean sauce
3 tbsp (45ml) hoisin sauce
6 green onions
white pepper

This joint can be cooked with its bones left in. If you get your butcher to remove the bones, be sure to add them to the saucepan with the braising liquid for greater flavor. Rub the pork belly with 1 tbsp (15ml) of salt and let it stand for 1 hour. Then carefully rinse the salt off. This helps to clean the pork and to firm it up by drawing out some of the meat's moisture. Dry the meat with paper towels.

Heat a wok or a large skillet over high heat until it is hot. Add the oil, and when it is very hot and slightly smoking, brown the pork belly, rind side only, until it is crisp and brown (cover the wok to prevent splattering). Add more oil if you feel it is necessary.

Put the braising liquid ingredients into a large saucepan or ovenproof casserole dish and season with 2 tsp (10ml) of white pepper. Bring the liquid to a simmer, then add the browned pork belly. Cover the pan and simmer slowly for 2–2½ hours, or until the pork is very tender.

When the pork is cooked, remove it from the pan and let it cool slightly. (The braising liquid can now be cooled and frozen for reuse. Remove any surface fat before transferring it to the freezer.) Slice the meat thinly. The Chinese would serve the pork rind and fat as well as the meat, but do remove it if you prefer. If you like, some of the braising liquid may be thickened with a little cornstarch and served as a sauce over the sliced pork. If you do this, be sure to remove all traces of fat from the liquid before thickening it.

Stuffed Beancurd

Beancurd is nutritious and inexpensive, but by itself it is rather bland. My mother used an old Chinese culinary trick of stuffing it with a pork and shrimp mixture, transforming the boring beancurd into quite a delicious dish. The trick is to hollow out the beancurd and press in the stuffing. It is not as hard as you may think, and can make a sensational talking point for any dinner party.

SERVES 4

1 lb (450g) fresh, firm beancurd

3 tbsp (45ml) peanut or
    vegetable oil

2 tbsp (30ml) finely chopped
    green onions or cilantro

FOR THE STUFFING

12 oz (350g) uncooked shrimp,
    peeled and minced coarsely

4 oz (100g) ground fatty pork

2 oz (50g) finely minced Parma
    ham

3 tbsp (45ml) finely chopped
    green onions

1 tbsp (15ml) finely chopped
    fresh ginger

2 tsp (10ml) Shaoxing rice wine
    or dry sherry

1 tsp (5ml) sugar

2 tsp (10ml) sesame oil

1 egg white, lightly beaten

salt and black pepper

FOR THE SAUCE

1 tbsp (15ml) light soy sauce

⅓ cup (85ml) Chicken Stock
    (page 75)

2 tbsp (30ml) oyster sauce

1 tbsp (15ml) Shaoxing rice
    wine or dry sherry

2 tsp (10ml) sesame oil

First make the stuffing by mixing all the ingredients together in a bowl and seasoning with 2 tsp (10ml) of salt and some black pepper to taste.

Cut the pieces of beancurd diagonally into triangles. Take one of the triangles and gently scoop out the center, making a pocket in the beancurd as deep as you can without breaking the sides. Gently, using a small spoon, press some of the stuffing into the pocket you have created. Continue to do this until you have used up all the beancurd.

Heat a skillet until it is hot and add the oil. Turn down the heat and pan-fry the beancurd triangles on all sides, until they are lightly browned.

Blot the excess oil with paper towels, then add all the sauce ingredients and simmer over low heat for 5 minutes, or until the sauce is heated through.

Add the chopped green onions or cilantro and serve straightaway.

Hot and Sour Kidneys

Pig's kidneys are tender and tasty when stir-fried in this hot and sour sauce. The contrasting flavors of the sauce perfectly complement the strong taste of the kidneys. As with Stir-fried Lamb's Kidneys (page 139), I suggest you marinate the kidneys first in baking soda and then toss them in vinegar and salt. This dish is inexpensive to make, and is delicious served with plain steamed rice and any stir-fried vegetable.

SERVES 4

1 lb (450g) pig's kidneys
1 tsp (5ml) baking soda
2 tsp (10ml) Chinese white rice
    vinegar or cider vinegar
salt
1 tbsp (15ml) peanut or
    vegetable oil
1 tbsp (15ml) finely chopped
    fresh ginger

FOR THE SAUCE

2 tsp (10ml) finely chopped
    garlic
2 tsp (10ml) finely chopped
    fresh ginger
1 tbsp (15ml) chili bean sauce
1 tbsp (15ml) Chinese white rice
    vinegar or cider vinegar
2 tsp (10ml) sugar
1 tbsp (15ml) dark soy sauce
1 tsp (5ml) roasted and ground
    Sichuan peppercorns
    (page 29), optional
1½ tbsp (22ml) Chicken Stock
    (page 75) or water

FOR THE GARNISH

2 tbsp (30ml) chopped green
    onions

Using a sharp knife, remove the thin outer membrane from the kidneys. Then, with a sharp cleaver or knife, split the kidneys in half horizontally. Cut away the small knobs of fat and any tough membrane surrounding them, then score the kidneys in a crisscross pattern and cut them into 1 in (2.5cm) slices. Toss the kidney slices with the baking soda and let them sit for about 20 minutes. Then rinse them thoroughly with cold water and toss them with the vinegar and 1 tsp (5ml) of salt. Put them into a colander and let them drain for at least 30 minutes, preferably longer.

Blot the kidney slices dry with paper towels. Heat a wok or a large skillet over high heat until it is hot. Add the oil, and when it is very hot and slightly smoking, stir-fry the ginger for about 20 seconds to flavor the oil. Then add the kidney slices and stir-fry them for approximately 1 minute. Now add the sauce ingredients and toss everything together well. Continue to stir-fry the mixture for about 2 minutes, or until the edges of the kidneys begin to curl. Turn the mixture onto a warm serving platter, garnish with the green onions and serve at once.

Steamed Beef Meatballs

Since my days as an apprentice in our family restaurant, I have always enjoyed these steamed meatballs. The secret of making them light and fluffy lies in the egg white and cornstarch. We used to mince the beef by hand with two cleavers, one in each hand, adding egg white and cornstarch as we chopped until it was all fully incorporated into the meat. Then we added the seasonings and continued to chop until the meat was almost a light paste. Such chopping requires concentration! But when we finished, we all sat about chatting as we rolled the meat into balls. Today, with a blender or food processor, this long process takes only a few minutes. The texture will be smoother, of course, but it does mean a lot less work. The meatballs reheat well by steaming until heated through, and are perfect for dinners or parties.

SERVES 4

12 oz (350g) minced beef
2 egg whites
5 tbsp (75ml) very cold water
1½ tbsp (22ml) light soy sauce
1 tbsp (15ml) sesame oil
3 tbsp (45ml) finely chopped
  fresh cilantro
3 tbsp (45ml) finely chopped
  spring onions
1 tsp (5ml) cornstarch
2 tsp (10ml) sugar
salt and black pepper

Mix the beef in a food processor for a few seconds. Slowly add the egg whites and cold water and mix for a few more seconds, until they are fully incorporated into the meat. Then add the rest of the ingredients and season with 1 tsp (5ml) of salt and 2 tsp (10ml) of black pepper. Mix for about 1 minute, until the mixture has become a light paste.

Using your hands, form the mixture into 1½ in (4cm) balls — about the size of a golf ball. (This recipe will make about 12 balls.) Next, set up a steamer, or put a rack into a wok or deep saucepan, and fill it with 2 in (5cm) of water. Bring the water to a boil over high heat. Put the meatballs on a heatproof plate and carefully lower it into the steamer or onto the rack. Turn the heat to low and cover the wok or saucepan tightly. Steam the meatballs gently for about 15 minutes. Pour off any liquid that has accumulated on the plate. Put the steamed meatballs on a platter and serve.

Rainbow Beef in Lettuce Cups

This dish is great for a dinner party. Each guest puts a helping of each ingredient into a hollow lettuce leaf and eats it with their fingers. Serve with a bowl of hoisin sauce.

SERVES 4–6

1 lb (450g) ground beef
1 tbsp (15ml) Shaoxing rice
  wine or dry sherry
1 tbsp (15ml) light soy sauce
2 tsp (10ml) sesame oil
2 tsp (10ml) cornstarch
½ oz (15g) Chinese dried
  mushrooms
4 oz (100g) carrots
4 oz (100g) bamboo shoots
4 oz (100g) zucchinis
4 oz (100g) red bell pepper
  (about 1)
8 oz (225g) iceberg lettuce
1¼ cups (300ml) peanut or
  vegetable oil
1 oz (25g) bean thread
  (transparent) noodles

FOR THE STIR-FRY SAUCE

1 tbsp (15ml) finely chopped
  garlic
1 tbsp (15ml) finely chopped
  shallots
3 tbsp (45ml) finely chopped
  green onions
2 tsp (10ml) dark soy sauce
2 tsp (10ml) Shaoxing rice wine
  or dry sherry
2–3 tbsp (45ml) hoisin sauce
2 tbsp (30ml) oyster sauce
salt and black pepper

Put the ground beef into a bowl with the rice wine, light soy sauce, sesame oil and cornstarch. Mix well and let it marinate for about 20 minutes.

Soak the dried mushrooms in warm water for 20 minutes, then drain them and squeeze out any excess liquid. Trim off the stems and shred the caps into 2-in (5cm) long strips. Meanwhile, peel the carrots and cut into fine shreds 2 in (5cm) long. Cut the bamboo shoots, zucchinis and bell peppers into similar fine shreds. Separate and wash the lettuce leaves, wiping off any excess water, and set them aside.

In a large wok or a deep-fat fryer, heat the 1¼ cups (300ml) of oil until it is slightly smoking. Deep-fry the noodles until they are crisp and puffed up, then drain them on paper towels. Set aside 2 tbsp (30ml) of the oil — the rest can be cooled and kept for future use.

Put 1 tbsp (15ml) of the reserved oil into a very hot wok or skillet, and when it begins to smoke, stir-fry the beef mixture for about 1 minute. Remove the beef and put it into a bowl. Wipe the wok or skillet clean.

Reheat the wok or skillet over high heat, and when it is hot, add the remaining 1 tbsp (15ml) of oil. When it is smoking slightly, add the garlic, shallots and green onions and stir-fry for 10 seconds. Then add the shredded carrots and stir-fry for another minute. Now add the remaining vegetables (except the lettuce), along with the soy sauce, rice wine, hoisin sauce, oyster sauce, ½ tsp (2ml) of salt and ¼ tsp (1ml) of black pepper. Stir-fry the mixture for 3 minutes, then return the beef to the mixture and stir so that it is just coated. Turn onto a platter. Arrange the lettuce and noodles on separate platters, put some hoisin sauce into a small bowl and serve at once.

Stir-fried Beef with Orange

This is a dish from northern and western China. I have adapted it by substituting fresh orange peel for dried tangerine peel, which is sometimes hard to find. The Chinese always use dried peel. The older the skin, the more prized the flavor. It's quite easy to make your own dried peel (page 24), but I find the tartness of fresh orange peel works just as well to balance the robust taste of the beef. This is an easy dish to make and the flavor is a pleasant change from the usual stir-fried beef recipes. Serve it with steamed rice.

SERVES 4

1 lb (450g) beef fillet
1 tbsp (15ml) light soy sauce
1 tbsp (15ml) Shaoxing rice
   wine or dry sherry
1½ tsp (7ml) finely chopped
   fresh ginger
2 tsp (10ml) cornstarch
4 tsp (20ml) sesame oil
5 tbsp (75ml) peanut or
   vegetable oil
2 dried red chilies, halved
   lengthwise
1 tbsp (15ml) fresh or dried
   orange peel, soaked and
   coarsely chopped (page 24)
2 tsp (10ml) roasted and finely
   ground Sichuan peppercorns
   (page 29), optional
1 tbsp (15ml) dark soy sauce
1½ tsp (7ml) sugar
salt and black pepper

Cut the beef into thick slices 2 in (5cm) long, cutting against the grain. Put them into a bowl with the soy sauce, rice wine, ginger, cornstarch and 2 tsp (10ml) of sesame oil. Mix well, then let the mixture marinate for about 20 minutes.

Heat a wok or a large skillet over high heat until it is very hot. Add the peanut or vegetable oil, and when it is very hot and slightly smoking, remove the beef from the marinade with a slotted spoon, add it to the wok and stir-fry for 2 minutes, until it browns. Remove the meat and leave to drain in a colander or sieve. Pour off most of the oil, leaving about 2 tsp (10ml).

Reheat the wok or skillet over high heat, add the dried chilies, and stir-fry them for 10 seconds. Then return the beef to the wok, add the remaining 2 tsp (10ml) of sesame oil and the rest of the ingredients, and season with ½ tsp (2ml) each of salt and black pepper. Stir-fry for 4 minutes, mixing well. Serve the dish at once.

Beef in Oyster Sauce

This was one of the most popular dishes in our family's restaurant. It is easy to make and delicious served with plain steamed rice and a stir-fried vegetable dish.

SERVES 4

1 lb (450g) beef fillet
1 tbsp (15ml) light soy sauce
2 tsp (10ml) sesame oil
1 tbsp (15ml) Shaoxing rice
    wine or dry sherry
2 tsp (10ml) cornstarch
3 tbsp (45ml) peanut oil
3 tbsp (45ml) oyster sauce
FOR THE GARNISH
1½ tbsp (22ml) finely chopped
    green onions

Cut the beef fillet into thick slices 2 in (5cm) long and put them into a bowl. Add the soy sauce, sesame oil, rice wine and cornstarch and let the mixture marinate for 20 minutes.

Heat a wok or a large skillet until it is very hot. Add the peanut oil, and when it is very hot and slightly smoking, add the beef slices and stir-fry for 5 minutes, or until they are lightly browned. Remove them and drain them well in a colander set over a bowl. Discard the drained oil.

Wipe the wok or skillet clean and reheat it over high heat. Add the oyster sauce and bring to a simmer. Return the drained beef slices and toss them thoroughly with the sauce. Turn the mixture onto a serving platter, garnish with the green onions, and serve at once.

Stir-fried Beef with Ginger

This typical Cantonese dish is one of the quickest and tastiest ways to cook beef.

SERVES 4

1 lb (450g) beef fillet
2 tsp (10ml) light soy sauce
2 tsp (10ml) Shaoxing rice wine
    or dry sherry
1 tsp (5ml) sesame oil
1 tsp (5ml) cornstarch
salt and white pepper
1½ tbsp (22ml) peanut oil, plus
    2 tsp (10ml)
3 tbsp (45ml) finely shredded
    fresh ginger
2 tbsp (30ml) Chicken Stock
    (page 75) or water
1 tsp (5ml) sugar

Put the beef into the freezer for 20 minutes. This will firm it slightly and make it easier to cut. Then cut it into thin slices 1½ in (4cm) long. Put them into a bowl and add the soy sauce, rice wine, sesame oil, cornstarch and ½ tsp (2ml) of salt. Mix well, and leave for about 15 minutes.

Heat a wok or a large skillet until it is very hot. Add the 1½ tbsp (22ml) of oil, and when it is very hot and slightly smoking, remove the beef from the marinade with a slotted spoon and stir-fry it for about 2 minutes. When all the beef is cooked, remove it, wipe the wok or skillet clean and reheat it. Add the 2 tsp (10ml) of oil and when it is very hot and slightly smoking, stir-fry the shredded ginger for a few seconds. Add the stock or water, sugar, 1½ tsp (7ml) of salt and 1 tsp (5ml) of white pepper, then quickly return the meat to the skillet and stir well. Turn the mixture onto a platter and serve at once.

Stir-fried Pepper Beef with Snow Peas

This is my adaptation of a stir-fried beef dish that is popular in Chinese restaurants in the West. What makes this recipe so adaptable is that any fresh vegetable can be substituted for the snow peas. This dish is extremely simple to make.

SERVES 4

1 lb (450g) beef fillet
2 tsp (10ml) light soy sauce
2 tsp (10ml) Shaoxing rice wine
  or dry sherry
2 tsp (10ml) sesame oil
2 tsp (10ml) cornstarch
salt and black pepper
4 oz (100g) red or green bell
  peppers (about 1)
3 tbsp (45ml) peanut oil
8 oz (225g) snow peas, trimmed
⅔ cup (150ml) Chicken Stock
  (page 75) or water
3 tbsp (45ml) oyster sauce

Cut the beef into thick slices 2 in (5cm) long. Put them into a bowl and add the soy sauce, rice wine, sesame oil, cornstarch, ½ tsp (2ml) of salt and ¼ tsp (1ml) of black pepper. Mix well with the beef and allow the mixture to marinate for 15 minutes. Cut the red or green bell peppers into 2 in (5cm) strips.

Heat a wok or a large skillet until it is very hot. Add the oil and when it is very hot and slightly smoking, stir-fry the beef for 3 minutes. Remove the beef and drain in a colander or sieve, reserving the oil.

Wipe the wok or skillet clean, then reheat it and return 1 tbsp (15ml) of the drained oil. When it is hot, stir-fry the bell pepper strips and snow peas for 2 minutes. Then add the chicken stock and oyster sauce and bring the mixture to a boil. Return the cooked beef to the wok and stir well. Turn onto a serving platter and serve at once.

Ground Beef with Scrambled Eggs

Eggs are found in many home-cooked dishes in China and are an inexpensive and easy-to-prepare food. Although they are rather bland on their own, they combine well with many ingredients to make hearty dishes. Here ground beef is marinated, stir-fried, then mixed with the stir-fried eggs. It is akin to a Western-style omelet in that it makes for a quick and delicious meal. Serve it with plain rice and stir-fried vegetables on the side.

SERVES 4

8 oz (225g) ground beef
2½ tbsp (37ml) peanut or
   vegetable oil
6 eggs, beaten
2 tsp (10ml) sesame oil
1 tsp (5ml) light soy sauce
4 tbsp (60ml) finely chopped
   green onions
salt and black pepper
FOR THE MARINADE
2 tsp (10ml) light soy sauce
2 tsp (10ml) Shaoxing rice wine
   or dry sherry
2 tsp (10ml) sesame oil
1 tsp (5ml) sugar
FOR THE GARNISH
finely chopped green onions

Combine the ground beef with the marinade ingredients and ½ tsp (2ml) of salt and ¼ tsp (1ml) of black pepper. Set aside for a few minutes.

Heat a wok or a large skillet over high heat until it is hot. Add 1 tbsp (15ml) of oil, and when it is very hot and slightly smoking, add the beef. Stir-fry the mixture for 2 minutes, then drain well in a colander or sieve.

Combine the eggs with the sesame oil, light soy sauce, green onions and ¼ tsp (1ml) each of salt and black pepper.

Wipe the wok clean and reheat it over a high heat until it is hot. Add the remaining 1½ tbsp (22ml) of oil, and when it begins to slightly smoke, swirl the oil around all sides of the wok. Add the egg mixture and stir-fry over high heat, folding and lifting the egg mixture, until the egg begins to set slightly. Return the beef to the wok and continue to stir-fry for another minute to finish cooking the eggs and to reheat the beef.

Turn the mixture onto a platter, garnish with green onions and serve at once.

Stewed Beef Northern Style

Beef in China is often tough, and braising is therefore the preferred method of cooking it. Chinese cooks long ago learned to make a virtue of this necessity by using spices and seasonings during the long braising process to imbue the meat with subtle and complex flavors. One of the ingredients is Chinese white radish, sometimes called mooli, which can be bought in many greengrocers and in Chinese and Asian grocers. If you cannot find it you could use turnips or carrots instead. Plain steamed rice is a perfect accompaniment.

SERVES 4–6

3 lb (1.5kg) stewing beef, such
   as brisket or shin

4 green onions

2 tbsp (30ml) peanut or
   vegetable oil

6 slices of ginger

4 garlic cloves, lightly crushed

4 dried red chilies

1 lb (450g) Chinese white
   radish (mooli)

FOR THE BRAISING SAUCE

3⅔ cups (900ml) Chicken
   Stock (page 75)

4 tbsp (60ml) Chinese rock
   sugar or granulated sugar

1½ tbsp (22ml) light soy sauce

2 tbsp (30ml) dark soy sauce

3 tbsp (45ml) Shaoxing rice
   wine or dry sherry

4 whole star anise

2 tsp (10ml) five-spice powder

5 tbsp (75ml) hoisin sauce

1 tbsp (15ml) whole yellow
   bean sauce

2 tbsp (30ml) fermented
   beancurd

Cut the meat into 2 in (5cm) cubes. Slice the green onions at a slight diagonal into 2 in (5cm) segments.

Heat a wok or a large skillet until it is hot. Add the oil, and when it is very hot and slightly smoking, add the beef and pan-fry until it is brown (this should take about 10 minutes). Pour off any excess fat, leaving 1 tbsp (15ml) of oil in the wok. Add the green onions, ginger, garlic and whole chilies and stir-fry with the beef for about 5 minutes.

Transfer this mixture to a large ovenproof casserole dish or saucepan and add the braising sauce ingredients. Bring the liquid to a boil, skim off any fat from the surface and turn the heat as low as possible. Cover and braise for 1½ hours.

Peel the Chinese white radish and cut it at a slight diagonal into 2 in (5cm) chunks. Add these to the meat and continue to cook the mixture for another 30 minutes, or until the beef is quite tender.

Then turn the heat up to high and rapidly reduce the liquid for about 15 minutes. The sauce should thicken slightly. The dish can be served immediately or cooled and reheated later.

Stewed Curry Beef Brisket

Traditional and hearty food has not been forgotten in Hong Kong's open receptivity to new cuisines. This stew is among the many old favorites you can still find there in homes and restaurants. The influence here comes originally from India via southeast Asia — curry, but in a mild form, not the hot and spicy curries of Indonesia or of India itself. The Western influence, however, can be seen in the use of potatoes and carrots, both of which are relative newcomers in Chinese cuisine. This is cool-weather food that is always welcomed. Leftovers can easily be frozen and reheated.

SERVES 6–8

3 lb (1.4kg) beef brisket or shank
3 tbsp (45ml) peanut or vegetable oil
1½ lb (675g) carrots
1½ lb (675g) potatoes

FOR THE CURRY

2 tbsp (30ml) finely chopped garlic
2 tbsp (30ml) finely chopped fresh ginger
3 tbsp (45ml) light soy sauce
6 tbsp (90ml) Madras curry powder or paste
3 tbsp (45ml) whole yellow bean sauce
3 tbsp (45ml) finely chopped green onions
2 tbsp (30ml) Shaoxing rice wine or dry sherry
2 tbsp (30ml) sugar

Cut the brisket or shank into large chunks and blanch them for 15 minutes in a large saucepan of boiling water. Drain well and blot dry with paper towels.

Heat a wok or a large skillet until it is hot and add the oil. Brown the meat for 10 minutes, then add the curry ingredients. Turn the mixture into a large clay pot or ovenproof casserole dish, cover and simmer for 1½ hours.

Meanwhile peel the carrots and potatoes. Cut the carrots into 2 in (5cm) pieces and the potatoes into large cubes. Leave them in cold water until you are ready to use them. Add the vegetables to the beef after 1½ hours and continue to cook for another 35–40 minutes, or until the meat is meltingly tender.

Red-cooked Oxtail Stew

Oxtail can make a rich and tasty dish because it lends itself to long stewing. This long cooking process allows it both to impart and absorb flavors slowly. Chinese aromatics and spices are a perfect foil for the strong taste of the oxtail. The beauty of this dish is that it can be made days ahead and is even better reheated.

SERVES 4

3 tbsp (45ml) peanut or
   vegetable oil
3 lb (1.5kg) oxtail, separated
   into sections
1 lb (450g) carrots

FOR THE SAUCE

2 tbsp (30ml) coarsely chopped
   garlic
6 cubes of red fermented
   beancurd or chili fermented
   beancurd
3 slices of fresh ginger
3 tbsp (45ml) Shaoxing rice
   wine or dry sherry
6 tbsp (90ml) hoisin sauce
5 tbsp (75ml) dark soy sauce
1 tbsp (15ml) five-spice powder
1 tbsp (15ml) whole yellow bean
   sauce
3 whole star anise
3 pieces of Chinese cinnamon
   bark or cinnamon stick
4 tbsp (60ml) Chinese rock
   sugar or granulated sugar
11¼ cups (2.8L) water
salt and black pepper

Heat a wok or a large skillet over high heat until it is hot. Add the oil, and when it is very hot and slightly smoking, add the oxtail, turn the heat down and brown the meat. Remove the oxtail and set aside. Drain off most of the oil and fat from the wok, leaving 1 tbsp (15ml). Discard the rest of the oil.

Reheat the wok and the 1 tbsp (15ml) of oil, and when it is hot, add the garlic and fermented beancurd and stir-fry the mixture for 30 seconds. Add the rest of the sauce ingredients along with some salt and black pepper and bring the mixture to a simmer, then transfer the sauce to a large ovenproof casserole dish and add the oxtail. Bring to a boil, then turn the heat to very low, cover, and cook for 2 hours, or until the meat is very tender.

While the oxtail is cooking, peel the carrots and cut them into 2 in (5cm) segments. When the meat is cooked, add the carrots and cook for an additional 40 minutes. Skim off all the surface fat, then put the stew on a platter and serve at once.

Beijing (Peking) Braised Lamb

The Chinese usually cook mutton and goat for this dish rather than lamb, which is scarce, and have many exciting ways of braising both these meats with spices. This tasty and filling lamb version is a great family dish that is perfect for the winter. It goes well with plain steamed rice or wrapped inside Chinese Pancakes (page 324).

SERVES 4

1 lb (450g) boned shoulder of lamb
2 green onions
2 slices of fresh ginger
1 tbsp (15ml) peanut or vegetable oil
1 small onion, finely chopped

FOR THE BRAISING SAUCE

3⅔ cups (900ml) Chicken Stock (page 75)
2 whole star anise
4 tbsp (60ml) Chinese rock sugar or granulated sugar
3 tbsp (45ml) dark soy sauce
3 tbsp (45ml) Shaoxing rice wine or dry sherry
1 piece of Chinese cinnamon bark or cinnamon stick
2 tbsp (30ml) sesame paste or peanut butter
2 tbsp (30ml) hoisin sauce

Cut the meat into 2 in (5cm) cubes. Next, blanch the lamb by plunging it into boiling water for 5 minutes. Then remove the meat and discard the water. Slice the green onions at a slight diagonal into 3 in (7.5cm) pieces.

Heat a wok or a large skillet over high heat until it is hot. Add the oil, and when it is very hot and slightly smoking, add the pieces of lamb and stir-fry them until they are brown. Add the green onions, ginger and onion to the pan and continue to stir-fry for 5 minutes. Transfer this mixture to a large ovenproof casserole dish or saucepan and add the braising sauce ingredients. Bring the liquid to a boil, skim off any fat from the surface, and turn the heat down as low as possible. Cover and braise for 1½ hours, or until the lamb is quite tender, skimming off any surface fat from the sauce.

Arrange the cooked meat on a platter and serve with the sauce. Any leftover sauce can be frozen.

Mongolian Hot Pot

The Chinese use a special charcoal-burning "fire pot" for this northern dish — similar in style to a European fondue — but you could use either a large fondue pot or a small portable electric element and saucepan or ovenproof casserole dish instead.

SERVES 4–6

2–3 lb (900g–1.5kg) lean lamb
  fillets or boneless lamb loin
6 oz (175g) bean thread
  (transparent) noodles
8 oz (225g) spinach
8 oz (225g) Chinese leaves
5 cups (1.2L) Chicken Stock
  (page 75)
2 tbsp (30ml) light soy sauce
2 tsp (10ml) dark soy sauce
1½ tbsp (22ml) Shaoxing rice
  wine or dry sherry
1 tbsp (15ml) sesame oil
1 tsp (5ml) sugar
2 tsp (10ml) finely chopped
  fresh ginger
3 tbsp (45ml) finely chopped
  green onions
1 tbsp (15ml) chopped garlic
3 tbsp (45ml) finely chopped
  fresh cilantro
salt

FOR THE DIPPING SAUCE

3 tbsp (45ml) sesame paste or
  peanut butter
1½ tbsp (22ml) light soy sauce
1 tbsp (15ml) dark soy sauce
2 tbsp (30ml) Shaoxing rice
  wine or dry sherry
1 tbsp (15ml) chili bean sauce
1 tbsp (15ml) sugar

Using a cleaver or a sharp knife, cut the lamb into very thin slices. Soak the bean thread (transparent) noodles in warm water for 5 minutes, then drain and cut them into 5 in (13cm) lengths. Separate the spinach leaves from the stalks and wash them well. Discard the stalks. Cut the Chinese leaves into 3 in (7.5cm) pieces.

Combine all the ingredients for the dipping sauce in a small bowl, add 1 tbsp (15ml) of hot water and mix them well.

Everyone should have their own small portion of dipping sauce. Serve each guest a plate containing their share of lamb, spinach and Chinese leaves. When you are ready to begin, bring the stock to a boil and light the fondue pot. Ladle the stock into the pot and add the soy sauces, rice wine, sesame oil, sugar, ginger, green onions, garlic, cilantro and 1 tsp (5ml) of salt.

Each person selects a piece of food and cooks it quickly in the pot. When all the meat and vegetables have been eaten, add the noodles to the pot, let them heat through, then ladle the soup into soup bowls.

This dish also works successfully with other foods such as steak, fish balls, oysters, shrimp, squid, mushrooms and lettuce, although then it would be more like the Cantonese Chrysanthemum Pot than a Mongolian hot pot.

Stir-fried Liver in Spicy Sauce

Pig's liver is a Chinese speciality that is delicious when it is properly prepared. My uncle used to make a delectable pig's liver dish with vegetables. His secret was to cut the liver into thin slices, stir-fry them quickly and then drain them to get rid of any bitter juices. My personal preference, however, is for calf's liver, and this dish is an adaptation of the traditional pig's liver recipe. Here is it paired with a robust and tasty sauce containing spices that help to balance the rich flavor of the liver. Cooked this way, the liver tastes a little like beef. I like to serve it with plain steamed rice and some green vegetables.

SERVES 4

8 oz (225g) fresh liver, such as calf's or pig's

3 green onions

⅔ cup (150ml) peanut or vegetable oil

FOR THE MARINADE

1 egg white

1 tbsp (15ml) Shaoxing rice wine or dry sherry

2 tsp (10ml) sesame oil

2 tsp (10ml) finely chopped fresh ginger

2 tsp (10ml) cornstarch

salt and white pepper

FOR THE SAUCE

2 tsp (10ml) light soy sauce

2 tsp (10ml) Shaoxing rice wine or dry sherry

2 tsp (10ml) sugar

1½ tbsp (22ml) whole yellow bean sauce

2 tsp (10ml) chili bean sauce

Cut the liver into thin slices 3 in (7.5cm) long. Mix the marinade ingredients together in a bowl with 2 tsp (10ml) of salt and ½ tsp (2ml) of white pepper. Add the liver slices and coat them thoroughly with the marinade. Cover the bowl tightly with plastic wrap and let it sit in the fridge for at least 20 minutes.

Meanwhile, cut the green onions diagonally into 2 in (5cm) pieces. In a separate bowl, mix together the sauce ingredients.

Heat a wok or a large skillet until it is hot. Add the oil, and when it is very hot and slightly smoking, remove the liver from the marinade with a slotted spoon and stir-fry it for 2 minutes. Drain the cooked liver in a colander or sieve, leaving about 2 tsp (10ml) of the oil in the wok. (Discard the rest of the oil.)

Reheat the wok or skillet and add the green onions. Stir-fry them for 1 minute, then add the sauce ingredients. When the sauce comes to a boil, return the liver to the wok or skillet and toss it well, coating it with the sauce. Stir-fry for 30 seconds, then turn it onto a platter and serve.

Stir-fried Lamb with Garlic

Lamb is especially delicious when it is stir-fried. This way of preparing it with a lot of garlic and green onions to balance its strong taste is a popular one. The tenderest parts of the lamb, such as fillet or steaks, are best for this dish.

SERVES 4

1 lb (450g) lean lamb steaks or fillet

1 tbsp (15ml) Shaoxing rice wine or dry sherry

2 tsp (10ml) dark soy sauce

1 tbsp (15ml) light soy sauce

2 tsp (10ml) sesame oil

2 tsp (10ml) cornstarch

1 tbsp (15ml) peanut or vegetable oil

3 tbsp (45ml) finely chopped green onions, white part only

6 garlic cloves, peeled and thinly sliced

2 tsp (10ml) finely chopped fresh ginger

1 tsp (5ml) roasted and ground Sichuan peppercorns (page 29)

Cut the lamb into thin slices and put them into a bowl. Add the rice wine, soy sauces, sesame oil and cornstarch and let the meat marinate for 20 minutes. Then drain off the marinade.

Heat a wok or a large skillet until it is hot. Add the oil, and when it is very hot and slightly smoking, add the marinated lamb pieces and stir-fry for 2 minutes over high heat. Now add the green onions, garlic and ginger and continue to stir-fry for another 3 minutes. Turn onto a serving platter, sprinkle with the ground peppercorns and serve immediately.

Stir-fried Lamb's Kidneys

Lamb's kidneys are delicious when they are simply stir-fried. As a young cook, I was taught a wonderful technique for cleaning kidneys that I use to this day. First, the kidneys should be scored and tossed in baking soda; this helps to tenderize them and to neutralize their acidity. Then the baking soda should be rinsed off and the kidneys tossed in a mixture of vinegar and salt to remove any remaining bitterness. The result is a clean and fresh-tasting kidney, and rather delicious, I might add. This dish can also be made with pig's kidneys.

SERVES 4

1 lb (450g) lamb's or pig's
　kidneys
1½ tsp (7ml) baking soda
2 tsp (10ml) Chinese white rice
　vinegar or cider vinegar
salt
1 tbsp (15ml) peanut or
　vegetable oil
3 dried red chilies, 2 whole,
　1 halved lengthwise
1 tbsp (15ml) finely chopped
　garlic
1 tbsp (15ml) dark soy sauce
2 tsp (10ml) Shaoxing rice wine
　or dry sherry
½ tsp (2ml) roasted and finely
　ground Sichuan peppercorns
　(page 29), optional
1 tsp (5ml) sugar
1 tsp (5ml) sesame oil
FOR THE GARNISH
2 tsp (10ml) finely chopped
　green onions

Using a sharp knife, remove the thin outer membrane from the kidneys. Then, with a sharp cleaver or knife, split the kidneys in half by cutting them horizontally. Cut away the small knobs of fat and any tough membrane surrounding them, then score the kidneys in a crisscross pattern and cut them into thin slices. Toss the kidney slices with the baking soda and let them sit for about 20 minutes. Then rinse them thoroughly with cold water and toss them with the vinegar and 1 tsp (5ml) of salt. Put them into a colander and drain for at least 30 minutes, preferably longer.

Blot the kidney slices dry with paper towels. Heat a wok or a large skillet over high heat until it is hot. Add the oil, and when it is very hot and slightly smoking, add the dried chilies. Stir-fry to flavor the oil for about 20 seconds. Then add the kidney slices and stir-fry for about 1 minute, coating the kidneys with the oil. Now add the rest of the ingredients, season with ½ tsp (2ml) of salt and toss everything together well. Continue to stir-fry the mixture for about 2 minutes, or until the edges of the kidneys begin to curl. Turn the mixture onto a warm serving platter, garnish with the green onions and serve at once.

POULTRY

Poultry is highly regarded in China, and the offering of a chicken to a guest is considered an act of great honor and respect. Poultry of all types — be it meat or egg — forms a central part of Chinese cuisine.

Cashew Chicken

This dish exemplifies the Chinese penchant for contrasting textures. Here, tender, succulent pieces of chicken are used with sweet, crunchy cashews. The original Chinese version would have been made with peanuts because cashews are not widely used in Chinese cookery. Nevertheless, this dish uses the best Chinese cooking principles: velveting to seal in the juices of the chicken, then stir-frying with spices to flavor it.

SERVES 4

1 lb (450g) boneless, skinless
  chicken breasts
1 egg white
2 tsp (10ml) cornstarch
salt
1¼ cups (300ml) peanut or
  vegetable oil, or water, plus
  2 tsp (10ml) oil
2 oz (50g) roasted cashews
1 tbsp (15ml) Shaoxing rice
  wine or dry sherry
1 tbsp (15ml) light soy sauce
FOR THE GARNISH
1 tbsp (15ml) finely chopped
  green onions

Cut the chicken breasts into ½ in (1cm) cubes. Combine them with the egg white, cornstarch and 1 tsp (5ml) of salt in a small bowl, and put into the fridge for about 20 minutes.

Heat a wok or a large skillet until it is very hot and then add the 1¼ cups (300ml) of oil (if using water, see below). When it is very hot, remove the wok from the heat and immediately add the chicken pieces, stirring vigorously to keep them from sticking. After about 2 minutes, when the chicken has turned white, quickly drain it in a stainless steel colander set over a bowl. Discard the oil.

If you choose to use water instead of oil, bring it to a boil in a saucepan. Remove the saucepan from the heat and immediately add the chicken pieces, stirring vigorously to keep them from sticking. After about 2 minutes, when the chicken has turned white, quickly drain it in a stainless steel colander set over a bowl. Discard the water.

If you have used a wok or skillet to cook the chicken, wipe it clean with paper towels. Heat it until it is very hot, then add the remaining 2 tsp (10ml) of oil. Add the cashews and stir-fry them for 1 minute, then add the rice wine and soy sauce. Return the chicken to the wok and stir-fry the mixture for another 2 minutes. Garnish with the green onions and serve at once.

Lemon Chicken

The southern Chinese have made a speciality of chicken cooked with lemon. The tart lemon sauce goes very well indeed with the receptive flavor of chicken. Unlike many versions that employ an overly sweet sauce, this recipe balances tartness with sweetness. Sometimes the lemon chicken is steamed, but I think it is equally good stir-fried, especially if the chicken is velveted beforehand.

SERVES 4

1 lb (450g) boneless, skinless
   chicken breasts
1 egg white
1 tsp (5ml) sesame oil
2 tsp (10ml) cornstarch
salt
1¼ cups (300ml) peanut or
   vegetable oil, or water

FOR THE SAUCE

5 tbsp (75ml) Chicken Stock
   (page 75) or water
3 tbsp (45ml) fresh lemon juice
1 tbsp (15ml) sugar
1 tbsp (15ml) light soy sauce
1½ tbsp (22ml) Shaoxing rice
   wine or dry sherry
1 tbsp (15ml) finely chopped
   garlic
1 tsp (5ml) dried red chili flakes
1 tsp (5ml) cornstarch, blended
   with 1 tsp (5ml) water
2 tsp (10ml) sesame oil

FOR THE GARNISH

2 tbsp (30ml) finely chopped
   green onions

Cut the chicken breasts into strips 3 in (7.5cm) long. Combine them with the egg white, sesame oil, cornstarch and 1 tsp (5ml) of salt in a bowl, and put it into the fridge for about 20 minutes.

Heat a wok or large skillet until it is very hot and then add the oil (if using water, see below). When the oil is very hot, remove the wok from the heat and immediately add the chicken pieces, stirring vigorously to keep them from sticking together. After about 2 minutes, when the chicken has turned white, quickly drain it in a stainless steel colander set over a bowl. Discard the oil.

If you choose to use water instead of oil, bring it to a boil in a saucepan. Remove the saucepan from the heat and immediately add the chicken pieces, stirring vigorously to keep them from sticking together. After about 2 minutes, when the chicken has turned white, quickly drain it in a stainless steel colander set over a bowl. Discard the water.

Wipe the wok or skillet clean with paper towels and reheat it. Add all the sauce ingredients except for the cornstarch mixture and sesame oil. Bring to a boil over high heat and then add the cornstarch mixture. Simmer for 1 minute. Return the chicken strips to the sauce and stir-fry them long enough to coat them all with the sauce, then stir in the sesame oil and mix once again. Turn everything onto a platter, garnish with the green onions, and serve at once.

Walnut Chicken

This recipe pairs the crunchy texture of walnuts with the softness of chicken in a classic stir-fry dish. For a variation, try this recipe with other nuts such as pine nuts or almonds, but be sure the nuts you use are very fresh. Stale nuts tend to go soft and will spoil both the texture and the flavor of the dish.

SERVES 4

1 lb (450g) boneless, skinless
   chicken breasts
1 egg white
2 tsp (10ml) cornstarch
salt
3 oz (75g) walnuts, shelled
   halves or pieces
1¼ cups (300ml) peanut or
   vegetable oil, or water, plus
   1 tbsp (15ml) oil
2 tsp (10ml) finely chopped
   garlic
1 tsp (5ml) finely chopped fresh
   ginger
2 tbsp (30ml) finely chopped
   green onions
2 tbsp (30ml) Shaoxing rice
   wine or dry sherry
1½ tbsp (22ml) light soy sauce

Cut the chicken breasts into 1 in (2.5cm) cubes. Combine them with the egg white, cornstarch and 1 tsp (5ml) of salt in a small bowl, and put into the fridge for about 20 minutes. Blanch the walnuts in a small saucepan of boiling water for about 5 minutes, then drain them.

Heat a wok or a large skillet until it is very hot and add the 1¼ cups (300ml) of oil (if using water, see below). When the oil is very hot, remove the wok from the heat and immediately add the chicken pieces, stirring vigorously to keep them from sticking together. After about 2 minutes, when the chicken has turned white, quickly drain it in a stainless steel colander set over a bowl. Discard the oil.

If you choose to use water instead of oil, bring it to a boil in a saucepan. Remove the saucepan from the heat and immediately add the chicken pieces, stirring vigorously to keep them from sticking together. After about 2 minutes, when the chicken has turned white, quickly drain it in a stainless steel colander set over a bowl. Discard the water.

If you have used a wok or skillet to cook the chicken, wipe it clean with paper towels. Reheat it until it is very hot, and add the remaining 1 tbsp (15ml) of oil. Add the walnuts and stir-fry them for 1 minute, then remove and set aside. Add the garlic, ginger and green onions and stir-fry for a few seconds. Return the walnuts to the wok and add the rest of the ingredients, then return the chicken to the wok and stir-fry the mixture for another 2 minutes. Serve at once.

Shredded Chicken with Sesame Seeds

This is my version of a fragrant Sichuan dish popularly known as "Strange Taste Chicken" because it incorporates so many flavors, being hot, spicy, sour, sweet and salty all at the same time. It is delicious as a hot dish, but I also find it excellent served cold. I simply let it cool and serve it at room temperature. The sesame seeds add a crunchy texture that contrasts nicely with the tender chicken meat.

SERVES 4

1 lb (450g) boneless, skinless
  chicken breasts
1 egg white
2 tsp (10ml) cornstarch
salt
1¼ cups (300ml) peanut or
  vegetable oil, or water, plus
  1 tbsp (15ml) oil
1 tbsp (15ml) white sesame
  seeds

FOR THE SAUCE

2 tsp (10ml) dark soy sauce
2 tsp (10ml) Chinese black rice
  vinegar or cider vinegar
2 tsp (10ml) chili bean sauce
2 tsp (10ml) sesame oil
2 tsp (10ml) sugar
1 tbsp (15ml) Shaoxing rice
  wine or dry sherry
1 tsp (5ml) roasted Sichuan
  peppercorns (page 29)
1½ tbsp (22ml) finely chopped
  green onions

Cut the chicken breasts into strips about 3 in (7.5cm) long. Combine them with the egg white, cornstarch and ½ tsp (2ml) of salt in a small bowl, and place in the fridge for about 20 minutes.

Heat a wok or a large skillet until it is very hot and add the 1¼ cups (300ml) of oil (if using water, see below). When it is very hot, remove the wok from the heat and immediately add the chicken pieces, stirring vigorously to keep them from sticking together. After about 2 minutes, when the chicken has turned white, quickly drain it in a stainless steel colander set over a bowl. Discard the oil.

If you choose to use water instead of oil, bring it to a boil in a saucepan. Remove the saucepan from the heat and immediately add the chicken pieces, stirring vigorously to keep them from sticking together. After about 2 minutes, when the chicken has turned white, quickly drain it in a stainless steel colander set over a bowl. Discard the water.

If you have used a wok or skillet to cook the chicken, wipe it clean with paper towels. Heat it until it is hot, then add the remaining 1 tbsp (15ml) of oil. Immediately add the sesame seeds and stir-fry them for 30 seconds, or until they are slightly brown, then add all the sauce ingredients and bring to a boil. Return the cooked chicken to the wok and stir-fry the mixture for another 2 minutes, coating the pieces thoroughly with the sauce and sesame seeds. Serve at once.

Soy Sauce Chicken

My friends are often surprised at their first taste of Soy Sauce Chicken. Instead of the saltiness they expect, given the name of the dish, they taste tender, succulent chicken bathed in a rich and subtle sauce. The technique of steeping used here ensures that the chicken is moist and tender, and allows the rich flavors of the sauce to gently permeate the meat. The chicken may be served hot, but I think it is best when cooled and served at room temperature, or refrigerated and served cold. It makes a delicious picnic dish and a wonderful cold starter. The steeping liquid may be used as a sauce, and the rest may be frozen and reused for making more Soy Sauce Chicken.

SERVES 4–6

1 x 3–4lb (1.5–1.75kg) chicken
6 green onions
6 slices of fresh ginger
salt and black pepper
FOR THE SAUCE
7 cups (1.75L) Chicken Stock
   (page 75) or water
2⅓ cups (600ml) dark soy
   sauce
⅔ cup (150ml) light soy sauce
1¼ cups (300ml) Shaoxing rice
   wine or dry sherry, or ⅔ cup
   (150ml) dry sherry mixed
   with ⅔ cup (150ml) Chicken
   Stock (page 75)
¾ cup(175ml) Chinese rock
   sugar or granulated sugar
5 whole star anise
5 pieces of Chinese cinnamon
   bark or cinnamon sticks
3 tbsp (45ml) cumin seeds
FOR THE GARNISH
sprigs of fresh cilantro

First, make the sauce by combining all the sauce ingredients in a very large saucepan and bringing the liquid to a simmer. Stuff the cavity of the chicken with the whole green onions, ginger slices, 2 tbsp (30ml) of salt and 1 tsp (5ml) of black pepper. Put the chicken into the saucepan breast side down and add the sauce mixture. If the liquid does not cover the chicken, add a little more stock or water. Bring it back to a simmer, then leave to simmer for about 20 minutes, skimming any fat or scum that rises to the surface. Turn the chicken over so the breast is touching the bottom of the saucepan. Turn off the heat, cover the saucepan tightly and leave for 1 hour.

After this time, remove the chicken with a slotted spoon and put it on a plate to cool. It can now be put into the fridge or cut up into pieces. Remove any surface fat from the sauce and spoon the sauce over the chicken. Garnish with cilantro sprigs before serving.

Drunken Chicken

This dish is called Drunken Chicken with good reason! You do need quite a lot of rice wine to cover the bird during the steeping process, but it can be reused.

SERVES 4

5 cups (1.2L) Chicken Stock
   (page 75)
3 slices of fresh ginger
3 tbsp (45ml) light soy sauce
1 green onion
salt
1 x 3–4 lb (1.5–1.75kg) chicken
5 cups (1.2L) Shaoxing rice wine

Place the stock in a large ovenproof casserole dish, bring it to a boil, then add the ginger, soy sauce, whole green onion, 1 tsp (5ml) of salt and the chicken. If the chicken is not covered by the stock, add some more. Bring the liquid back to boiling point, then reduce the heat. Simmer for 30 minutes, skimming any fat or scum that rises to the surface. Turn the heat off, cover and leave the chicken in the liquid for about 30 minutes.

Remove the cooked chicken and let it cool. (The cooking liquid can now be skimmed of all fat and used as a base for stock or to cook rice.) Cut the chicken in half lengthwise and place the halves in a bowl. Cover with the rice wine and leave for 2 days in the fridge, turning from time to time.

After 2 days, remove the chicken from the bowl and place it on a serving platter. Pour some of the wine over to moisten it.

Yunnan Steamed Pot Chicken

I use a Yunnan ceramic steam pot — a squat, round, lidded vessel — for this succulent dish, but you may, of course, simply use a covered ovenproof casserole dish.

SERVES 4

1 x 4 lb (1.75kg) chicken
salt
6 slices of fresh ginger
2 green onions, cut into 2 in
   (5cm) pieces, plus extra to
   dip
2¾ cups (700ml) Chicken Stock
   (page 75)
2 tbsp (30ml) Shaoxing rice
   wine or dry sherry
FOR DIPPING
light soy sauce
chili bean sauce

Cut the chicken into pieces and blanch for 3 minutes in a large saucepan of boiling water, then remove and rinse thoroughly in cold running water. Place the chicken pieces around the Yunnan pot or on a rack set in a ovenproof casserole dish. Sprinkle the chicken with 1 tsp (5ml) of salt and scatter the ginger and green onions over the top. Pour in the chicken stock and rice wine. Cover and gently steam for 2 hours, replenishing the hot water from time to time if necessary.

Remove the ginger and green onion pieces, and with a spoon, remove all the surface fat. Ladle the soup into a tureen, and pass round the chicken on a separate platter with the extra green onions, soy sauce and chili bean sauce for dipping.

Curried Chicken with Bell Peppers

Curry blends well with chicken, especially when used in the style of southern Chinese cuisine, namely, as a light and subtle sauce that does not overpower the delicate chicken flavor. The chicken is velveted to preserve its juiciness and flavor. You can use the traditional oil method, or, for a less fattening alternative, substitute water instead. The bell peppers provide the dish with a crunchy texture that makes a wonderful complement to the soft, tender chicken.

SERVES 4

8 oz (225g) red or green bell peppers (about 2)

1 lb (450g) boneless, skinless chicken breasts

1 egg white

3 tsp (15ml) cornstarch

salt

1¼ cups (300ml) peanut or vegetable oil, or water, plus 1 tbsp (15ml) oil

1 tbsp (15ml) finely chopped garlic

⅔ cup (150ml) Chicken Stock (page 75)

1½ tbsp (22ml) Madras curry paste

2 tsp (10ml) sugar

1½ tbsp (22ml) Shaoxing rice wine or dry sherry

1½ tbsp (22ml) light soy sauce

Wash and seed the bell peppers, cut them into 1 in (2.5cm) cubes, and set aside. Cut the chicken breasts into 1 in (2.5cm) cubes. Combine them with the egg white, 2 tsp (10ml) of cornstarch and 1 tsp (5ml) of salt in a small bowl, and put the mixture into the fridge for about 20 minutes. Blend the remaining 1 tsp (5ml) of cornstarch with 2 tbsp (30ml) of water.

Heat a wok or skillet over high heat until it is hot, then add the 1¼ cups (300ml) of oil (if using water, see below). When the oil is very hot, remove the wok from the heat and immediately add the chicken pieces, stirring vigorously to keep them from sticking together. After about 2 minutes, when the chicken has turned white, quickly drain it in a stainless steel colander set over a bowl. Discard the oil.

If you choose to use water instead of oil, bring it to a boil in a saucepan. Remove the saucepan from the heat and immediately add the chicken pieces, stirring vigorously to keep them from sticking together. After about 2 minutes, when the chicken has turned white, quickly drain it in a stainless steel colander set over a bowl. Discard the water.

Wipe the wok or skillet clean with paper towels and reheat it until it is very hot. Add the remaining 1 tbsp (15ml) of oil, and when it is very hot, add the bell peppers and garlic and stir-fry for 2 minutes. Add the cornstarch mixture and the rest of the ingredients, and cook for another 2 minutes. Add the drained chicken and stir-fry for another 2 minutes, coating the chicken thoroughly with the sauce. Serve at once.

Salt-Roasted Chicken

This is a popular southern Chinese technique for cooking chicken. The result is not salty, but succulent and very tasty. The salt seals in the juices of the chicken as it slowly cooks, and filling the cavity with a savory sauce makes the chicken even tastier. It makes a delicious treat whether served hot or cold.

SERVES 4

1 x 3½–4 lb (1.5–1.75kg) chicken
5–6 lb (2.5–3kg) rock salt
FOR THE SAUCE
1 tbsp (15ml) peanut or
    vegetable oil
3 slices of fresh ginger
3 cloves of garlic, lightly
    crushed
5 green onions, cut into 3 in
    (7.5cm) segments
1 tbsp (15ml) whole yellow bean
    sauce
2 tbsp (30ml) light soy sauce
1½ tbsp (22ml) Shaoxing rice
    wine or dry sherry
1 tbsp (15ml) sugar
2 whole star anise
2 tsp (10ml) roasted Sichuan
    peppercorns (page 29)
⅔ cup (150ml) Chicken Stock
    (page 75)
a bunch of fresh cilantro, stems
    tied together

Wipe the chicken dry inside and out with paper towels and let it sit, loosely wrapped, in the fridge for at least 2 hours.

Preheat the oven to 325°F (160°C). Pour half the rock salt into a large roasting pan or ovenproof dish (big enough to hold the chicken), and heat it in the oven for at least 30 minutes. Pour the rest of the salt into a saucepan and heat it on low heat for at least 30 minutes.

Meanwhile, heat a wok or a large skillet over high heat until it is hot. Add the oil, and when it is very hot and slightly smoking, add the ginger, garlic and green onions and stir-fry for 2 minutes. Then add the rest of the sauce ingredients, turn down the heat and simmer the mixture for 5 minutes. Pour the mixture into a bowl and allow it to cool thoroughly before proceeding.

Put the cooled sauce into the cavity of the chicken and seal the cavity using bamboo skewers and kitchen string.

Turn the oven up to 350°F (180°C). Remove the salt from the oven and place the chicken on top, then pour over the hot salt from the saucepan. The salt should cover the chicken completely. Cover the roasting pan or ovenproof dish tightly and cook in the oven for 1½ hours.

When the chicken is cooked, carefully remove the hot salt. Let the chicken cool slightly, then drain the sauce from the cavity into a bowl. Carve the chicken and serve with the sauce on the side.

Crispy Chicken

This is one of my favorite chicken dishes. It was a standard at all family gatherings on special occasions. Although it is usually served in restaurants, it can easily be made at home. The many exotic ingredients give this dish a special taste experience. Although it requires a bit of patience to make, much of the work can be done the day before. Serve this as a centerpiece for a special dinner party.

SERVES 4–6

1 x 3–3½ lb (1.5kg) chicken
5 cups (1.2L) peanut or
    vegetable oil

FOR THE SIMMERING SAUCE

14 cups (3.5L) water
2 pieces of Chinese cinnamon
    bark or cinnamon sticks
1 cup (250ml) dark soy sauce
3 tbsp (45ml) light soy sauce
½ cup (120ml) Shaoxing rice
    wine or dry sherry
3 whole star anise
1 tbsp (15ml) fresh orange
    peel, finely chopped, or dried
    citrus peel, soaked and finely
    chopped
3 slices of fresh ginger
2 green onions
4 tbsp (60ml) Chinese rock
    sugar
    or granulated sugar

FOR THE GLAZE

3 tbsp (45ml) honey
1¼ cups (300ml) water
2 tbsp (30ml) dark soy sauce
2 tbsp (30ml) Chinese black
    rice vinegar or cider vinegar

FOR THE GARNISH

1 lemon, cut in wedges
Salt and Pepper Dip (page 37)

Combine all the ingredients for the simmering sauce in a large ovenproof casserole dish or saucepan and bring the mixture to a boil. Then turn the heat down to a simmer. Lower in the chicken, breast side down, and simmer it, uncovered, for 30 minutes. Remove the chicken, cut into halves lengthwise and let them cool on a rack for at least 3 hours. The skin of the chicken should be completely dried and should feel like parchment paper.

In a wok or saucepan, bring the glaze ingredients to a boil. Baste the skins of the dried chicken halves with the glaze and let the chicken dry again for another 2 hours, keeping it in a very cool and airy place, but not in the fridge. The dish can be prepared up to this point the day before you want to serve it.

Heat the oil in a deep-fat fryer or a large wok, and lower in one of the chicken halves, skin side down. Deep-fry it until it is a rich, dark brown color and very crisp. Remove from the wok and drain well on paper towels. Deep-fry the other half and drain. Cut the chicken into bite-sized pieces, and arrange on a warm platter. Serve with lemon wedges and the Salt and Pepper Dip.

Wine-flavored Chicken in a Clay Pot

I suspect that the origins of this dish probably lie in northern China. However, like many things in Hong Kong, where I first tasted this wonderful chicken, new dishes are readily adapted, and origins and distinctions are blurred. Hong Kong chefs have no qualms about changing a dish to suit their own taste or their patrons' wishes. This cold chicken is extremely delicate and tasty and, as a bonus, much of it can be made ahead of time. The Chinese rose wine adds a particularly attractive fragrance and is well worth the effort to obtain.

SERVES 4–6

1 x 3–3½ lb (1.5–1.6kg) chicken
FOR THE BRAISING LIQUID
3 tbsp (45ml) Chinese rose
   wine
½ cup (120ml) Shaoxing rice
   wine or dry sherry
4 tbsp (60ml) light soy sauce
4 tbsp (60ml) dark soy sauce
3 tbsp (45ml) sugar
2 pieces of Chinese cinnamon
   bark
1 piece of dried citrus peel or
   zest of 1 fresh orange
2 tbsp (30ml) coarsely chopped
   fresh ginger
3 whole star anise
1 tbsp (15ml) Sichuan
   peppercorns
salt

Place the braising liquid ingredients and 2 tsp (10ml) of salt in a large clay pot or ovenproof casserole dish and bring to a boil. Turn the heat down and leave to simmer for 20 minutes. Add the chicken and continue to simmer for 20 minutes more, rotating the chicken once or twice during the cooking time. Turn the heat off and let the chicken rest in the liquid until it is thoroughly cooled. This will take 2–3 hours.

Remove the chicken from the pot, cut it into slices and serve with some of the braising liquid.

Mango Chicken

This might be called "Nouvelle Hong Kong" or "Southeast Asia Meets Hong Kong." It is an exotic and unlikely combination. I have had this dish several times in Hong Kong and found it delicious every time. The rich sweetness and soft texture of the mango works extremely well with the delicate taste of the chicken. The mango is cooked for a short time, just enough to warm it through. Mangoes are very popular in Hong Kong. They are imported from Thailand and the Philippines. They are one of the best liked of all tropical fruits and, as this recipe indicates, they mix well with other distinctively flavored foods.

SERVES 4

1 lb (450g) boneless, skinless chicken breasts, cut into 1 in (2.5cm) pieces

1 egg white

2 tsp (10ml) cornstarch

2 tsp (10ml) sesame oil

salt and black pepper

2⅓ cups 600ml) peanut or vegetable oil, or water, plus 1½ tbsp (22ml) oil

1 tbsp (15ml) finely chopped fresh ginger

1 tbsp (15ml) finely chopped garlic

1½ tbsp (22ml) Shaoxing rice wine or dry sherry

2 mangoes, peeled and cut into 1 in (2.5cm) pieces

FOR THE GARNISH

1 tbsp (15ml) finely chopped fresh cilantro

Put the chicken pieces into a bowl with the egg white, cornstarch, 1 tsp (5ml) of sesame oil, 1 tsp (5ml) of salt and black pepper to taste. Mix well and refrigerate for about 20 minutes.

Heat a wok or large skillet until it is very hot and add the 2⅓ cups (600ml) of oil (if using water, see below). When it is very hot, remove the wok from the heat and immediately add the chicken pieces, stirring vigorously to keep them from sticking together. After about 2 minutes, when the chicken has turned white, quickly drain it in a stainless steel colander set over a bowl. Discard the oil.

If you choose to use water instead of oil, bring it to a boil in a saucepan. Remove the saucepan from the heat and immediately add the chicken pieces, stirring vigorously to keep them from sticking together. After about 2 minutes, when the chicken has turned white, quickly drain it in a stainless steel colander set over a bowl. Discard the water.

Add the remaining 1½ tbsp (22ml) of oil to the saucepan and reheat. Add the ginger and garlic and stir-fry for 30 seconds. Then add the rice wine, 1 tsp (5ml) of salt, the remaining 1 tsp (5ml) of sesame oil and the mango. Stir-fry gently for 2 minutes, or until the mango is heated through. Add the drained chicken and stir gently to mix well. Garnish with the cilantro, turn onto a platter and serve at once.

Smoked Chicken

Among the many methods the Chinese have for preserving food, as well as making it appetizing, perhaps the most appealing is smoking. We do not often practice this technique in our modern homes, but it is easier to do than you may think. The whole process is long, but the cooking itself is quite quick. The chicken is first marinated, then gently steamed, and finally lightly smoked. The result is a surprisingly succulent chicken with the savoriness one expects of smoked food. This dish can be served cold or warm. It is wonderful for a picnic, as well as an unusual starter for any meal.

SERVES 4

1 x 3½–4 lb (1.6kg–1.75kg) chicken
salt and white pepper
2 tbsp (30ml) roasted and ground Sichuan peppercorns (page 29)
2 tsp (10ml) five-spice powder
6 green onions
6 slices of fresh ginger

FOR THE SMOKING MIXTURE

2 oz (50g) black tea
4 tbsp (60ml) uncooked long-grain white rice
4 tbsp (60ml) brown sugar
3 whole star anise, broken into sections
2 pieces of Chinese cinnamon bark, broken into sections

Rub the chicken evenly inside and out with 2 tbsp (30ml) of salt, the Sichuan peppercorns, five-spice powder and 1 tsp (5ml) of white pepper. Wrap it well in plastic wrap and place it in the fridge overnight.

The next day, unwrap the chicken and place the green onions and ginger inside the cavity.

Next, set up a steamer, or put a rack into a wok or deep saucepan, and fill it with 2 in (5cm) of water. Bring the water to a boil over high heat. Put the chicken on a heatproof plate and carefully lower it into the steamer or onto the rack. Turn the heat to low and cover the wok or saucepan tightly. Steam gently for 1¼ hours, or until the chicken is cooked. Allow the chicken to cool thoroughly.

Line the inside of a wok with foil. Place the tea, rice, sugar, star anise and cinnamon on the bottom. Rub a rack with oil and place it over the smoking ingredients. Place the chicken on the rack. Now heat the wok over high heat until the mixture begins to burn. Turn the heat down to medium, cover the chicken with foil, and let it smoke for 15 minutes. Turn off the heat and allow it to sit, covered, for another 10 minutes. Remove the chicken from the wok and discard the smoking ingredients along with the foil. Carve or cut up the chicken and serve.

Paper-wrapped Chicken

This unusual method of cooking chicken is ingenious: a thin slice of chicken is sandwiched between flavorful ingredients and wrapped in wax paper, then deep-fried. As the package cooks, the mixture steams and the flavors meld, the result being a most delicious and unique starter. The package must be wrapped carefully so the oil does not seep in. Some Chinese restaurants cheat by using a quick marinade of hoisin and soy sauce, then wrapping the chicken in foil. Although this recipe takes a little more work, the outcome is worth the effort. It is one of those special dishes that is also a dinnertime conversation piece: the cook may modestly but justifiably boast of the achievement!

SERVES 6–10, AS A STARTER

8oz (225g) boneless, skinless chicken breasts
30 shreds of red chili, 1½ in (4cm) long
60 fresh cilantro leaves
30 pieces of Parma ham, 3 in (7.5cm) square
60 shreds of green onion, cut into 1½ in (4cm) pieces, on the diagonal
30 shreds of fresh ginger, cut into 1½ x ¼ in (4 x 0.5cm) pieces
30 thinly sliced pieces of fresh, peeled or canned water chestnut
5 cups (1.2L) peanut oil

FOR THE MARINADE

2 tbsp (30ml) oyster sauce
1 tbsp (15ml) light soy sauce
1 tbsp (15ml) dark soy sauce
1 tbsp (15ml) Shaoxing rice wine or dry sherry
2 tsp (10ml) sugar
1 tsp (5ml) sesame oil
salt and black pepper

Cut the chicken into 30 pieces about 1½ x ¼ in (4 x 0.5cm) and combine them with the marinade ingredients in a glass bowl. Leave to marinate in the fridge for at least 1 hour.

Cut out 30, 6 in (15cm) squares of wax paper. Place a wax paper square on a work surface, with a corner toward you, and fold the tip in slightly. In the center of the square place the following: a shred of chili, a fresh cilantro, a piece of marinated chicken, a square of Parma ham, 2 shreds of green onion, a shred of ginger, a slice of water chestnut, and finally, another fresh cilantro leaf. Fold the first corner over the ingredients, then fold in the sides. Then fold the entire package in half, leaving a flap at the corner furthest away from you. Finally tuck the flap in to secure the package. Repeat until all the packages are filled and the ingredients are used up.

Heat a wok over high heat until it is hot, then add the oil. When it is hot and slightly smoking, add about 10 packages and deep-fry for about 3 minutes. Remove them with a slotted spoon and drain well. Deep-fry the rest of the packages in 2 batches in the same manner.

When they are all ready, arrange them on a platter and let each guest unwrap his or her own packages.

Stir-fried Chicken Shreds

This is a simple recipe that is quick and easy to make and is very suitable for a family meal. The secret of cooking the chicken shreds without drying them out is to velvet them quickly in oil or water until they turn opaque, and then remove them at once. You can substitute other vegetables such as asparagus, carrots or peas for the ones I have used, if you prefer.

SERVES 4

1 lb (450g) boneless, skinless
 chicken breasts
1 egg white
2 tsp (10ml) cornstarch
salt and black pepper
6 oz (175g) fresh bean sprouts
4 oz (100g) snow peas, trimmed
6 oz (175g) fresh water
 chestnuts (or 4 oz/100g
 canned, drained weight)
4 green onions
1¼ cups (300ml) peanut or
 vegetable oil, or water, plus
 1 tbsp (15ml) oil
1 tbsp (15ml) light soy sauce
2 tsp (10ml) Shaoxing rice wine
 or dry sherry
1 tsp (5ml) sugar
2 tsp (10ml) sesame oil

Cut the chicken into very thin shreds and combine them with the egg white, cornstarch and 1 tsp (5ml) of salt in a bowl. Mix well and place in the fridge for about 20 minutes. Meanwhile, trim the bean sprouts, finely shred the snow peas lengthwise, shred or slice the water chestnuts and shred the green onions.

Heat a wok or a large skillet until it is very hot and add the 1¼ cups (300ml) of oil (if using water, see below). When the oil is very hot, remove the wok from the heat and immediately add the chicken pieces, stirring vigorously to keep them from sticking together. After about 2 minutes, when the chicken has turned white, quickly drain it in a stainless steel colander set over a bowl. Discard the oil.

If you choose to use water instead of oil, bring it to a boil in a saucepan. Remove the saucepan from the heat and immediately add the chicken pieces, stirring vigorously to keep them from sticking together. After about 2 minutes, when the chicken has turned white, quickly drain it in a stainless steel colander set over a bowl. Discard the water.

Heat the wok or large skillet until it is hot, add the remaining 1 tbsp (15ml) of oil, then add the vegetables and stir-fry for 1 minute. Add the soy sauce, rice wine, sugar, 1½ tsp (7ml) of salt and a little pepper to taste, and continue to stir-fry for 2 minutes. Return the drained chicken to the wok, stir to mix well, and add the sesame oil. Stir a few more times, then turn everything onto a warm serving platter and serve at once.

Garlic Chicken with Cucumber

Cucumbers are rarely served raw in China, and then only after they have been lightly pickled, but they are delicious cooked. In this recipe they are stir-fried with delicate chicken breasts and flavored with garlic and chili. This is an uncomplicated dish and is perfect for everyday dining.

SERVES 4

1 lb (450g) boneless, skinless
  chicken breasts
1 lb (450g) cucumber
salt
1 tbsp (15ml) peanut or
  vegetable oil
1½ tbsp (22ml) finely chopped
  garlic
1 tbsp (15ml) finely chopped
  green onions
1 tbsp (15ml) light soy sauce
1 tbsp (15ml) Shaoxing rice
  wine or dry sherry
2 tsp (10ml) chili bean sauce or
  chili powder
2 tsp (10ml) sesame oil

Cut the chicken into 1 in (2.5cm) cubes and set aside. Peel the cucumber, halve it and remove the seeds with 1 tsp (5ml). Then cut it into 1 in (2.5cm) cubes, season with 2 tsp (10ml) of salt and put the pieces into a colander to drain for 20 minutes. (This removes the excess moisture.) Rinse the cucumber cubes under cold running water and blot them dry with paper towels.

Heat a wok or a large skillet over high heat until it is hot. Add the oil, and when it is very hot and slightly smoking, add the chicken and stir-fry for a few seconds. Add all the other ingredients except the sesame oil and cucumber and continue to stir-fry for another 2 minutes. Now add the cucumber and keep stir-frying for another 3 minutes. Stir in the sesame oil and serve at once.

Chicken in Black Bean Sauce

This recipe is a favorite one for me, and not only because it evokes childhood memories of the fragrance of black bean sauce mixed with garlic that often greeted me at the door when I came home from school. My mother used to make this dish with chicken wings, one of the tastiest parts of the chicken. Wings are ideal for stir-frying because they cook quickly, but other parts of the chicken work just as well. Here I use another favorite: boneless chicken thighs. The tender, juicy flesh makes them ideal for this recipe.

SERVES 4

1 lb (450g) boneless chicken thighs

1 tbsp (15ml) peanut or vegetable oil

1 tbsp (15ml) finely chopped fresh ginger

1½ tbsp (22ml) finely chopped garlic

1 tbsp (15ml) finely chopped shallots

1½ tbsp (22ml) finely chopped green onions

2½ tbsp (37ml) black beans, rinsed and coarsely chopped

⅔ cup (150ml) Chicken Stock (page 75) or water

FOR THE MARINADE

1 tbsp (15ml) light soy sauce

1½ tbsp (22ml) Shaoxing rice wine or dry sherry

1 tsp (5ml) sugar

1 tsp (5ml) sesame oil

2 tsp (10ml) cornstarch

salt

FOR THE GARNISH

2 tbsp (30ml) finely chopped green onions

Cut the chicken thighs into 2 in (5cm) chunks. Mix the marinade ingredients together with ½ tsp (2ml) of salt and pour over the chicken pieces. Leave to marinate for about 1 hour, then drain the chicken and discard the marinade.

Heat a wok or a large skillet over high heat until it is hot. Add the oil, and when it is very hot and slightly smoking, add the chicken and stir-fry it for 5 minutes, or until it begins to brown. Add the ginger, garlic, shallots, green onions and black beans and stir-fry for 2 minutes. Then add the stock. Bring to a boil, then reduce the heat, cover the wok and simmer for 10 minutes, or until the chicken is cooked. Garnish with the green onions, and serve. This dish can be cooked ahead of time and reheated.

Sweet and Sour Chicken

This dish is often featured in the West, where it invariably appears as a sweet, gluey, reddish concoction in mediocre Chinese restaurants. Properly prepared, however, it has the perfect balance of sweet and sour paired with moist, succulent chicken meat.

SERVES 4

1 lb (450g) boneless, skinless chicken breasts

1 egg white

2 tsp (10ml) cornstarch

salt

8 oz (225g) red or green bell peppers

1¼ cups (300ml) peanut or vegetable oil, or water, plus 1 tbsp (15ml) oil

3 garlic cloves, peeled and finely sliced

5 green onions, cut into 2 in (5cm) sections

6 oz (175g) canned lychees, drained, or fresh orange segments

FOR THE SAUCE

⅔ cup (150ml) Chicken Stock (page 75)

1 tbsp (15ml) light soy sauce

2 tsp (10ml) dark soy sauce

2 tsp (10ml) sesame oil

2 tbsp (30ml) Chinese white rice vinegar or cider vinegar

1½ tbsp (22ml) sugar

2 tbsp (30ml) tomato paste or ketchup

salt and white pepper

2 tsp (10ml) cornstarch, mixed with 1 tbsp (15ml) water

Cut the chicken breasts into 1 in (2.5cm) cubes. Combine them with the egg white, cornstarch and ½ tsp (2ml) of salt in a small bowl, then put the mixture into the fridge for about 20 minutes. Wash and seed the red or green bell peppers and cut them into 1 in (2.5cm) cubes.

Heat a wok or a large skillet over high heat until it is hot, then add the 1¼ cups (300ml) of oil (if using water, see below). When it is very hot, remove the wok from the heat and immediately add the chicken pieces, stirring vigorously to keep them from sticking together. After about 2 minutes, when the chicken has turned white, quickly drain it in a stainless steel colander set over a bowl. Discard the oil.

If you choose to use water instead of oil, bring it to a boil in a saucepan. Remove the saucepan from the heat and immediately add the chicken pieces, stirring vigorously to keep them from sticking together. After about 2 minutes, when the chicken has turned white, quickly drain it in a stainless steel colander set over a bowl. Discard the water.

Wipe the wok or large skillet clean and reheat it until it is very hot. Then add the remaining 1 tbsp (15ml) of oil. When it is very hot, add the bell peppers, garlic and green onions and stir-fry for 2 minutes. Add all the sauce ingredients except the cornstarch mixture, season with ½ tsp (2ml) each of salt and white pepper and cook for 2 minutes. Then add the cornstarch mixture and cook for 1 minute. Add the drained chicken to the wok and stir-fry for another 2 minutes, coating the chicken thoroughly with the sauce. Add the lychees or orange segments, mix well and serve at once.

Beggar's Chicken

There are several legends concerning the origin of this recipe, but the most common is that a beggar, having stolen a chicken and eluding his pursuers, started to cook the chicken over a campfire by a river. When it was half cooked, he suddenly heard his pursuers in the distance. In a panic, he buried the chicken in the mud by the riverbank and ran off. Once the danger had passed, the beggar retrieved the mud-encased chicken, finished cooking it, and cracked it open to discover a succulent meal. Over the years, this ancient dish has evolved into the recipe below.

SERVES 4

1 x 3–3½ lb (1.5–1.6kg) chicken

4 oz (100g) ground pork

1 tsp (5ml) sesame oil

salt and white pepper

4 tsp (20ml) light soy sauce

2 tbsp (30ml) Shaoxing rice wine or dry sherry

2 oz (50g) Chinese black mushrooms

1 oz (25g) cloud ear or tree ear mushrooms

2 oz (50g) water chestnuts, fresh or canned

1½ tbsp (22ml) peanut or vegetable oil

3 tbsp (45ml) finely chopped green onions

1 tbsp (15ml) finely chopped fresh ginger

2 oz (50g) Sichuan preserved vegetables, rinsed and coarsely chopped

2 tsp (10ml) sugar

Dry the chicken thoroughly inside and out with paper towels.

Combine the pork in a small bowl with the sesame oil, ½ tsp (2ml) of salt, ½ tsp (2ml) of white pepper, 2 tsp (10ml) of the light soy sauce and 1 tbsp (15ml) of the rice wine.

Soak the black mushrooms in warm water for 20 minutes, drain them and squeeze out the excess liquid. Remove and discard the stems and coarsely chop the caps. Soak the cloud ears or tree ears in warm water for 20 minutes, drain them and rinse several times to remove any sand. Remove and discard any hard bits and chop coarsely. If you are using fresh water chestnuts, peel and chop them finely. If you are using canned water chestnuts, rinse them well, drain them and chop finely.

Heat a wok or a large skillet until it is hot. Add the oil, and when it is very hot, add the green onions and ginger and stir-fry for 10 seconds. Add the pork mixture and continue to stir-fry for 3 minutes, then add the mushrooms, cloud ears or tree ears, water chestnuts, Sichuan vegetables, the remaining 1 tbsp (15ml) of rice wine, the remaining 2 tsp (10ml) of light soy sauce and the sugar. Continue to stir-fry for 5 minutes. Turn into a bowl and allow the mixture to cool thoroughly.

Preheat the oven to 450°F (230°C). Put the cooled pork mixture into the cavity of the chicken and close with a skewer. Put the chicken, breast side down, in a roasting pan. Cook in the oven for 15 minutes, until it is brown, then turn down to 350°F (180°C). Continue to cook for another 35 minutes, then turn the chicken breast side up and cook for a further 15 minutes. Let the chicken rest for at least 20 minutes before carving and serving with the stuffing.

Hot Spiced Chicken

This hot and spicy chicken dish can easily be made ahead of time and reheated. It is a good example of the combination of contrasting flavors that characterize the spicy cuisine of western China. The finished dish has a wonderful fragrance and an equally delightful taste.

SERVES 4

1 lb (450g) boneless, skinless chicken thighs

salt

4 green onions

⅔ cup (150ml) peanut or vegetable oil, plus 1 tsp (5ml)

3 dried red chilies, halved lengthwise

2 tsp (10ml) finely chopped fresh ginger

1 tbsp (15ml) chili bean sauce

1¼ cups (300ml) Chicken Stock (page 75)

2 tsp (10ml) roasted and ground Sichuan peppercorns (page 29)

2 tsp (10ml) sugar

2 tbsp (30ml) dark soy sauce

Rub the chicken thighs with 1 tsp (5ml) of salt and let them sit for about 30 minutes. Then cut them into 1 in (2.5cm) cubes. Cut the green onions into 2 in (5cm) pieces.

Heat a wok or a large skillet over high heat until it is hot. Add the ⅔ cup (150ml) of oil, and when it is very hot and slightly smoking, add the dried chilies and stir to flavor the oil. When the chilies turn black, turn the heat down. At this point you may remove the chilies or leave them in as the Chinese do. Add the chicken pieces to the wok and brown slowly. Drain in a colander set over a bowl, then place them on paper towels.

Heat a clean wok or skillet over moderate heat and add the remaining 1 tsp (5ml) of oil. Fry the green onions, ginger and chili bean sauce, taking care not to have the heat too high or the sauce will burn. A few seconds later, add the chicken stock, Sichuan peppercorns, sugar and soy sauce. Turn the heat down low, and add the chicken pieces. Cover, and let the chicken finish cooking in the sauce, turning the pieces from time to time. This should take about 20 to 30 minutes. Remove any surface fat and serve the chicken with the sauce.

Crispy Shrimp Paste Chicken

I first enjoyed this chicken dish in the company of Willie Mark, perhaps Hong Kong's most knowledgeable food critic. We were at the Sun Tung Lok restaurant in Harbour City, and I was unprepared for the excellence of what I thought would be a simple fried chicken dish. I immediately set out to replicate the dish in my own kitchen, and ever since then I have incorporated it into the repertory of dishes I make frequently.

The distinctive flavor comes from the shrimp paste, which gives an aromatic and exotic taste: it must be used with care, as it is quite strong. The secret of the extra crispness of the chicken is in the double-frying. Marinated and then fried the first time, the chicken is fried again just before serving, making it ideal to serve at a dinner party. The use of a seafood paste to flavor chicken is a typically southern Chinese touch: a Chiu Chow inspiration.

The chicken is not boned; this helps the meat to remain flavorful and moist.

SERVES 4

1 x 2¼ lb (1kg) whole chicken
all-purpose flour or potato flour,
   for dusting
2⅓ cups (600ml) peanut or
   vegetable oil, for deep-frying

**FOR THE SHRIMP PASTE
   MARINADE**

2 tbsp (30ml) shrimp paste or
   sauce
1 tbsp (15ml) Shaoxing rice
   wine or dry sherry
1 tbsp (15ml) ginger juice,
   squeezed from 2 oz (50g)
   fresh ginger (page 25)
2 tsp (10ml) sugar
2 tsp (10ml) sesame oil
1 tsp (5ml) light soy sauce

FOR THE GARNISH

3 tbsp (45ml) finely chopped
   green onions

Chop the chicken into bite-sized pieces with a heavy knife or a Chinese cleaver. Mix the marinade ingredients in a bowl, then add the chicken pieces and let them sit at room temperature for 30 minutes.

Heat a wok or a large, deep skillet until it is hot and add the oil. Drain the chicken pieces, then lightly dust them with flour, shaking off any excess. When the oil is hot, put in half the chicken and deep-fry for 5 minutes, or until golden brown. Drain on paper towels, then fry the rest of the chicken the same way.

Just before serving, remove any debris from the oil with a fine mesh ladle. Reheat the oil until it is very hot and refry the chicken for 1 minute, or until golden brown and heated through. Drain on paper towels, sprinkle with the chopped green onions and serve at once.

Fragrant Crispy Chicken

This eastern Chinese flavored chicken is one of my favorites because it combines succulent meat with a simple but extremely tasty marinade. The method is to deep-fry the chicken twice, once at a lower temperature and then at a much higher temperature. The result is a crispy-textured chicken that is quickly cooked and very moist within.

SERVES 4

1½ lb (675g) boneless, skinless
  chicken thighs
2⅓ cups (600ml) peanut or
  vegetable oil
2 tsp (10ml) sesame oil
2 tbsp (30ml) finely chopped
  green onions
2 tsp (10ml) sugar

FOR THE MARINADE

3 tbsp (45ml) Shaoxing rice
  wine or dry sherry
1 tbsp (15ml) light soy sauce
2 tsp (10ml) dark soy sauce
3 green onions
2 slices of fresh ginger
1 tbsp (15ml) honey
1 tsp (5ml) five-spice powder
1 tsp (5ml) roasted and ground
  Sichuan peppercorns
  (page 29)
salt and black pepper

Place the chicken thighs between 2 pieces of plastic wrap and lightly pound them until they are evenly flat. Put them into a bowl and set aside.

To make the marinade, combine the rice wine, soy sauces, green onions and ginger in a blender and purée. Strain the purée over the chicken. Add the rest of the marinade ingredients, season with 1 tsp (5ml) of salt and ½ tsp (2ml) of black pepper and mix well. Let the chicken marinate for 45 minutes.

Remove the chicken from the bowl and reserve the marinade. Heat a wok or a large skillet over high heat until it is hot. Add the oil, and when it is very hot and slightly smoking, add the chicken and fry for 5 minutes. Remove the chicken and drain, then reheat the oil in the wok until it is very hot. Fry the chicken again until it is crispy and golden brown. Remove the chicken from the wok and drain well on paper towels. Drain off all the oil and discard. Cut the chicken into slices and arrange on a platter.

Reheat the wok over medium heat and add the reserved marinade, sesame oil, green onions and sugar. Bring this mixture to a boil and pour it over the chicken. Serve at once.

Steeped Chicken

This is a classic Cantonese chicken dish that my mother often made. The technique used is called steeping, which applies to delicate foods such as chicken. Here the gentlest possible heat is used so that the flesh of the chicken remains extremely moist and flavorful, with a satiny, almost velvet-like texture. It is not difficult to make. The chicken simmers in liquid for a few minutes, then the heat is turned off, the pan tightly covered, and the chicken left to steep to finish cooking. The water the chicken is steeped in can be saved for cooking rice or as a base for chicken stock.

The pure, simple flavors of Steeped Chicken call for a suitably pungent counterpoint in the dipping sauce. Green onions and root ginger, jolted to their full fragrance by a quick dousing of hot vegetable oil, offer the perfect flavor combination.

SERVES 4

1 x 3–4 lb (1.5–1.75kg) chicken
6 slices of fresh ginger
6 green onions
salt and black pepper
FOR THE CANTONESE-STYLE DIPPING SAUCE
4 tbsp (60ml) finely chopped green onions, white part only
2 tsp (10ml) finely chopped fresh ginger
salt
2 tbsp (30ml) peanut or vegetable oil

Fill a large wok or saucepan, big enough to hold the whole chicken, with water and bring it to a boil. Put in the chicken and add the ginger, green onions, 1 tbsp (15ml) of salt and some black pepper, tipping out any excess water, but leaving enough to cover the chicken. Bring the water to a simmer and cook for 20 minutes, then turn off the heat, cover the wok tightly and leave for 1 hour. After 1 hour, remove the chicken from the liquid and allow it to cool. Strain, saving the liquid, which can be used as a base for making stock or for cooking rice.

Put the chicken on a chopping board. Cut it into bite-sized pieces and arrange them on a platter. To make the sauce, place all the ingredients except the oil in a bowl, season with 2 tsp (10ml) of salt and mix well. Heat a wok until it is hot, then add the oil. When it is very hot and smoking, pour it on to the sauce ingredients and mix well. Serve with the chicken.

Steamed Chicken with Chinese Sausage

My mother used to make this often. It is uncomplicated, tasty and, above all, easy.

SERVES 4

1 lb (450g) boneless, skinless
   chicken breasts
2 Chinese sausages, finely sliced
1 tbsp (15ml) light soy sauce
1 tbsp (15ml) Shaoxing rice
   wine or dry sherry
2 tsp (10ml) sesame oil
salt and white pepper

Make thin cuts in the chicken breast without cutting all the way through. Push the sliced sausages into these cuts.

Place the chicken on a heatproof plate. In a small bowl, mix the soy sauce, rice wine, sesame oil and a little salt and pepper. Pour this mixture evenly over the chicken.

Set up a steamer, or put a rack into a wok or deep saucepan, and fill it with 2 in (5cm) of water. Bring the water to a boil, then carefully lower the chicken, still on its plate, into the steamer or onto the rack. Turn the heat to low and cover the wok or saucepan. Steam gently for 20 minutes, or until the chicken is cooked. Serve at once.

Sichuan Peppercorn Chicken

If you can't find shrimp paste, you can use shrimp sauce for the marinade and sauce.

SERVES 4

1½ lb (700g) boneless, skinless
   chicken thighs
2 tbsp (30ml) peanut oil
FOR THE MARINADE
1 tsp (5ml) dark soy sauce
1 tsp (5ml) shrimp paste
1 tsp (5ml) cornstarch
½ tsp (2ml) sesame oil
FOR THE SAUCE
1 green onion
½ tsp (2ml) roasted and ground
   Sichuan peppercorns
   (page 29)
1 tsp (5ml) shrimp paste
2 tsp (10ml) Shaoxing rice wine
   or dry sherry
1 tsp (5ml) dark soy sauce
1 tsp (5ml) sesame oil

Place the chicken thighs between 2 sheets of plastic wrap and pound gently to tenderize. Then cut the meat into 1 x 3 in (2.5 x 7.5cm) strips. Put the chicken strips into a bowl with the marinade ingredients, stir and leave to marinate for around 30 minutes before draining.

Finely chop the green onion. Heat a wok or a large skillet until it is hot. Add the oil, and when it is quite hot, quickly stir-fry the chicken strips for about 3 minutes. Add all the sauce ingredients except the sesame oil to the wok or skillet and continue to stir-fry for another 3 minutes, or until the chicken is cooked. Stir in the sesame oil and serve at once.

Bean Sauce Chicken

This straightforward chicken dish, redolent with the aroma of rich yellow bean sauce and enlivened by the textural crunch of nuts, is easy to make. You may substitute your own favorite ingredients. Simply follow the same procedure for a delicious result.

SERVES 4

1 lb (450g) boneless, skinless
   chicken breasts
1 egg white
2 tsp (10ml) cornstarch
salt
6 oz (175g) water chestnuts,
   fresh or canned
8 oz (225g) red pepper
   (about 2), seeded
2 cups (450ml) peanut or
   vegetable oil or water, plus
   1 tbsp (15ml) oil
4 oz (100g) raw peanuts
1 tbsp (15ml) light soy sauce
2 tsp (10ml) Shaoxing rice wine
   or dry sherry
1½ tbsp (22ml) whole yellow
   bean sauce
2 tbsp (30ml) hoisin sauce
2 tsp (10ml) sesame oil

Cut the chicken into ½ in (1cm) cubes and combine them with the egg white, cornstarch and 1 tsp (5ml) of salt in a bowl. Mix well and place in the fridge for about 20 minutes.

Meanwhile, if you are using fresh water chestnuts, peel them and chop them into roughly ½ in (1cm) dice. If you are using canned water chestnuts, first rinse them well in cold water. Drain in a colander and then chop them into roughly ½ in (1cm) dice. Do the same with the red bell pepper.

Heat a wok until it is very hot and add the 2 cups (450ml) of oil (if using water, see below). When it is very hot, remove the wok from the heat and immediately add the chicken cubes, stirring vigorously to keep them from sticking together. After about 2 minutes, when the chicken has turned white, quickly drain it in a stainless steel colander set over a bowl. Discard the oil.

If you choose to use water instead of oil, bring it to a boil in a saucepan. Remove the saucepan from the heat and immediately add the chicken pieces, stirring vigorously to keep them from sticking together. After about 2 minutes, when the chicken has turned white, quickly drain it in a stainless steel colander set over a bowl. Discard the water.

Heat the wok until it is hot, add the remaining 1 tbsp (15ml) of oil, then add the peanuts and stir-fry for 1 minute, or until they are lightly browned. Add the vegetables and stir-fry for 1 minute. Finally, add the soy sauce, rice wine, yellow bean sauce and hoisin sauce and continue to stir-fry for 2 minutes. Return the drained chicken to the wok, stir to mix well and add the sesame oil. Give the mixture a few more stirs, and then turn it onto a warm serving platter. Serve at once.

Twice-cooked Chicken

This eastern Chinese recipe involves a two-step cooking process. First the chicken is marinated and steamed. This cooks the flesh but retains the moisture and flavor of the bird. The chicken pieces are then dried and deep-fried to a golden, crispy brown. The shrimp paste in the marinade adds a fragrant and unusual touch to the dish.

SERVES 4–6

1½ lb (750g) boneless, skinless chicken thighs, cut into 2 in (5cm) cubes

2⅓ cups (600ml) peanut or vegetable oil

cornstarch, for dusting

FOR THE MARINADE

1 tbsp (15ml) Shaoxing rice wine or dry sherry

1½ tbsp (22ml) light soy sauce

1 tbsp (15ml) dark soy sauce

1 tbsp (15ml) shrimp paste or sauce

1 tbsp (15ml) finely chopped green onions

2 tsp (10ml) finely chopped fresh ginger

1 tsp (5ml) roasted and ground Sichuan peppercorns (page 29)

2 tsp (10ml) sugar

salt

FOR DIPPING

Salt and Pepper Dip (page 37)

Combine all the marinade ingredients in a bowl and add 2 tsp (10ml) of salt. Rub the marinade all over the chicken pieces and let them sit in a cool place for an hour.

Next, set up a steamer, or put a rack into a wok or deep saucepan, and fill it with 2 in (5cm) of water. Bring the water to a boil over high heat. Put the chicken on a heatproof plate and carefully lower it into the steamer or onto the rack. Turn the heat to low and cover the wok or saucepan tightly. Steam gently for 30 minutes.

Remove the cooked chicken from the saucepan and let it cool and dry completely. This may take up to 1 hour or more. (The dish can be made a day ahead up to this point.)

Heat the oil in a deep-fat fryer or large wok until it is hot. Dust the pieces of dried, steamed chicken with cornstarch, shaking off any excess. Then deep-fry the chicken, a few pieces at a time, until the pieces are golden brown and heated right through. Drain the pieces on paper towels. Serve the chicken hot with the Salt and Pepper Dip on the side.

Whole Stuffed Chicken Skin

This is the most spectacular recipe in the book, in which the skin of the chicken is removed, stuffed, shaped and deep-fried. Keep the skinned chicken for use elsewhere.

SERVES 6–8

1 quantity Savory Glutinous
Rice Stuffing (page 303)
1 x 4–4½ lb (1.75kg–2kg)
chicken
6 cups (1.5L) peanut or
vegetable oil

First, skin the chicken. With your fingers, begin to loosen the skin, starting from the neck end. Work until you have reached the end and gently begin to separate the skin where it is attached to the breast area. Find the joint where the wing is attached to the body, and with poultry shears cut it from the body, but leave the wing intact. Now do the other side of the wing joint. Then with a small, sharp knife, starting at the back of the neck, cut away the skin from the backbone with your knife edge toward the bone, gently pulling the skin back. As the skin begins to loosen, pull it gently over the chicken as if to turn it inside out. Continue to cut against the bone and gently pull the skin from the back. Remove the tail from the chicken, but leave it attached to the rest of the skin. Very gently pull the skin over the thighs and legs, using a knife to scrape the fibers attached to the leg and free the skin. Cut the final end joint of the leg and leave it intact with the skin. Do the same to the other leg. At this point, turn the complete chicken skin right side out.

Skewer the neck end and gently stuff the cold rice stuffing in through the tail end. Continue to push in the stuffing so as to "re-form" the chicken — do not overstuff, though, as it should be rather loose. Skewer the tail and place on a heatproof plate.

Next, set up a steamer, or put a rack into a wok or deep saucepan, and fill it with 2 in (5cm) of water. Bring the water to a boil. Lower the stuffed chicken, still on its plate, into the steamer or onto the rack. Turn the heat to low, cover and steam gently, making sure you replenish the water from time to time. After 1 hour, pour off all the liquid that has accumulated and allow the chicken to cool. Once cooled, it can be loosely wrapped in plastic wrap and refrigerated.

When you are ready to serve, heat a large wok and add the oil. When it is hot, carefully lower the chicken into the oil breast side up. Baste the chicken with the hot oil until it is brown and crispy. Remove and drain on paper towels to serve. Congratulations, you deserve a glass of wine!

Crispy Sichuan Duck

In my family, and in typical Chinese custom, duck was a treat reserved for special occasions and family banquets. I always remembered such feasts long afterwards. This duck recipe is one of my favorites, and it is not surprising that it is so popular in Chinese restaurants in the West. Don't be intimidated by the long preparation process. Most of the steps are quite simple and can be done up to a day ahead, and the results are well worth the labor. This is a dish for a special dinner party and is great served with Steamed Buns (page 322) and Salt and Pepper Dip (page 37).

SERVES 4–6

1 x 3½-4 lb (1.6–1.75kg) duck, fresh or frozen and thawed
2 tbsp (30ml) five-spice powder
2½ oz (60g) Sichuan peppercorns, crushed
1 oz (25g) whole black peppercorns, crushed
3 tbsp (45ml) cumin seeds
7 oz (200g) rock salt
4 slices of fresh ginger
4 green onions
cornstarch or potato flour, for dusting
5 cups (1.2L) peanut or vegetable oil

TO SERVE
Steamed Buns (page 322)
Salt and Pepper Dip (page 37)
green onions, sliced lengthwise

Blot the duck with paper towels until it is thoroughly dry, then rub it inside and out with the five-spice powder, Sichuan peppercorns, black peppercorns and cumin seeds. Cover the outside of the duck with the rock salt, making sure it is rubbed on evenly. Wrap the duck well in plastic wrap and place in the fridge for 24 hours.

After this time, brush the salt from the duck. Cut the ginger into slices 3 x ¼ in (7.5 x 0.5cm). Cut the green onions into 3 in (7.5cm) lengths. Stuff the ginger and green onions into the cavity of the duck, and put it on an ovenproof china or glass plate.

Next, set up a steamer, or put a rack into a wok or deep saucepan, and fill it with 2 in (5cm) of water. Bring the water to a boil. Carefully lower the duck, still on its plate, into the steamer or onto the rack. Turn the heat to low and cover the wok or saucepan. Steam gently for 2 hours, pouring off the excess fat from time to time. Be sure to replenish the water as necessary. Remove the duck and pour off all the fat and liquid that may have accumulated. Discard the ginger and green onions. Put the duck on a platter and leave in a cool, dry place for about 2 hours, until it has thoroughly dried and cooled. At this point the duck can be refrigerated.

Just before you serve it, cut the duck into quarters. Dust them with cornstarch or potato flour, shaking off the excess. Heat the oil in a deep-fat fryer or wok and, when it is hot, deep-fry the quarters until crisp and warmed right through. Drain on paper towels, then chop into smaller serving pieces.

To eat, dip a piece of duck meat in the Salt and Pepper Dip, then put the meat into a Steamed Bun — rather like a sandwich.

Cantonese Roast Duck

One of the most delicious ways to cook duck is this Cantonese method of roasting it with a flavorful marinade inside the cavity. It makes a spectacular centerpiece.

SERVES 4–6

1 x 3½–4 lb (1.6–1.75kg) duck, fresh or frozen and thawed

FOR THE MARINADE

1 tbsp (15ml) peanut oil

3 tbsp (45ml) chopped fresh ginger

5 unpeeled garlic coves, crushed

6 green onions, cut into 3 in (7.5cm) pieces

1 tbsp (15ml) whole yellow bean sauce

2 tbsp (30ml) light soy sauce

2 tbsp (30ml) Shaoxing rice wine or dry sherry

1½ tbsp (22ml) crushed Chinese rock sugar or granulated sugar

3 whole star anise

1 tbsp (15ml) roasted Sichuan peppercorns (page 29)

⅔ (150ml) Chicken Stock (page 75)

10 sprigs of cilantro

FOR THE BASTING MIXTURE

6 tbsp (90ml) honey

4 tbsp (60ml) dark soy sauce

3 tbsp (45ml) Shaoxing rice wine or dry sherry

2 tbsp (30ml) black rice vinegar or cider vinegar

Rinse the duck well and blot it completely dry with paper towels, then insert a meat hook near the neck.

Heat a wok or a large skillet over high heat until it is hot. Add the oil, and when it is very hot and slightly smoking, add the ginger and garlic and stir-fry for 10 seconds. Then add the rest of the marinade ingredients. Bring the mixture to a simmer and remove it from the heat. Allow the marinade to cool thoroughly.

Pour the marinade into the cavity of the duck and skewer the tail opening with a bamboo or steel skewer. Tie up the opening with strong string.

Combine the basting mixture ingredients with 5 cups (1.2L) of water in a medium saucepan and bring to a boil. Using a large ladle or spoon, pour this over the duck several times, as if to bathe it, until the skin is completely coated. Hang the duck in a cool, well-ventilated place to dry overnight, or alternatively, hang it in front of a cold fan for about 4–5 hours, longer if possible. (Be sure to put a baking sheet or roasting pan underneath to catch any drips.) Once the duck has dried, the surface of the skin will feel like parchment paper.

Preheat the oven to 475°F (240°C). Place the duck on a roasting rack in a roasting pan, breast side up. Put ⅔ cup (150ml) of water into the roasting pan. (This will prevent the fat from splattering.) Now put the duck into the oven and roast it for 15 minutes. Then turn the heat down to 350°F (180°C) and roast for a further 1 hour and 10 minutes.

Remove the duck from the oven and let it sit for at least 10 minutes before you carve it. Carefully remove the skewer and drain the marinade into a bowl. Skim any fat from the top. Using a cleaver or a sharp knife, cut the duck into serving portions and arrange them on a warm platter. Serve the marinade separately as a sauce.

Eight Jewel Duck

Although time-consuming, the end results of this dish are well worth the effort.

SERVES 6–8

1 x 3½–4 lb (1.6–1.75kg) duck, fresh or frozen and thawed

cornstarch or potato flour, for dusting

5 cups (1.2L) peanut or vegetable oil

FOR THE RICE

8 oz (225g) glutinous rice, soaked in water for 4 hours

4 Chinese sausages, coarsely chopped

FOR THE STUFFING

8 whole chestnuts

4 oz (100g) water chestnuts, fresh or canned

2 oz (50g) Chinese black mushrooms

2 tbsp (30ml) peanut or vegetable oil

4 oz (100g) Parma ham or lean smoked bacon, coarsely diced

2 tbsp (30ml) coarsely chopped cilantro

3 oz (75g) ginkgo nuts

1 oz (25g) bamboo shoots, coarsely chopped

3 tbsp (45ml) finely chopped green onions

2 tbsp (30ml) Shaoxing rice wine or dry sherry

1 tbsp (15ml) light soy sauce

salt and black pepper

Mix the soaked glutinous rice with the Chinese sausage and place on an ovenproof plate. Set up a steamer, or put a rack into a wok or deep saucepan, and fill it with 2 in (5cm) of water. Bring the water to a boil and lower the plate into the steamer or onto the rack. Turn the heat to low and cover the wok or saucepan. Steam gently for 30 minutes, or until the rice is cooked, then allow to cool.

Peel and quarter the chestnuts and, if you are using fresh water chestnuts, peel and chop them coarsely (if you are using canned water chestnuts rinse and chop them). Soak the mushrooms in warm water until soft, then squeeze out the excess water, cut off the tough stems and coarsely chop.

Heat a wok until hot, then add the 2 tbsp (30ml) of oil. When the oil is smoking, add all the stuffing ingredients and stir-fry for 10 minutes. Add the cooked rice and sausage, mix well and allow to cool thoroughly.

Now, bone the duck. Using your fingers and a small knife, cut along the skin of the neck to expose the wishbone. This is connected with the wing joints. With poultry shears, cut both wing joints free. Working with your knife, carefully cut against the bone, pulling the meat away with your hands. When you have reached the thigh joint, cut the carcass away from both joints. Work until the end, keeping the tail attached to the skin and meat while detaching the backbone. Scrape the meat away from the thigh and cut at the tip of each leg.

Stuff the duck with the rice stuffing, then skewer the neck and tail. Put the duck on a heatproof plate and steam (just as you did with the rice and sausage) for 1½ hours, occasionally pouring off excess fat and replenishing the water.

After 1½ hours, remove the duck, pour off any fat and liquid and leave the duck for at least 2 hours to dry and cool.

Just before you serve, dust the duck with cornstarch or potato flour, shaking off the excess. Heat the oil in a deep-fat fryer or wok. When it is almost smoking, lower in the duck, basting it until it is crispy. Drain on paper towels and serve.

Cantonese Pressed Duck

This Cantonese speciality is said to have originated in northern China and to have been brought south during the Ming dynasty, when the Manchu invaded China and the Emperor and his court fled south. In the traditional method, a boned duck was literally flattened and cured with various spices before cooking.

Much of the work here is in the preparation. The duck is braised, then boned, steamed and finally fried. The result is an unusual and delicious duck, unlike any you have ever had. Fortunately, much of the preparation can be done ahead of time. It makes a superb main course for a dinner party, as well as for a special family meal.

SERVES 4

1 x 3½–4 lb (1.6–1.75kg) duck, fresh or frozen and thawed
2 eggs, beaten
cornstarch or potato flour, for dusting
5 cups (1.2L) peanut or vegetable oil

FOR THE BRAISING LIQUID

3⅔ cups (900ml) Chicken Stock (page 75)
3⅔ cups (900ml) dark soy sauce
2 cups (450ml) light soy sauce
2 cups (450ml) Shaoxing rice wine or dry sherry
½ cup (120g) Chinese rock sugar or granulated sugar
5 whole star anise
3 pieces of Chinese cinnamon bark or cinnamon sticks

Cut the duck in half lengthwise and dry with paper towels.

Combine all the braising ingredients in a large saucepan and bring the mixture to a boil. Add the duck halves and turn the heat down to a simmer. Cover the saucepan and slowly braise the duck for 1 hour, or until it is tender.

Skim off the large amount of surface fat that will be left when the duck is cooked, and allow the duck to cool. Once cooled, take the duck out of the pan, remove any lingering surface fat from the liquid and set the liquid aside.

Carefully remove all the bones from the duck, keeping the meat and skin intact. Place the duck halves between 2 pieces of plastic wrap and press the meat and skin together. Baste the duck halves with the beaten egg and dust with cornstarch or potato flour.

Next, set up a steamer, or put a rack into a wok or deep saucepan, and fill it with 2 in (5cm) of water. Bring the water to a boil over high heat. Put the duck on a heatproof plate and carefully lower it into the steamer or onto the rack. Turn the heat to low and cover the wok or saucepan tightly. Steam gently for 20 minutes. Allow the duck to cool thoroughly. The dish can be completed to this stage a day in advance.

When you are ready to serve the duck, heat a wok or a large skillet over high heat until it is hot. Add the oil, and when it is very hot and slightly smoking, add the duck halves and deep-fry until they are crispy. Remove and drain well on paper towels. Heat some of the reserved braising liquid and serve with the duck as a sauce.

Beijing (Peking) Duck

Preparing Beijing (Peking) Duck is a time-consuming task, but I have devised a simpler method that closely approximates to the real thing. Just give yourself plenty of time and the results will be good enough for an emperor. Traditionally, Beijing (Peking) Duck is served with Chinese pancakes, green onions cut into brush shapes and sweet bean sauce. In Hong Kong and in the West, hoisin sauce is used instead. It is very similar to sweet bean sauce but contains vinegar. Each guest spoons some sauce onto a pancake. Then a helping of crisp skin and meat is placed on top with a green onion brush, and the entire mixture is rolled up like a stuffed pancake.

SERVES 4–6

1 x 3½–4 lb (1.6–1.75kg) duck, fresh or frozen and thawed

FOR THE HONEY SYRUP
1 lemon
5 cups (1.2L) water
3 tbsp (45ml) honey
3 tbsp (45ml) dark soy sauce
⅔ cup (150ml) Shaoxing rice wine or dry sherry

TO SERVE
Chinese Pancakes (page 324)
8–12 green onions, cut into brushes (page 45)
6 tbsp (90ml) hoisin sauce or sweet bean sauce

Rinse the duck well and blot it completely dry with paper towels, then insert a meat hook near the neck.

Using a sharp knife, cut the lemon into ¼ in (5mm) slices, leaving the rind on. Combine the lemon slices with the rest of the honey syrup ingredients in a large saucepan and bring the mixture to a boil. Turn the heat to low and simmer for about 20 minutes. Using a large ladle or spoon, pour this mixture over the duck several times, as if to bathe it, until the skin of the duck is completely coated.

Hang the duck in a cool, well-ventilated place to dry overnight, or alternatively, hang it in front of a cold fan for about 4–5 hours, longer if possible. (Be sure to put a baking sheet or roasting pan underneath to catch any drips.) Once the duck has dried, the surface of the skin will feel like parchment paper.

Preheat the oven to 475°F (240°C). Place the duck on a rack in a roasting pan, breast side up. Put ⅔ cup (150ml) of water into the roasting pan. (This will prevent the fat from splattering.) Now put the duck into the oven and roast it for 15 minutes. Then turn the heat down to 350°F (180°C) and continue to roast for a further 1 hour 10 minutes.

Remove the duck from the oven and let it sit for at least 10 minutes before you carve it. Using a cleaver or a sharp knife, cut the meat and skin into pieces and arrange them on a warm platter. Serve at once with Chinese pancakes, green onion brushes and a bowl of hoisin sauce or sweet bean sauce.

Tea-smoked Duck

I loved the first time I tasted the smoky rich taste of a tea-smoked duck. The flavor of duck fat interacts very well with the smoky aroma of the tea, giving the duck a taste that reminds me of ham. You can eat this either with Steamed Buns (page 322) or with Chinese Pancakes (page 324). Either way you will be in duck-lover heaven. Much of the work can be done ahead of time, which makes the whole process a lot easier, leaving just the smoking to be done on the day.

SERVES 4–6

1 x 3½–4 lb (1.6–1.75kg) duck, fresh or frozen and thawed

2 tbsp (30ml) roasted and ground Sichuan peppercorns (page 29)

2 tsp (10ml) five-spice powder

salt and white pepper

6 green onions

6 slices of fresh ginger

FOR THE SMOKING MIXTURE

2 oz (50g) black tea

4 tbsp (60ml) uncooked long-grain white rice

4 tbsp (60ml) brown sugar

3 whole star anise, broken into sections

2 pieces of Chinese cinnamon bark, broken into sections

TO SERVE

Steamed Buns (page 322)

Chinese Pancakes (page 324)

Rub the duck evenly inside and out with the Sichuan peppercorns, five-spice powder, 1 tbsp (15ml) of salt and 1 tsp (5ml) of white pepper. Wrap it well in plastic wrap and place in the fridge overnight. The next day, unwrap the duck and place the green onions and ginger inside the cavity.

Next, set up a steamer, or put a rack into a wok or deep saucepan, and fill it with 2 in (5cm) of water. Bring the water to a boil over high heat. Put the duck on a heatproof plate and carefully lower it into the steamer or onto the rack. Turn the heat to low and cover the wok or saucepan tightly. Steam gently for 1 hour and 15 minutes, or until the duck is cooked. Pour off any juices and fat and discard. Allow the duck to cool thoroughly before you proceed.

Line the inside of a wok with foil. Place the tea, rice, sugar, star anise and cinnamon on the bottom. Rub a rack with oil and place it over the smoking ingredients. Place the duck on the rack. Now heat the wok over high heat until the mixture begins to burn. Turn the heat down to moderate, cover with foil and a lid, and let the duck smoke for 15 minutes. Turn off the heat and allow it to sit, covered, for another 10 minutes. Remove the duck from the wok and discard the smoking ingredients, along with the foil. Carve or cut up the duck and serve with Steamed Buns or Chinese Pancakes.

Braised Duck

The braising sauce used for this duck recipe is similar to the one used for Soy Sauce Chicken (page 147). The sauce can be frozen and reused. Unlike chicken, duck needs long braising to cook it thoroughly and render out the fat in the skin. You can see this braised duck in food shops in China, southeast Asia, Taiwan, Hong Kong, and in Chinatowns in the US and the UK, hanging picturesquely from hooks.

It is easy to make at home and reheats well, although I think it is best served at room temperature.

SERVES 4–6

1 x 3½–4 lb (1.6–1.75kg) duck, fresh or frozen and thawed
5 cups (1.2L) peanut or vegetable oil
Garlic and Vinegar Dipping Sauce (page 37)

FOR THE BRAISING SAUCE

5 cups (1.2L) Chicken Stock (page 75) or water
5 cups (1.2L) dark soy sauce
1¼ cups (300ml) light soy sauce
2 cups (450ml) Shaoxing rice wine or dry sherry, or 1 cup (250ml) dry sherry mixed with 1 cup (250ml) Chicken Stock (page 75)
½ cup (120ml) Chinese rock sugar or granulated sugar
5 whole star anise
3 pieces of Chinese cinnamon bark or cinnamon sticks
2 tbsp (30ml) fennel seeds
1 tbsp (15ml) cumin seeds

FOR THE GARNISH

cilantro sprigs

Cut the duck in half, lengthwise. Dry the halves thoroughly with paper towels. Heat the oil in a wok or a large skillet until it is almost smoking, and deep-fry the two halves of the duck, skin side down. Turn the heat to medium and continue to fry slowly until the skin is browned. This should take about 15–20 minutes. Do not turn the pieces over, but baste the duck as it fries. Drain the lightly browned duck on paper towels.

Combine all the braising sauce ingredients in a large saucepan and bring to a boil. Add the duck halves and turn the heat down to a simmer. Cover the saucepan and slowly braise the duck for 1 hour, or until it is tender.

Skim off the large amount of surface fat that will be left when the duck is cooked. This procedure will prevent the duck from becoming greasy. Now remove the duck halves from the sauce with a slotted spoon. Let them cool, then chop them into smaller pieces. Arrange on a warm platter, garnish with the cilantro and serve at once, with the Garlic and Vinegar Sauce. Alternatively, you can let the duck cool thoroughly and serve it at room temperature. Once the braising sauce has cooled, remove any lingering surface fat. It can now be frozen and reused to braise duck or chicken. This dish reheats beautifully.

Five-spice Red Braised Pigeons

In this recipe, the five-spice powder gives the pigeons a delicious flavor, while the soy braising sauce endows them with a rich brown color. Chinese cooks often blanch pigeons before braising them to rid them of any impurities. Braising is a good technique to use, as it keeps the pigeons moist. If you prefer, you can substitute quails or other small game birds. This dish is excellent served cold and is perfect for an exotic picnic treat.

SERVES 4, AS A STARTER

2 x ¾–1 lb (350–450g)
   squab pigeons, cut in half
   lengthwise

FOR THE SAUCE

2 cups (450ml) dark soy sauce
⅔ cup (150ml) light soy sauce
3 tbsp (45ml) hoisin sauce
2 tbsp (30ml) five-spice powder
⅔ cup (150ml) Shaoxing rice
   wine or dry sherry
4 tbsp (60ml) Chinese rock
   sugar or granulated sugar

FOR THE GARNISH

2 tbsp (30ml) finely chopped
   green onions
1 tbsp (15ml) finely chopped
   fresh ginger

Blanch the pigeons by immersing them in a large saucepan of boiling water for about 5 minutes. Remove them with a slotted spoon and discard the water.

Combine the sauce ingredients in a medium-sized saucepan and bring to a boil. Turn the heat down to a simmer and add the pigeons. Cover the saucepan and braise the birds over low heat for about 35 minutes, or until they are tender.

Remove the pigeons from the saucepan with a slotted spoon and let them cool. (The braising sauce may be saved and frozen for the next time you cook this dish.) Chop the pigeons into bite-sized pieces and arrange them on a warm serving platter. Sprinkle the green onions and ginger on top and serve at once. If you want to serve the dish cold, let the pigeon pieces cool and then sprinkle them with the garnish ingredients. Refrigerate, wrapped in plastic wrap, until you are ready to serve.

Crispy Fried Pigeons

On Sundays in Hong Kong one of the most popular outings is to Shatin, a town in the New Territories, to play the famous Chinese game Mahjong and to eat pigeon. Pigeons have a rich, gamey taste. The southern Chinese like to braise them quickly, let them dry and deep-fry them just before serving. The result is moist, highly flavored pigeon with crisp skin. The secret of this dish lies in the braising liquid, which is used over and over again. In some restaurants it is used for years, like a vintage stock.

This dish takes time and patience, but it is not difficult to make and much of the work can be done several hours in advance. It is an impressive dish for a special dinner party.

SERVES 4, AS A STARTER

2 x 8–12 oz (225–350g) squab
   pigeons, halved lengthwise
4 slices of fresh ginger
3²⁄₃ cups (900ml) peanut oil
lemon wedges
Salt and Pepper Dip (page 37)
FOR THE BRAISING SAUCE
5 cups (1.2L) Chicken Stock
   (page 75)
5 tbsp (75ml) dark soy sauce
3 tbsp (45ml) light soy sauce
²⁄₃ cup (150ml) Shaoxing rice
   wine or dry sherry
3 tbsp (45ml) Chinese rock
   sugar or granulated sugar
6 pieces of fresh orange peel,
   finely chopped, or dried
   citrus peel, soaked and finely
   chopped (page 24)
3 pieces of Chinese cinnamon
   bark or cinnamon sticks
3 whole star anise
2 tsp (10ml) sesame oil
salt and white pepper

Bring a large saucepan of water to a boil. Blanch the pigeons in the boiling water for about 2 minutes. This method helps to rid them of impurities and tightens the skin. Remove the pigeons from the saucepan and discard the water.

Combine all the braising sauce ingredients in a large saucepan with a seasoning of 1 tsp (5ml) each of salt and white pepper, and bring to a boil. Add the pigeons and the ginger. Lower the heat to a simmer and cover the saucepan tightly. Let it simmer for about 30 minutes, or until the pigeons are just tender. Remove them with a slotted spoon and let them dry on a plate, or hang them up in a cool, dry, airy place for at least 2 hours. The braising liquid, once cooled, can be stored in a plastic container and frozen for future use.

After 2 hours, the skin of the pigeons should feel like parchment paper. Just before you are ready to serve them, heat the oil in a deep-fat fryer or a large wok. When it is hot, lower in the pigeons and deep-fry them until they are crisp and deep brown in color, turning them over frequently with a slotted spoon so that all sides are thoroughly cooked and browned. This should take about 10 minutes. Drain the cooked pigeons on paper towels and let them cool for a few minutes. Using a heavy cleaver or knife, chop them into 4–6 pieces and arrange them on a warm serving platter. Serve at once with lemon wedges and the Salt and Pepper Dip.

Barbecued Quails

I enjoy being in southern China or Hong Kong in autumn because this is the season for rice birds. These very small birds are caught with nets in the rice fields and then simply barbecued on skewers with a zesty sauce. Unable to find rice birds in Europe, I discovered an excellent alternative — quails. They are easy to prepare, and as they are also delicious cold they make a wonderful dish for a picnic.

SERVES 4

4 x 4 oz (100g) quails, fresh or
   frozen and thawed
salt

FOR THE SAUCE

3 tbsp (45ml) hoisin sauce
1 tbsp (15ml) Shaoxing rice
   wine or dry sherry
1 tbsp (15ml) light soy sauce
2 tsp (10ml) sesame oil
salt and white pepper

Preheat the oven to 475°F (240°C).

Dry the quails well with paper towels, then rub each one inside and out with a little salt.

Mix the sauce ingredients in a small bowl with ½ tsp (2ml) each of salt and white pepper. Rub the quails inside and out with this sauce and place them in a small roasting pan. Put them into the oven for 5 minutes, then turn the heat down to 350°F (180°C) and continue to roast the birds for another 20 minutes. Turn off the oven and leave them there for another 5 minutes. Take them out of the oven and let them rest for another 10 minutes before serving.

Serve the quails whole or, if you wish to serve them Chinese-style, use a cleaver or a heavy knife to chop each one into 4–6 pieces. Arrange on a warm platter and serve.

Stir-fried Quails

Quails are popular in southeast as well as southern China because of their excellent flavor and their suitability for stir-frying. This technique seals in the taste and juices of the game birds and precludes overcooking. The bamboo shoots and water chestnuts provide a crunchy texture that complements the tenderness of the quail meat.

This recipe is an adaptation of a banquet dish from the former Lee Gardens Rainbow Room Restaurant in Hong Kong. The robust flavors and rich colors of the dish make it a perfect main course for a dinner party.

SERVES 4, AS STARTER

4 x 4 oz (100g) quails, fresh or frozen and thawed
8 oz (225g) water chestnuts, fresh or canned (drained weight)
8 oz (225g) canned bamboo shoots
6 green onions
⅔ cup (150ml) peanut or vegetable oil
1¼ cups (300ml) Chicken Stock (page 75)
2 tbsp (30ml) oyster sauce
2 tsp (10ml) sugar
2 tsp (10ml) cornstarch, mixed with 2 tsp (10ml) water

FOR THE MARINADE

2 tbsp (30ml) Shaoxing rice wine or dry sherry
2 tbsp (30ml) light soy sauce
1 tbsp (15ml) cornstarch
2 tsp (10ml) sesame oil
salt and white pepper

Dry the quails inside and out with paper towels. Then, using a cleaver or a heavy sharp knife, cut each quail into about 6 pieces. Put them into a bowl along with the marinade ingredients and ½ tsp (2ml) each of salt and white pepper. Mix them well and leave them to marinate for 20 minutes.

Next, prepare the vegetables. If you are using fresh water chestnuts, peel and slice them (if you are using canned water chestnuts, rinse them thoroughly in cold water first). Rinse the bamboo shoots in cold water and slice these too. Cut the green onions at a diagonal into 3 in (7.5cm) segments.

Remove half the quail pieces from the marinade using a slotted spoon. Heat a wok or large skillet and when it is very hot, add half the oil. When it is smoking slightly, stir-fry the quail pieces for about 5 minutes until they are brown. Transfer them to a colander or sieve to drain and discard the cooking oil. Reheat the wok or skillet and stir-fry the rest of the quail pieces in the same manner, using the other half of the peanut oil. Again, drain in a colander or sieve, but leave about 1 tbsp (15ml) of oil in the wok.

Reheat the wok or skillet over high heat. Add the green onions, fresh water chestnuts if you are using them and bamboo shoots, and stir-fry them for about 2 minutes. Then add the rest of the ingredients and bring the mixture to a boil. Return the quail pieces to the wok and cook for about 3 minutes. Make sure you coat them thoroughly with the sauce. If you are using canned water chestnuts, add these now and cook for 2 more minutes. Serve at once.

Meat-filled Omelet

This hearty dish is representative of the type of Chinese home cooking I love.

SERVES 4

4 large eggs, beaten
3 tbsp (45ml) all-purpose flour
1 tbsp (15ml) sesame oil
salt and black pepper

FOR THE FILLING

1 tbsp (15ml) fresh ginger
3 tbsp (45ml) green onions
8 oz (225g) minced pork
1 tbsp (15ml) light soy sauce
2 tbsp (30ml) Shaoxing rice
  wine or dry sherry
2 tsp (10ml) sesame oil
1 egg white, beaten
2 tsp (10ml) cornstarch
1 tsp (5ml) roasted ground
  Sichuan peppercorns
  (page 29)

FOR THE SAUCE

1½ tbsp (22ml) peanut oil
4 garlic cloves
3 tbsp (45ml) green onions
1 oz (25g) dried lily buds,
½ oz (15g) dried cloud ear
  mushrooms
2 tbsp (30ml) Shaoxing rice
  wine or dry sherry
1 tbsp (15ml) light soy sauce
1 tbsp (15ml) dark soy sauce
2 tsp (10ml) sugar
1 tsp (5ml) roasted and ground
  Sichuan peppercorns
1¼ cup (300ml) Chicken Stock
  (page 75)
2 tsp (10ml) sesame oil

First, for the sauce, leave the dried lily buds and cloud ear mushrooms in separate bowls of warm water to soak for about 20 minutes. When they are soft, remove them from the water, rinse them and remove the ends of the lily buds.

Mix 3 of the eggs with the flour, sesame oil and a pinch of salt in a blender until it is a smooth batter with no lumps. Put the batter through a fine sieve or strainer.

Heat a wok over medium heat until it is hot, then use paper towels to grease the surface of the wok with peanut oil. Put in 2 tbsp (30ml) of the egg batter and tilt the wok in all directions to coat the bottom. When the batter has set, carefully peel it off and lay it on a plate. Repeat the process until you have used up all the batter.

Finely chop the ginger and green onions for the filling. Combine all of the filling ingredients in a bowl, season with ½ tsp (2ml) each of salt and black pepper and mix well. Put about 2 tbsp (30ml) of filling in the center of each omelet. Moisten the edges with the remaining beaten egg and fold over one-half of the omelet to seal. It should be like a half-moon-shaped dumpling. Repeat the process until you have used up the omelets and filling. Leftover filling can be used in the sauce.

For the sauce, heat a wok over high heat until it is hot, then add the oil. Finely slice the garlic and green onions and, when the oil is hot and slightly smoking, add them to the wok. Stir-fry for 20 seconds, then add the lily buds and cloud ear mushrooms and stir-fry for 1 minute. Add the rest of the sauce ingredients, apart from the sesame oil. Bring the sauce to a boil and add the omelet dumplings. Turn the heat to very low, cover and simmer for 15 minutes. When the dumplings are cooked, add the sesame oil, turn out onto a platter and serve at once.

Home-style Omelet

This home-style omelet is a good example of a quick, easy and appetizing dish that can serve as a main course or be part of a meal.

SERVES 2–4

6 large eggs, beaten

6 tbsp (90ml) finely chopped green onions

6 oz (175g) ground pork

2 oz (50g) Sichuan preserved vegetables, rinsed thoroughly and finely chopped

white pepper

3 tbsp (45ml) peanut or vegetable oil

1 tsp (5ml) sesame oil

2 tsp (10ml) Shaoxing rice wine or dry sherry

2 tsp (10ml) light soy sauce

1 tsp (5ml) sugar

In a large bowl, combine the eggs with half the green onions, pork, preserved vegetables and ¼ tsp (1ml) of white pepper.

Heat a wok or a large skillet over high heat until it is hot. Add the oil, and when it is very hot and slightly smoking, add the egg mixture and fry until it is brown. Carefully turn it over and fry the other side. Remove it from the oil and drain well on paper towels.

Pour off most of the oil from the wok and discard, leaving 1 tbsp (15ml) in the wok. Reheat the wok until it is hot. Add the remaining green onions, pork and preserved vegetables, along with the sesame oil, rice wine, light soy sauce and sugar, and stir-fry for 2 minutes. Transfer the omelet to a plate, pour over the mixture from the wok and serve at once.

Four-color Omelet

This is a recipe for an adventurous cook, but it will repay you with a beautiful meal.

SERVES 4

1 preserved egg (thousand-year-old egg)

1 salted duck egg

4 eggs, beaten

2 tbsp (30ml) finely chopped green onions

1 tbsp (15ml) finely chopped cilantro

white pepper

2 tbsp (30ml) peanut or vegetable oil

Shell the preserved egg and cut into small dice, then set aside. Crack the salted duck egg and add the egg white to the beaten eggs. Cut the yolk up into small dice and combine with the preserved egg.

Combine the beaten eggs with the green onions, cilantro and pepper.

Heat a wok or a large skillet until it is hot and add the oil. Add the beaten eggs and stir-fry gently. When the eggs have barely set, add the preserved egg mixture. Continue to cook for a few minutes, until the eggs are warmed through and cooked. Serve at once.

Stir-fried Eggs with Tomatoes

Anyone who travels to the remoter parts of China is guaranteed some surprises. I experienced one in Yunnan province when I visited the tiny village of Yi Liang Gou Jie, a place even my friends who live in the province had never been to. It is a colorful place, teeming with activity, and yet looking like something out of the sixteenth century. Everywhere our party went (my photographer, his assistant, the driver and me), crowds would surround us, peering at us as if were alien beings — which, of course, we were, with our Western garb, high-tech equipment and strange language. And whenever we smiled, they would break out into congenial laughter.

After some hours of walking around the town, we were famished. We stumbled upon a rustic tea house/restaurant, quite unpretentious, with no sign or nameplate, but with someone's goat tethered in front. We ordered the speciality of the house, Yunnan duck, along with several seasonal vegetable dishes, and this delectable stir-fry of eggs and tomatoes — quite a repast in the middle of nowhere at the no-name café. The delicate flavor of the eggs is nicely balanced by the sweet acidity of the tomatoes, and both ingredients should be as fresh as possible.

SERVES 4

6 eggs, beaten
2 tsp (10ml) sesame oil
1 tsp (5ml) salt
1 lb (450g) fresh tomatoes
6 green onions
1½ tbsp (22ml) peanut or
    vegetable oil
salt and white pepper

In a medium-sized bowl, combine the eggs with the sesame oil and salt. Set aside.

Cut the tomatoes into quarters and then into eighths. With the flat of a cleaver or knife, crush the green onions and then finely shred them.

Heat a wok or a large skillet until it is hot. Add the oil, ½ tsp (2ml) of salt, a little white pepper and the green onions and stir-fry for 30 seconds. Then add the tomatoes and eggs and continue to cook, stirring continually, until the eggs are set, about 5 minutes. Place on a platter and serve at once.

Eggs with Stir-fried Vegetables

This easy-to-make home-style dish utilizes only a few prosaic ingredients but transforms them into a wholesome and delicious meal. It illustrates the versatility and imagination of Chinese cooking. This recipe can easily be altered to accommodate any leftover vegetables and meat you may have in your fridge.

SERVES 4

1 oz (25g) Chinese black
  mushrooms
2 tbsp (30ml) peanut or
  vegetable oil
4 oz (100g) minced pork
4 oz (100g) bamboo shoots,
  shredded
4 oz (100g) green beans, finely
  sliced at a slight diagonal
4 green onions, finely shredded
1 tbsp (15ml) light soy sauce
1 tbsp (15ml) Shaoxing rice
  wine or dry sherry
2 tsp (10ml) sesame oil
salt and white pepper
6 eggs, beaten

Soak the mushrooms in warm water for 20 minutes, then drain them and squeeze out the excess liquid. Remove and discard the stems and slice the caps into thin strips.

Heat a wok or a large skillet over high heat until it is hot. Add the oil, and when it is very hot and slightly smoking, add the pork and stir-fry for 2 minutes. Then add the mushrooms, bamboo shoots, green beans and green onions and stir-fry for another 3 minutes. Add the soy sauce, rice wine, sesame oil, 1 tsp (5ml) of salt and ½ tsp (2ml) of white pepper and stir-fry for 1 minute. Now add the beaten eggs and stir-fry gently until the eggs are cooked and slightly browned. Remove the mixture to a platter and serve at once.

Steamed Egg Custard with Meat Sauce

This is a delectable dish with an ambrosial aroma and a satisfying and unusual silky texture. The contrast of the hearty meat sauce and the smooth custard makes this dish a great favorite of many cooks. The eggs, lightened by the chicken stock, stand up well against the robust sauce. It is easy to make and goes well with plain rice.

SERVES 4

1½ oz (40g) Chinese black
   mushrooms
1½ tbsp (22ml) peanut or
   vegetable oil
12 oz (350g) ground pork
3 tbsp (45ml) finely chopped
   green onions
1½ tbsp (22ml) Shaoxing rice
   wine or dry sherry
2 tsp (10ml) sesame oil
2 tbsp (30ml) dark soy sauce
1 tsp (5ml) five-spice powder
1 tsp (5ml) sugar
salt and white pepper peanut
   or vegetable oil, for frying
FOR THE CUSTARD
4 eggs
2⅓ cups (600ml) Chicken Stock
   (page 75)
salt
FOR THE GARNISH
3 tbsp (45ml) finely chopped
   green tops of green onions

Soak the mushrooms in warm water for 20 minutes, then drain them and squeeze out the excess liquid. Remove and discard the stems and finely chop the caps.

Heat a wok or a large skillet over high heat until it is hot. Add the oil, and when it is very hot and slightly smoking, add the pork and stir-fry for 2 minutes. Drain the pork, then return it to the wok. Add the green onions, rice wine, sesame oil, soy sauce, five-spice powder, sugar, mushrooms, 1 tsp (5ml) of salt and ½ tsp (2ml) of white pepper and continue to stir-fry for 3 minutes. Remove from the heat and set aside.

Mix the custard ingredients in a bowl with 1 tsp (5ml) of salt. Rub a heatproof shallow bowl with peanut or vegetable oil and pour in the custard mixture.

Next, set up a steamer, or put a rack into a wok or deep saucepan, and fill it with 2 in (5cm) of water. Bring the water to a boil over high heat. Carefully lower the bowl into the steamer or onto the rack. Turn the heat to low, and cover the wok or saucepan tightly. Steam gently for 10–12 minutes, or until the custard has set. Add the stir-fried meat mixture and spread it over the top of the custard. Cover and steam for another 4 minutes. Remove the bowl of custard from the steamer, sprinkle with the green green onion tops and serve at once.

Steamed Egg Custard with Clams

There are many different varieties of clams harvested off the coast of eastern China. A favorite way to prepare them is to steam them whole, then crack them at the table and dip them in vinegar and sugar. In this Shanghai-inspired dish, cooked clams are mixed with beaten egg and steamed. The result is a savory velvet- or satin-textured custard. Only the freshest live clams should be used for this dish because the taste of the clams must not overwhelm the delicate custard.

SERVES 4

⅔ cup (150ml) water
1 lb (450g) fresh live clams,
   well scrubbed

FOR THE CUSTARD

3 eggs
1¼ cups (300ml) Chicken Stock
   (page 75)
1 tbsp (15ml) finely shredded
   fresh ginger
1½ tbsp (22ml) Shaoxing rice
   wine or dry sherry
salt and white pepper

FOR THE GARNISH

3 tbsp (45ml) finely chopped
   green onions, white part only
1 tbsp (15ml) peanut or
   vegetable oil

Bring the water to a boil in a large saucepan and add the clams. When they begin to open, remove them immediately and drain. Finish opening them by hand, reserving any clam juices, which will give an added depth of flavor.

Mix the custard ingredients in a bowl and add the reserved clam juices, 1 tsp (5ml) of salt and ½ tsp (2ml) of white pepper. Pour this mixture into a heatproof shallow bowl and arrange the cooked clams attractively around it.

Next, set up a steamer, or put a rack into a wok or deep saucepan, and fill it with 2 in (5cm) of water. Bring the water to a boil over high heat. Carefully lower the bowl with the clams into the steamer or onto the rack. Turn the heat to low and cover tightly. Steam gently for 10 minutes, or until the custard has set. Remove the custard and sprinkle with the green onions. Heat the oil in a small saucepan until it begins to smoke, pour this over the custard and serve at once.

Marbled Tea Eggs

This unique method of cooking eggs in spiced tea derives its name from the marbled texture and web of cracks that appear on the surface of the eggs when they are shelled. Traditionally, tea eggs are served cold, and they make a wonderful and easy garnish for cold platters. Not only are they delicious but they are also beautiful to look at.

Eggs are rarely eaten as a plain dish by themselves in Chinese cuisine. However, they do lend themselves to imaginative combinations. These marbled eggs are one such unusual and delicious treat. They are best left overnight in the liquid, so that the flavors can permeate the eggs and, once cooled, they can be kept in the tea liquid and stored in the fridge for up to 2 days. They are also wonderful to take along on picnics.

SERVES 4–6, AS A STARTER

7 cups (1.75L) water
6 eggs, at room temperature
FOR THE TEA MIXTURE
6 tbsp (90ml) black tea,
  preferably Chinese
3 tbsp (45ml) dark soy sauce
1½ tbsp (22ml) light soy sauce
1 tbsp (15ml) five-spice powder
2 tsp (10ml) roasted and ground
  Sichuan peppercorns
  (page 29)
3 pieces of Chinese cinnamon
  bark or cinnamon sticks
3 whole star anise
3⅔ cups (900ml) water
salt

Bring the 7 cups (1.75L) of water to a boil in a large saucepan and cook the eggs for 5 minutes. Remove them from the saucepan and immediately plunge them into cold water, then gently crack the shells with a large spoon under cold running water, until the entire shell is a network of cracks. Let them sit in the cold running water for at least 10 minutes.

Put the tea mixture ingredients into the empty saucepan with 2 tsp (10ml) of salt and bring to a simmer, then return the cracked eggs to the saucepan. Cook them in the mixture for 10 minutes, making sure the liquid covers the eggs completely, remove the saucepan from the heat and let the eggs and liquid cool.

Leave the cooked eggs in the liquid and put them into the fridge overnight. When you are ready to serve the eggs, remove them from the cooled liquid and gently peel off the cracked shells. You should have a beautiful marble-like web on each egg. Serve them cut in half or quarters as a snack with other cold dishes, or use them as a garnish.

Stir-fried Milk

I have sampled many versions of this dish in Hong Kong and in Guangdong, a province in Southern China. My most special memory of stir-fried milk, however, was at the Qing Hui Yuan restaurant, in Shunde, Guangdong. This is really a thick custard, stir-fried with shrimp, barbecued Chinese pork and pine nuts, a perfect combination of taste and textures. I was told by the residents of the town that cows are abundant in the area and that milk-based dishes have been part of the local cuisine for a long time.

In a country with almost no "dairy," Cantonese milk dishes date from the Portuguese influence of over 300 years ago. Exposed to the European tradition, the Cantonese created dishes that make milk both digestible and exceptionally tasty. In any event, this is a delightful and venerable dish.

SERVES 4

2 cups (450ml) milk
4 tbsp (60ml) cornstarch
salt and white pepper
1½ tbsp (22ml) peanut or
    vegetable oil, plus 1 tbsp
    (15ml) for oiling the pan
8 oz (225g) Barbecued Roast
    Pork (page 104) or cooked
    ham, coarsely chopped
4 oz (100g) uncooked shrimp,
    peeled and coarsely chopped
4 oz (100g) pine nuts

Combine the milk and cornstarch with 1 tsp (5ml) of salt and ½ tsp (2ml) of white pepper in a medium-sized saucepan and mix until smooth. Simmer the mixture over low heat for 8 minutes, or until it has thickened to a consistency of soft scrambled eggs. Oil a heatproof dish, pour in the cooked milk mixture, and allow it to cool thoroughly. Cover with plastic wrap and refrigerate. This can be done the day before.

Heat a wok or a large skillet until it is hot and add the oil and 1 tsp (5ml) of salt. Add the barbecued pork or ham and the shrimp, and stir-fry the mixture for 1 minute. Add the milk mixture and the pine nuts, and stir-fry for 3 minutes, or until everything is heated through. Serve at once.

FISH & SHELLFISH

In my family, fish and seafood have always been regarded with a special affection, something I still maintain today. The Chinese prefer to cook whole fish, something that is seen as a symbol of prosperity, but fillets are a perfectly acceptable substitute.

Braised Fish

Onions in all forms are popular in Chinese cookery, but shallots are especially prized for their distinctive flavor. I think they complement fish beautifully. If you can't get shallots for this recipe you can use green onions instead. A firm white fish such as cod, haddock or sea bass will work better here than delicate ones such as plaice. Plain steamed rice and a fresh green vegetable would go well with this dish.

SERVES 4

1 lb (450g) firm white fish
  fillets, such as cod or halibut
salt
⅔ cups (150ml) peanut or
  vegetable oil
10 oz (275g) small shallots,
  peeled and left whole, or
  green onions
2 tbsp (30ml) finely chopped
  fresh ginger
1 tbsp (15ml) light soy sauce
1 tbsp (15ml) dark soy sauce
2 tsp (10ml) sugar
2 tbsp (30ml) Shaoxing rice
  wine or dry sherry
⅔ cup (150ml) Chicken Stock
  (page 75)
2 tsp (10ml) sesame oil

Pat the fish fillets dry with paper towels. Rub each side with 1 tsp (5ml) of salt and cut them into 1½ in (3.5cm) wide diagonal strips. Set the fish aside for 20 minutes, then pat them dry again. The salt will have extracted some of the excess moisture from the fish. If you are using green onions, cut them into 3 in (7.5cm) segments.

Heat a wok or a large skillet over high heat until it is hot. Add the oil, and when it is very hot and slightly smoking, turn the heat down to medium and brown the fish in 2 batches, draining each cooked batch on paper towels. Drain all but 1 tbsp (15ml) of oil from the wok and discard the rest of the oil.

Reheat the wok or skillet and add the shallots and ginger. Stir-fry them for 1 minute, then add the rest of the ingredients. Bring to a boil, then turn the heat down to a simmer and cook for 5 minutes, or until the shallots are tender. Return the fish to the wok, cover, and simmer for 2 minutes until the fish is heated through. Using a slotted spoon, gently remove the fish and shallots and arrange them on a warm platter. Pour the sauce over the top and serve at once.

Sweet and Sour Fish

A sweet and sour sauce is a perfect foil for fish. The sugar and vinegar in the sauce contrast well with the distinctive flavor of the fish. The dish is at its most impressive when a whole fish is used, but it can be just as successfully made with fish fillets, as here. The best fish to use are cod, haddock or sea bass. The sauce can be made in advance and reheated.

SERVES 4

1 lb (450g) fish fillets, such as cod, haddock or sea bass, at least 1 in (2.5cm) thick

salt and white pepper

4 oz (100g) carrots

4 oz (100g) peas

4 oz (100g) snow peas, trimmed

cornstarch, for dusting

1 egg

1 tsp (5ml) sesame oil

5 cups (1.2L) peanut or vegetable oil

FOR THE SAUCE

2 tbsp (30ml) finely chopped green onions

1½ tbsp (22ml) finely chopped fresh ginger

1¼ cups (300ml) Chicken Stock (page 75)

1 tbsp (15ml) light soy sauce

2 tbsp (30ml) Shaoxing rice wine or dry sherry

1½ tbsp (22ml) tomato paste

2 tbsp (30ml) Chinese white rice vinegar or cider vinegar

2 tbsp (30ml) sugar

2 tsp (10ml) cornstarch, blended with 2 tsp (10ml) water

salt and white pepper

Remove the skin from the fish fillets, then, using a sharp knife or cleaver, make crisscross slashes across the top of each fillet. Do not cut right through, but keep the fillets intact. Rub them evenly with 2 tsp (10ml) of salt and 1 tsp (5ml) of white pepper and set aside.

Peel and dice the carrots. Blanch the carrots, peas and snow peas in a saucepan of boiling water for about 4 minutes each. Plunge them into cold water, then drain them. Put all the blanched vegetables into a saucepan with all the sauce ingredients and season with 1 tsp (5ml) of salt and ½ tsp (2ml) of white pepper. Bring the mixture to a simmer and remove the saucepan from the heat.

Coat the fish fillets well with cornstarch, shaking off any excess. In a small bowl, combine the egg and sesame oil. Spread this over the fillets and dust again with cornstarch, shaking off any excess. Heat the oil in a deep-fat fryer or a large wok until it is almost smoking and deep-fry the fillets in 2 batches until crisp and brown. Drain on paper towels.

Bring the sauce back to a simmer. Arrange the fish fillets on a warm serving platter and pour the sauce over the top. Serve at once.

Fish in Hot Sauce

I love to make this quick and easy Sichuan-inspired dish when I am particularly in the mood for fish. A firm white fish such as cod, sea bass, halibut or haddock is most suitable for shallow-frying because it is meaty and holds its shape during the cooking process. In China, carp would be the preferred fish for this recipe. Serve with plain rice and any stir-fried vegetable.

SERVES 4

1 lb (450g) fresh, firm white fish
    fillets, such as cod, sea bass
    or halibut
salt
cornstarch, for dusting
3 green onions
⅔ cup (150ml) peanut or
    vegetable oil
1 tbsp (15ml) finely chopped
    garlic
2 tsp (10ml) finely chopped
    fresh ginger

FOR THE SAUCE

⅔ cup (150ml) Chicken Stock
    (page 75)
2 tsp (10ml) whole yellow bean
    sauce
1 tbsp (15ml) chili bean sauce
2 tbsp (30ml) Shaoxing rice
    wine or dry sherry
2 tsp (10ml) dark soy sauce
2 tsp (10ml) sesame oil
salt and white pepper

Sprinkle the fish fillets evenly on both sides with 1 tsp (5ml) of salt. Cut the fish into strips 2 in (5cm) wide and let them sit for 20 minutes. Then dust them with the cornstarch.

Cut the green onions into 2 in (5cm) diagonal slices. Heat a wok or a large skillet over high heat until it is hot. Add the oil, and when it is very hot and slightly smoking, turn the heat down. Fry the fillets on both sides until they are partially cooked. Then remove and drain the fish on paper towels. Pour off most of the oil, leaving about 1 tbsp (15ml) in the wok.

Reheat the wok or skillet and add the green onions, garlic and ginger. Stir-fry them for 30 seconds, then add the sauce ingredients and season with about ½ tsp (2ml) of salt and ¼ tsp (1ml) of white pepper. Bring the mixture to a boil. Turn the heat down to a simmer and return the fish to the wok. Simmer for about 2 minutes, then turn the fish and sauce onto a platter and serve.

West Lake Fish

I remember sitting in a restaurant right on the fish-laden West Lake in the beautiful city of Hangzhou and eating this famous dish. The carp was perfectly poached (or steeped) and covered with a most deliciously mild sweet and sour sauce. The earthy flavor of the carp is a perfect contrast for the sauce. If you are unable to find carp, you can easily substitute a fat sea trout or sea bass.

SERVES 4–6

1 oz (25g) dried Chinese wood
    ear mushrooms

salt and black pepper

2 slices of fresh ginger

2 green onions

1 whole carp or trout or sea
    bass, about 2¼ lb (1kg),
    cleaned

1 tbsp (15ml) peanut or
    vegetable oil

2 garlic cloves, peeled and
    crushed

1½ lb (675g) baby spinach

FOR THE SAUCE

⅔ cup (150ml) Chicken Stock
    (page 75)

⅓ cup (85ml) Chinese rock
    sugar or granulated sugar

⅔ cup (150ml) Chinese black
    vinegar or 4 tbsp (60ml) cider
    vinegar

1 tbsp (15ml) dark soy sauce

1 tbsp (15ml) Shaoxing rice
    wine or dry sherry

2 tbsp (30ml) finely chopped
    fresh ginger

3 tbsp (45ml) finely chopped
    Parma ham or lean smoked
    bacon

Soak the wood ear mushrooms in warm water for about 20 minutes, until soft. Rinse well in cold water and squeeze out the excess liquid. Remove any hard stems and finely shred the mushrooms.

Fill a large wok or saucepan with water. Add 2 tsp (10ml) of salt and the ginger and green onions and bring to a boil. Gently lower the fish into the water until it is fully covered, adding more water if necessary. Bring the mixture to a simmer. Cover the wok tightly, then turn off the heat and let it sit for about 15 minutes.

Meanwhile, put all the sauce ingredients into a medium saucepan, simmer for 5 minutes and set aside.

Heat a wok or a large skillet until it is hot. Add the oil, and when it is hot add the garlic and stir-fry for 15 seconds, or until it is slightly browned. Add the wood ear shreds and stir-fry for 3 minutes, then add the spinach and stir-fry for another 3 minutes, or until it is wilted. Season with salt and pepper. Remove to a platter.

Gently remove the fish from the liquid and place it on top of the spinach and wood ear mixture. Pour the sauce over the fish and serve at once.

Fish in Wine Sauce

This is an elegant Shanghai fish dish served in many homes as well as in the best restaurants. Even though it calls for a rich wine sauce, it is surprisingly easy to make. The fish is coated with an egg white mixture and then gently cooked in oil, or you can use water; then it is drained and mixed with the sauce. The dried mushrooms add a rich, smoky flavor, a nice accompaniment to the subtle taste of the fish fillets. Because it is so delicious and so easy to make, this is an excellent recipe for a special dinner party.

SERVES 4

2 oz (50g) Chinese dried
 mushrooms
1 lb (450g) fresh firm white fish,
 such as sea bass, halibut or
 cod
1 egg white
2 tsp (10ml) cornstarch
salt and white pepper
2⅓ cups (600ml) peanut or
 vegetable oil or water

FOR THE WINE SAUCE

3 tbsp (45ml) Shaoxing rice
 wine or dry sherry
2 tsp (10ml) dark soy sauce
1 tsp (5ml) light soy sauce
1½ tbsp (22ml) Chinese rock
 sugar or granulated sugar
⅔ cup (150ml) Chicken Stock
 (page 75)
2 tsp (10ml) cornstarch, mixed
 with 1 tbsp (15ml) water
salt and white pepper

Soak the mushrooms in warm water for 20 minutes. Then drain them and squeeze out the excess liquid. Remove and discard the stems and finely shred the caps.

Cut the fish into 2 in (5cm) pieces and combine them with the egg white, cornstarch, 1 tsp (5ml) of salt and ½ tsp (2ml) of white pepper in a medium-sized bowl. Mix well and refrigerate for 20 minutes.

Heat a wok until it is very hot and add the oil (if using water, see below). When it is very hot, remove the wok from the heat and immediately add the fish, stirring vigorously to keep the pieces from sticking together. After about 2 minutes, when the fish has turned white, quickly drain it in a stainless steel colander set over a bowl. Discard the oil.

If you choose to use water instead of oil, bring it to a boil in a saucepan. Remove the saucepan from the heat and immediately add the fish pieces, stirring vigorously to keep them from sticking together. After about 2 minutes, when the fish has turned white, quickly drain it in a stainless steel colander set over a bowl. Discard the water.

Put the sauce ingredients with 1 tsp (5ml) each of salt and white pepper in a saucepan and bring to a simmer. Add the mushrooms and cook for about 2 minutes, then add the fish pieces and heat through. Serve at once.

Smoked Fish

The smoking process gives delicate fish a subtle new dimension. This Shanghai-inspired recipe requires no great expertise. It makes a wonderful cold dish but is equally tasty when served warm.

SERVES 4

1–1½ lb (450–675g) firm white
 fish fillets, such as cod or
 sole, or a whole fish such as
 sole or turbot

1½ tbsp (22ml) finely chopped
 fresh ginger

1½ tbsp (22ml) Shaoxing rice
 wine or dry sherry

2 tbsp (30ml) light soy sauce

3 tbsp (45ml) finely chopped
 green onions

peanut or vegetable oil,
 for greasing

FOR THE SMOKING MIXTURE

2 oz (50g) brown sugar

2 oz (50g) uncooked long-grain
 white rice

2 oz (50g) black tea

3 whole star anise, broken into
 sections

2 tsp (10ml) five-spice powder

2 tbsp (30ml) Sichuan
 peppercorns

2 pieces of Chinese cinnamon
 bark, broken into sections

If you are using a whole fish, remove the gills. Pat the fish or fish fillets dry with paper towels. In a small bowl, mix the ginger, rice wine, soy sauce and green onions well until they are almost a paste. You can use a food processor or blender for this. Rub this mixture evenly on both sides of the fish and set aside for 30 minutes.

Next, set up a steamer, or put a rack into a wok or deep saucepan, and fill it with 2 in (5cm) of water. Bring the water to a boil over high heat. Put the fish on a heatproof plate and carefully lower it into the steamer or onto the rack. Cover the wok tightly and gently steam the fish for 5 minutes, then remove the plate of semi-cooked fish and allow it to cool slightly.

Line the inside of a wok with foil. Place the sugar, rice, tea, star anise, five-spice powder, Sichuan peppercorns and cinnamon on the bottom. Rub a rack with oil and place it over the smoking ingredients. Place the fish on the rack. Now heat the wok over high heat until the mixture begins to burn. Turn the heat down to moderate, cover and let it smoke for 5 minutes. Turn off the heat and allow it to sit, covered, for another 5 minutes. Remove the fish and discard the smoking ingredients and the foil. Serve at once.

Fish in Hot and Sour Sauce

The combination of hot and sour is a popular one in the Sichuan region. A quick and simple dish, this is perfect for a light family meal.

SERVES 4

1 lb (450g) fresh, firm white fish
  fillets, such as sole or plaice
cornstarch, for dusting
⅔ cup (150ml) peanut or
  vegetable oil

**FOR THE HOT AND SOUR
  SAUCE**

⅔ cup (150ml) Chicken Stock
  (page 75)
2 tbsp (30ml) Shaoxing rice
  wine or dry sherry
1½ tbsp (22ml) dark soy sauce
1 tbsp (15ml) tomato paste
2 tsp (10ml) chili bean sauce
2 tbsp (30ml) Chinese black
  rice vinegar or cider vinegar
2 tsp (10ml) sugar
white pepper

FOR THE GARNISH

3 tbsp (45ml) finely chopped
  green onions

If you are using plaice, have your fishmonger remove the dark skin of the fish or else remove it yourself, using a small, sharp knife. Cut the fish fillets, across the width and at a slight diagonal, into 1-in (2.5cm) wide strips. Dust the pieces with cornstarch, shaking off any excess.

Heat a wok or a large skillet over high heat until it is hot. Add the oil, and when it is very hot and slightly smoking, turn the heat down to medium. Fry the fish strips gently for 2–3 minutes, until they are golden brown. You may have to do this in batches. Drain the cooked fish strips on paper towels.

Discard the oil, wipe the wok or skillet clean and reheat it. Add all the sauce ingredients, season with ½ tsp (2ml) of white pepper and bring to a boil, then lower the heat to a simmer. Add the fried fish strips and simmer them in the sauce for 2 minutes. Serve garnished with the green onions.

Red-cooked Fish

"Red-cooked" usually means dishes that are braised for a long time, so that the food takes on the reddish tones of the soy sauce mixture. This is more difficult to do with fish, as quick cooking is usually the rule and does not allow time for absorption of color. However, in this case the fish is pan-fried beforehand, and it is then braised briefly in the sauce. Serve this with fried rice and a vegetable dish.

SERVES 4

2 x 8 oz (225g) fillets of
    haddock or halibut
salt
cornstarch for dusting
3 tbsp (45ml) peanut or
    vegetable oil

FOR THE SAUCE

1½ tbsp (22ml) peanut or
    vegetable oil
1 tbsp (15ml) finely chopped
    garlic
1 tbsp (15ml) finely chopped
    fresh ginger
2 tbsp (30ml) Shaoxing rice
    wine or dry sherry
1½ tbsp (22ml) hoisin sauce
1 tbsp (15ml) dark soy sauce
2 tsp (10ml) ground bean sauce
1 tbsp (15ml) Chinese rock
    sugar or granulated sugar
⅔ cup (150ml) Chicken Stock
    (page 75)
2 tsp (10ml) cornstarch, mixed
    with 1 tbsp (15ml) water
2 tsp (10ml) sesame oil

FOR THE GARNISH

green onions, sliced lengthwise

Put the fish fillets on a baking sheet. Sprinkle 2 tsp (10ml) of salt and cornstarch evenly over the fish, shake off any excess.

Heat a wok or a large skillet over high heat until it is hot, then add the oil. When it is slightly smoking, slide the fish in and gently pan-fry for 2 minutes, or until golden brown. Carefully turn the fish over and fry the other side. Remove it from the wok and drain on paper towels. Wipe the wok clean.

Now make the sauce. Reheat the wok over high heat until it is hot, and add the oil. When it is hot and slightly smoking, add the garlic and ginger and stir-fry for 20 seconds. Then add the rest of the sauce ingredients apart from the cornstarch mixture and the sesame oil. Stir-fry for 1 minute, then add the cornstarch mixture and, when the sauce boils, turn the heat to low. Carefully slide the fillets into the sauce and simmer for 3–5 minutes, basting constantly.

Remove the fish from the wok and arrange on a platter. Stir the sesame oil into the sauce, pour over the fish and garnish with the green onions. Serve at once.

Fried Fish with Ginger

In this easy dish, ginger imparts a subtle fragrance and is a counterpoint to the fish.

SERVES 4

1 lb (450g) firm white fish
    fillets, such as cod, sea bass
    or halibut
salt and white pepper
cornstarch, for dusting
⅔ cup (150ml) peanut or
    vegetable oil
3 tbsp (45ml) finely shredded
    fresh ginger
2 tbsp (30ml) Chicken Stock
    (page 75) or water
2½ tbsp (37ml) Shaoxing rice
    wine or dry sherry
2 tsp (10ml) sugar
2 tsp (10ml) sesame oil

Sprinkle the fish fillets evenly on both sides with 1 tsp (5ml) of salt. Cut the fish into strips 1 in (2.5cm) wide and let them sit for 20 minutes. Then dust them with the cornstarch.

Heat a wok or a large skillet over high heat until it is hot. Add the oil, and when it is very hot and slightly smoking, add the ginger and, a few seconds later, the fish. Shallow-fry the fish strips until they are firm and partially cooked. Remove them with a slotted spoon and drain on paper towels.

Pour off all the oil and discard it. Wipe the wok or skillet clean and add 1 tsp (5ml) of salt, ½ tsp (2ml) of white pepper and the rest of the ingredients. Bring them to a boil, then return the fish strips to the wok and coat them with the sauce. Turn the fish gently in the sauce for 1 minute, taking care not to break up the fish. Remove to a platter and serve at once.

Fried Fish with Garlic and Green Onions

This is a simple dish, easy to make, and works especially well with any flat fish.

SERVES 4

1 lb (450g) sole or plaice fillets
salt and white pepper
2 eggs
2 oz (50g) cornstarch
⅔ cup (150ml) peanut or
    vegetable oil
3 tbsp (45ml) sliced garlic
2 tbsp (30ml) finely chopped
    green onions
2 tbsp (30ml) Shaoxing rice
    wine or dry sherry
2 tsp (10ml) sesame oil

If you are using plaice, have your fishmonger remove the dark skin or else remove it yourself, using a small, sharp knife. Cut the fish fillets into 1 in (2.5cm) strips. Sprinkle the strips with 1 tsp (5ml) of salt and let them sit for 15 minutes. Beat the egg and pepper in a small bowl. Dip the pieces of fish into the cornstarch and then into the beaten egg.

Heat a wok or a large skillet until it is hot. Add the oil, and when it is very hot, turn the heat down to medium. Shallow-fry the fish pieces on each side, in several batches, until they are golden brown, then drain them on paper towels. Pour off the oil and discard it. Wipe the wok or skillet clean and add 1 tsp (5ml) of salt, ¼ tsp (1ml) of white pepper and the rest of the ingredients. Simmer for 2 minutes. Put the fried fish on a serving platter and pour over the hot sauce.

Fish Balls with Broccoli

We often made this dish in our family restaurant, but usually just for the Chinese customers. My uncle thought that his non-Chinese diners would not enjoy it. I remember how laborious it was, mincing the fish until it was smooth and like a paste. Now, thanks to modern kitchen equipment, it can be easily prepared at home in minutes. And I eventually discovered how much my Western friends love it!

SERVES 4–6

1 lb (450g) white fish fillets, such as cod, sea bass or halibut
1 egg white
2 tsp (10ml) cornstarch
2 tsp (10ml) sesame oil
salt and white pepper
1 lb (450g) broccoli
1½ tbsp (22ml) peanut oil
3 tbsp (45ml) finely shredded fresh ginger
2 oz (50g) Parma ham, or lean smoked bacon, finely shredded
1 tbsp (15ml) light soy sauce
2 tbsp (30ml) Shaoxing rice wine or dry sherry
1¼ cups (300ml) Chicken Stock (page 75)
2 tsp (10ml) cornstarch, blended with 2 tsp (10ml) water
2 tsp (10ml) sesame oil

Remove the skin from the fish fillets and cut them into small pieces about 1 in (2.5cm) square. Combine the fish, egg white, cornstarch and sesame oil with about 2 tsp (10ml) of salt and 1 tsp (5ml) of white pepper in a food processor, and blend until you have a smooth paste. If you are using a blender, pulse by turning the blender on and off until the mixture is well mixed, otherwise the paste will turn out rubbery.

Bring a large saucepan of salted water to simmering point. Take spoonfuls of the fish paste and form the mixture into balls about 1 in (2.5cm) in diameter. Poach them in the boiling water until they float to the top. (This should take about 3–4 minutes.) Remove them with a slotted spoon and drain them on paper towels.

Divide the broccoli heads into small florets. Peel the skin off the stems, as they are often fibrous and stringy, and cut them into thin slices at a slight diagonal. This will ensure that the stems cook evenly with the florets. Bring a saucepan of water to a boil, add the broccoli florets and stems and cook for about 5 minutes. Drain them, plunge them into cold water, and drain again.

Heat a wok or a large skillet over high heat until it is hot. Add the oil, and when it is very hot and slightly smoking, add the ginger and the ham or bacon and stir-fry for 30 seconds. Add the soy sauce, rice wine, stock and the cornstarch mixture. Bring to a boil, then add the broccoli and the poached fish balls. Stir gently over high heat for 1 minute, then add the sesame oil and turn the mixture onto a serving platter. Serve at once.

Fried Sesame Seed Fish

This is a quick and delicious way to cook fish fillets, with the crunchy sesame seeds giving the fish a crispy coating. Serve this with a noodle dish and a fast stir-fry vegetable dish as an unusual twist for lunch or dinner.

SERVES 4

1 lb (450g) fresh, firm white fish
    fillets, such as cod, halibut or
    sea bass
3 slices of fresh ginger
3 green onions
2 tbsp (30ml) Shaoxing rice
    wine or dry sherry
salt and black pepper
cornstarch or potato flour, for
    dusting
1 egg, beaten
4 oz (100g) white sesame seeds
4 oz (100g) black sesame seeds
1¼ cups (300ml) peanut or
    vegetable oil

Cut the fish fillets into strips 1 in (2.5cm) wide. In a blender or food processor, mix the ginger, green onions, rice wine, salt and pepper. Strain this mixture over the fish and leave to marinate for 25 minutes.

Drain the fish and blot dry with paper towels. Dust with cornstarch or potato flour. Dip each piece of fish into the beaten egg and coat one side with white sesame seeds and the other side with black sesame seeds.

Heat a wok until it is hot, then add the oil. When the oil is moderately hot, fry the fish pieces for 2 minutes. Drain on paper towels and serve at once.

Crispy Fish Roll

This is a wonderful dish that we used to serve at banquets at my uncle's restaurant. A savory fish paste was wrapped in sheets of caul fat, then dusted with cornstarch and fried. It was then sliced and served with lemon wedges and a salt and pepper dip. This unusual appetizer was extremely popular. It is quite easy to make.

SERVES 4–6

4 pieces of caul fat, about 12 in (30cm) square
Cornstarch or potato flour, for dusting
3⅔ cups (900ml) peanut or vegetable oil

FOR THE FILLING

1 lb (450g) white fish fillets, such as cod, sea bass or halibut
1 tbsp (15ml) finely chopped fresh ginger
2 tbsp (30ml) finely chopped green onions
1 egg white
2 tsp (10ml) cornstarch
2 tsp (10ml) sesame oil

FOR THE GARNISH

lemon wedges
Salt and Pepper Dip (page 37)

In a food processor, mix all the filling ingredients with 2 tsp (10ml) of salt and 1 tsp (5ml) of white pepper until the mixture forms a paste.

Spread out the caul fat sheets on a work surface and divide the fish filling into 4 equal parts. Place a portion of fish filling at the end of each piece of caul fat, close up the sides, and roll up the caul fat, encasing the filling. When you have made 4 rolls, dust them with cornstarch or potato flour, shaking off any excess.

Heat a wok or large skillet until it is very hot. Add the oil, and when it is hot, deep-fry the rolls for about 5 minutes, or until they are very crispy and slightly browned. Drain on paper towels.

When they are cool enough to handle, cut the rolls into slices and serve them immediately, with the lemon wedges and the Salt and Pepper Dip.

Pan-fried Fish with Lemon Sauce

This simple-to-make fish recipe perfectly combines the fish with a subtle lemon sauce. Unlike many versions made in the West, this version has just enough sauce to coat and never to drown the fish pieces.

SERVES 4

1 lb (450g) fillets of any firm
  white fish
3 tbsp (45ml) peanut oil
FOR THE MARINADE
2 tsp (10ml) ginger juice
  (page 25)
1 tbsp (15ml) rice wine
1 tbsp (15ml) light soy sauce
2 tsp (10ml) cornstarch
FOR THE SAUCE
1 tbsp (15ml) green onions
1 lemon, halved
2 tsp (10ml) peanut oil
3 garlic cloves, crushed
½ tsp (2ml) cornstarch
4 tbsp (60ml) Chicken Stock
  (page 75)
1 tsp (5ml) light soy sauce
1 tsp (5ml) sugar
salt

Cut the fish into large pieces. Combine with the marinade ingredients in a large bowl and leave for 30 minutes.

Heat a wok or a large skillet until it is hot and add the oil. When it is moderately hot, pan-fry the fish until lightly brown. Remove and drain on paper towels. Arrange on a warm platter.

To make the sauce, begin by finely chopping the green onions and slicing half of the lemon. Reheat the wok and add the oil. When it is hot, add the garlic and stir-fry for 30 seconds. Mix the cornstarch with ½ tsp (2ml) of water, then add it to the wok along with 3 tbsp (45ml) of juice from the uncut half of lemon, and the rest of the sauce ingredients. Season with ½ tsp (2ml) of salt and bring to a simmer. Pour this sauce over the fish and serve.

Squirrel Fish

Chinese chefs are masters at making foods appear different from what they are supposed to be, and this playful attitude is apparent in this delightful dish. It is all in the technique used in the preparation of the fish. Once fried, the fish curls up like a squirrel's tail, hence its name. This is the classic presentation as a banquet dish for a sweet and sour fish. It is worth doing and is impressive to say the least.

SERVES 4–6

1 whole sea bass, about 2¼ lb
  (1kg), cleaned
cornstarch or potato flour, for
  dusting
3⅔ cup (900ml) peanut or
  vegetable oil
salt and black pepper

FOR THE SAUCE

1¼ cups (300ml) Chicken Stock
  (page 75)
4 tbsp (60ml) Shaoxing rice
  wine or dry sherry
6 tbsp (90ml) light soy sauce
3 tsp (45ml) dark soy sauce
3 tbsp (45ml) tomato paste
6 tbsp (90ml) Chinese white
  rice vinegar or cider vinegar
2 tbsp (30ml) sugar
2 tbsp (30ml) cornstarch,
  blended with 4 tbsp (60ml)
  water

First cut off the fish head behind the gills and set aside. With a sharp knife, fillet the fish on one side and cut until you reach the tailbone. Do the same with the other side. Gently pull away the 2 fillets intact and attached to the tailbone. Cut the bone that is attached to the tailbone. You should have 2 fillets held together by the tailbone. Alternatively, you could have your fishmonger do this for you.

Now score each fillet on the flesh side in a crisscross pattern. Season the fish with salt and pepper. Dust the fish and the reserved fish head thoroughly with cornstarch or potato flour, shaking off any excess.

Make the sauce by combining all the ingredients except the cornstarch mixture in a saucepan and bringing to a simmer. Slowly thicken the sauce with the cornstarch mixture and set aside.

Heat a large wok or skillet until it is very hot. Add the oil and when it is slightly smoking, quickly deep-fry the fish until it is crisp and cooked. Drain on paper towels. Now deep-fry the fish head and drain on paper towels.

Set the fish and the head on a platter, pour the sauce over and serve at once.

Steamed Fish Cantonese Style

Steaming fish is a great southern Chinese tradition, and it is my favorite method of cooking fish. Because it is such a gentle cooking technique, nothing masks the fresh taste of the fish, which remains moist and tender at the same time, and you can savour the combination of the other ingredients. Always ask your fishmonger for the freshest possible fish.

SERVES 4

1 lb (450g) firm white fish
  fillets, such as seabass or cod,
  or a whole fish such as turbot
1 tsp (5ml) coarse sea salt or
  plain salt
1½ tbsp (22ml) finely shredded
  fresh ginger
3 tbsp (45ml) finely shredded
  green onions
1 tbsp (15ml) light soy sauce
2 tsp (10ml) dark soy sauce
1 tbsp (15ml) peanut or
  vegetable oil
2 tsp (10ml) sesame oil
FOR THE GARNISH
cilantro sprigs

If you are using a whole fish, remove the gills. Pat the fish or fish fillets dry with paper towels. Rub with the salt on both sides, then set aside for 30 minutes. This helps the flesh to firm up and draws out any excess moisture.

Next, set up a steamer, or put a rack into a wok or deep saucepan, and fill it with 2 in (5cm) of water. Bring the water to a boil over high heat. Put the fish on a heatproof plate and scatter the ginger evenly over the top. Lower the plate of fish into the steamer or onto the rack. Cover the wok tightly and gently steam the fish until it is just cooked. Flat fish will take about 5 minutes to cook. Thicker fish or fillets such as sea bass will take 12–14 minutes.

Remove the plate of cooked fish from the wok and sprinkle with the green onions and the light and dark soy sauces. Heat the two oils together in a small saucepan. When they are hot and smoking, pour the hot oil on top of the fish and garnish with the cilantro sprigs. Serve at once.

Steamed Salmon with Black Beans

The virtues of fish and seafood most brilliantly shine forth against a backdrop of piquant flavors. In this case, we rely on the pungent seasoning of black beans, which add zest and depth without overwhelming the subtle character of the fish. We use salmon here, which is not a Chinese fish, although it is growing in popularity in cosmopolitan cities like Beijing, Shanghai and Canton. This is a most delicious way to prepare fish. Serve with plain rice and another stir-fry dish and you have a complete meal.

SERVES 4

1 lb (450g) skinless, boneless
  salmon fillet, divided into
  4 equal pieces
salt and white pepper
2 tbsp (30ml) black beans,
  rinsed and chopped
1½ tbsp (22ml) finely chopped
  garlic
1 tbsp (15ml) finely chopped
  fresh ginger
1½ tbsp (22ml) Shaoxing rice
  wine or dry sherry
1 tbsp (15ml) light soy sauce
2 tbsp (30ml) light soy sauce
3 green onions, finely shredded
a small handful of cilantro
1½ tbsp (22ml) peanut or
  vegetable oil

Sprinkle the salmon pieces evenly with 1 tsp (5ml) of salt and pepper to taste. Combine the black beans, garlic and ginger in a small bowl. Put the salmon on a heatproof plate and evenly scatter the black bean mixture over the top. Now pour the rice wine and soy sauce over the fish.

Next, set up a steamer, or put a rack into a wok or deep saucepan, and fill it with 2 in (5cm) of water. Bring the water to a boil over high heat. Carefully lower the fish, on its plate, into the steamer or onto the rack. Turn the heat to low and cover the wok or saucepan tightly. Steam gently for 8–10 minutes, depending on the thickness of the fillets, replenishing the water in the steamer from time to time as necessary. When the fish is cooked, remove from the wok and drain off any liquid.

Pour over the soy sauce and scatter the green onions and cilantro on top of the fish. Heat a small saucepan over high heat until it is hot. Add the oil, and when it is very hot and slightly smoking, pour it over the fillets. Serve at once.

Sizzling Rice Shrimp

This is a dramatic dish that is sure to earn you compliments. It is moderately easy to make, but requires organization and some experience of Chinese cooking. The key to success is that the shrimp sauce mixture and the rice cake should both be fairly hot. You will then be sure to achieve a dramatic sizzle when the two are combined. You can buy dried rice pieces at Chinese grocers.

SERVES 6

1 lb (450g) uncooked shrimp

5 cups (1.2L) peanut oil, plus 2 tbsp (30ml)

1 tbsp (15ml) finely chopped fresh ginger

1½ tbsp (22ml) finely chopped garlic

3 tbsp (45ml) finely chopped green onions

8 squares of shop-bought dried rice pieces

FOR THE SAUCE

4oz (100g) green or red bell pepper (about 1), diced

1½ tbsp (22ml) cider vinegar or Chinese black rice vinegar

1 tbsp (15ml) dark soy sauce

2 tsp (10ml) light soy sauce

1½ tbsp (22ml) chili bean sauce

1½ tbsp (22ml) tomato paste

2 tbsp (30ml) Shaoxing rice wine or dry sherry

2 tsp (10ml) sugar

1¼ cups (300ml) Chicken Stock (page 75)

1 tbsp (15ml) cornstarch, blended with 2 tbsp (30ml) water

1 tbsp (15ml) sesame oil

If required, peel the shrimp and discard the shells. Using a small, sharp knife, split the shrimp in half but leave them still attached at the back so that they splay out like butterflies. If you are using large, uncooked shrimp, remove the fine digestive cord. Rinse the shrimp well in cold water and blot them dry with paper towels.

Heat a wok or a large skillet over high heat until it is hot. Add the 2 tbsp (30ml) of oil, and when it is very hot and slightly smoking, add the ginger and stir it quickly for a few seconds, then add the garlic and green onions. A few seconds later add the shrimp and stir-fry them quickly until they become firm. Then add all the sauce ingredients except the cornstarch mixture and sesame oil. Bring the mixture to a boil, remove it from the heat and stir in the cornstarch mixture. Bring back to a boil, stir in the sesame oil, then reduce the heat to a very slow simmer.

Now you are ready to fry the rice pieces. Heat a wok over high heat until it is hot, or heat the oil in a deep-fat fryer. Add the 5 cups (1.2L) of oil, and when it is very hot and slightly smoking, drop in a small piece of the dried rice cake to test the heat. It should bubble all over and immediately come up to the surface. Now deep-fry the pieces of rice cake for about 1–2 minutes, until they puff up and brown slightly. Remove them immediately with a slotted spoon and set them to drain on a plate lined with paper towels.

Quickly transfer the pieces of hot rice cake to a platter and pour the hot shrimp and sauce over them. It should sizzle dramatically. Once you are skilled at preparing this dish, you can try this trick at the dinner table. (The oil used for cooking the rice pieces can be saved and reused once it has cooled. Filter it through coffee filter paper before storing it.)

Stir-fried Shrimp with Egg

This dish is commonly known in the West as Egg Fu Yung. It is popular because it is light and delicious, is easy to make and uses familiar ingredients. You can substitute crab, fish or even ground pork or beef for the shrimp. However, I think it is at its best made with good-quality shrimp.

SERVES 4

8 oz (225g) uncooked shrimp

1 egg white

salt and white pepper

1 tsp (5ml) sesame oil

2 tsp (10ml) cornstarch

6 large eggs, beaten

2 tsp (10ml) sesame oil

3 tbsp (45ml) Chicken Stock
(page 75) or water

1 tbsp (15ml) Shaoxing rice
wine or dry sherry

1 tbsp (15ml) light soy sauce

1 tsp (5ml) sugar

2 tbsp (30ml) peanut oil

FOR THE GARNISH

3 tbsp (45ml) finely chopped
green tops of green onions
tops

If required, peel the shrimp and, if you are using large, uncooked ones, cut them down the back and remove the fine digestive cord. Wash the shrimp and pat them dry with paper towels. Put the shrimp into a bowl and add the egg white, 1 tsp (5ml) of the sesame oil, cornstarch, 1 tsp (5ml) of salt and ½ tsp (2ml) of white pepper. Let the mixture sit in the fridge for 20 minutes.

Put the eggs, remaining sesame oil and the rest of the ingredients except the peanut oil into a bowl.

Heat a wok or a large skillet over high heat until it is hot. Add half the peanut oil, and when it is very hot and slightly smoking, add the shrimp and stir-fry them for 2 minutes. Remove them to a plate with a slotted spoon.

Wipe the wok clean, reheat it over high heat, then put the rest of the oil into the wok. Quickly add the egg mixture and stir-fry for 1 minute, or until the egg begins to set. Add the shrimp to the egg mixture and stir-fry for 1 minute more. Garnish with the green onion tops and serve.

Sichuan Shrimp in Chili Sauce

Sichuan cooking is popular throughout China. I can see why — next to Cantonese, it is one of my favorite culinary regions of Chinese cookery. This is one of the best-known dishes from that area, but beware of versions that tend to err on the side of excessive sweetness. The dish is quick and easy and makes a wholesome and delicious meal served with a stir-fried vegetable and steamed rice.

SERVES 4

1 lb (450g) uncooked shrimp
1½ tbsp (22ml) peanut oil
2 tsp (10ml) finely chopped
    fresh ginger
2 tsp (10ml) finely chopped
    garlic
2 tbsp (30ml) finely chopped
    green onions

FOR THE SAUCE

1 tbsp (15ml) tomato paste
2 tsp (10ml) chili bean sauce
1 tsp (5ml) Chinese black
    vinegar or cider vinegar
1 tsp (5ml) sugar
2 tsp (10ml) sesame oil
salt and black pepper

FOR THE GARNISH

green onions, sliced lengthwise

If required, peel the shrimp, and if you are using large, uncooked ones, cut them down the back and remove the fine digestive cord. Wash them and pat them dry with paper towels.

Heat a wok or a large skillet over high heat until it is hot. Add the oil, and when it is very hot and slightly smoking, add the ginger, garlic and green onions. Stir-fry for 20 seconds and then add the shrimp. Stir-fry the shrimp for about 1 minute. Add the sauce ingredients, season with ½ tsp (2ml) each of salt and black pepper and continue to stir-fry for another 3–5 minutes over high heat. Garnish with the green onions and serve at once.

Sweet and Sour Shrimp

A very popular Chinese dish in the West, the sweet and pungent flavors of the sauce in this dish combine well with the firm and succulent shrimp. It is simple to make and can be served as part of a Chinese meal or on its own as a starter for a Western meal.

SERVES 4

1 lb (450g) uncooked shrimp
8 oz (225g) water chestnuts,
   fresh or canned
4 oz (100g) red or green bell
   pepper (about 1)
4 green onions
1½ tbsp (22ml) peanut oil
1 tbsp (15ml) finely chopped
   garlic
2 tsp (10ml) finely chopped
   fresh ginger

FOR THE SAUCE

⅔ cup (150ml) Chicken Stock
   (page 75)
2 tbsp (30ml) Shaoxing rice
   wine or dry sherry
3 tbsp (45ml) light soy sauce
2 tsp (10ml) dark soy sauce
1½ tbsp (22ml) tomato paste
3 tbsp (45ml) Chinese white
   rice vinegar or cider vinegar
1 tbsp (15ml) sugar
1 tbsp (15ml) cornstarch,
   blended with 2 tbsp (30ml)
   water

TO SERVE

Perfect Steamed Rice
   (page 288)

If required, peel the shrimp, and if you are using large, uncooked ones, cut them down the back and remove the fine digestive cord. Wash them and pat dry with paper towels. If you are using fresh water chestnuts, peel and slice them. If you are using canned water chestnuts, first rinse them well in cold water. Drain in a colander and then slice them. Cut the bell pepper into 1 in (2.5cm) squares, and slice the green onions diagonally into 1½ in (4cm) pieces.

Heat a wok or a large skillet over high heat until it is hot. Add the oil, and when it is very hot and slightly smoking, add the garlic, ginger and green onions and stir-fry for just 20 seconds. Add the shrimp to the wok and stir-fry them for 1 minute. Then add the bell peppers and water chestnuts and stir-fry for 30 seconds. Now add the sauce ingredients. Bring the mixture to a boil, then turn the heat down and simmer for 4 minutes. Serve immediately with steamed rice.

Mango Shrimp

This exotic and unlikely combination is yet another example of how Chinese food practices have evolved in Hong Kong, with the new and the foreign joining the venerable and the native. The fresh sea fragrance and delicate taste of the shrimp work perfectly with the sweet, soft mango.

SERVES 4

1 lb (450g) uncooked shrimp

1 egg white

2 tsp (10ml) cornstarch

salt and white pepper

3 tsp (45ml) sesame oil

1 lb (450g) ripe mangoes

2 cups (450ml) peanut or
    vegetable oil, or water, plus
    1½ tbsp (22ml) oil

1½ tbsp (22ml) finely chopped
    fresh ginger

2 tsp (10ml) finely chopped
    garlic

1 tbsp (15ml) Shaoxing rice
    wine or dry sherry

FOR THE GARNISH

2 tbsp (30ml) finely chopped
    green onions

If required, peel the shrimp, and if you are using large, uncooked ones, cut them down the back and remove the fine digestive cord. Wash them and pat them dry with paper towels. Combine the shrimp with the egg white, cornstarch, 1 tsp (5ml) of salt, ½ tsp (2ml) of white pepper and 1 tsp (5ml) of the sesame oil. Mix well and leave in the fridge for about 20 minutes.

Peel the mangoes and remove the stones. Cut the flesh into 1 in (2.5cm) dice.

Heat a wok or a large skillet until it is very hot and add the 2 cups (450ml) of oil (if using water, see below). When it is very hot, remove the wok from the heat and immediately add the shrimp, stirring vigorously to keep them from sticking together. After about 2 minutes, when the shrimp have turned white, quickly drain them in a stainless steel colander set over a bowl. Discard the oil.

If you choose to use water instead of oil, bring it to a boil in a saucepan. Remove from the heat and immediately add the shrimp, stirring vigorously to keep them from sticking together. After about 2 minutes, when the shrimp have turned white, quickly drain them in a stainless steel colander set over a bowl. Discard the water.

Reheat the wok or skillet over high heat until it is hot. Add the remaining 1½ tbsp (22ml) of oil, and when it is very hot and slightly smoking, add the ginger and garlic and stir-fry for 10 seconds. Then return the shrimp to the wok with the rice wine and 1 tsp (5ml) of salt and ½ tsp (2ml) of pepper. Stir-fry the mixture for 1 minute. Now add the mango pieces and stir gently for 1 minute to warm them through. Finally, stir in the remaining 2 tsp (10ml) of sesame oil.

Turn onto a platter, garnish with the green onions and serve at once.

Shrimp with Honey-glazed Walnuts

This exotic and unlikely combination is one of the best examples of how Chinese food practices evolve in Hong Kong and spread throughout China. Here a classical dish is given a refreshing new dimension. I have enjoyed this dish in several different ways in Shanghai and Beijing.

Here, the rich sweetness and crunchy texture of the walnuts work extremely well with the fresh, delicate taste and soft texture of the shrimp. Although it takes a bit of time, it is well worth making for a special occasion or as the main course of a dinner party. If you have the time, make the caramelized walnuts the day before.

SERVES 4

1 x quantity of Caramelized
  Walnuts (page 64)
1 lb (450g) uncooked shrimp
1 egg white
2 tsp (10ml) cornstarch
3 tsp (45ml) sesame oil
salt and white pepper
2 cups (450ml) peanut or
  vegetable oil or water, plus
  1½ tbsp (22ml) oil
1 tbsp (15ml) finely chopped
  fresh ginger
2 tsp (10ml) finely chopped
  garlic
1 tbsp (15ml) Shaoxing rice
  wine or dry sherry

TO GARNISH

2 tbsp (30ml) finely chopped
  green onions

Peel the shrimp, and if you are using large, uncooked ones, cut them down the back to remove the fine digestive cord. Wash them and pat them dry with paper towels. Combine the shrimp with the egg white, cornstarch, 1 tsp (5ml) of the sesame oil, 1 tsp (5ml) of salt and ½ tsp (2ml) of white pepper. Mix well and let them sit in the fridge for 20 minutes.

Heat a wok until it is very hot and add the 2 cups (450ml) of oil (if using water, see below). When it is very hot, remove the wok from the heat and immediately add the shrimp, stirring vigorously to keep them from sticking together. After about 2 minutes, when the shrimp have turned white, drain them in a stainless steel colander set over a bowl. Discard the oil.

If you choose to use water instead of oil, bring it to a boil in a saucepan. Remove the saucepan from the heat and immediately add the shrimp, stirring vigorously to keep them from sticking together. After about 2 minutes, when the shrimp have turned white, quickly drain them in a stainless steel colander set over a bowl. Discard the water.

Reheat the wok or a large skillet over high heat until it is hot. Add the remaining 1½ tbsp (22ml) of oil, and when it is very hot and slightly smoking, add the ginger and garlic and stir-fry for 10 seconds. Then return the shrimp to the wok with the rice wine, 1 tsp (5ml) of salt and ½ tsp (2ml) of white pepper. Stir-fry the mixture for 1 minute. Now add the caramelized walnuts and stir gently for 1 minute to mix well. Stir in the remaining sesame oil.

Serve in bowls and garnish with the green onions.

Beijing (Peking) Shrimp

This is my adaptation of a favorite northern Chinese shrimp dish.

SERVES 4

1 lb (450g) uncooked shrimp
⅓ cup (85ml) all-purpose flour
½ cup (120ml) toasted
   breadcrumbs
1 egg
2 tsp (10ml) sesame oil
salt and white pepper
1¼ cups (300ml) peanut oil
FOR THE DIPPING SAUCE
2 tbsp (30ml) hoisin sauce
1 tsp (5ml) sesame oil

If required, peel the shrimp, leaving the tail shell on if you can. Using a sharp knife, split each shrimp lengthwise but leave it still attached at the back. Open the shrimp out so that it splays out flat in a butterfly shape and remove the fine digestive cord. Rinse the shrimp and pat dry with paper towels.

Spread out the flour and breadcrumbs on separate plates. Beat the egg in a small bowl, then add the sesame oil, 1 tsp (5ml) of salt and ½ tsp (2ml) of white pepper; mix well.

Heat the oil in a wok or a deep skillet. Dip the shrimp into the flour, then into the egg mixture, then into the breadcrumbs and shallow-fry the shrimp. Drain on paper towels. Mix the sauce ingredients in a small dish and serve.

Braised Shrimp

Try this with cooked shrimp, but reduce the cooking time so they just heat through.

SERVES 4

1 lb (450g) uncooked shrimp
FOR THE SAUCE
1 tsp (5ml) cornstarch
2 tbsp (30ml) green onions
1 tbsp (15ml) fresh ginger
2 tsp (10ml) garlic
⅔ cup (150ml) Chicken Stock
   (page 75)
1 tbsp (15ml) Shaoxing rice
   wine or dry sherry
1 tbsp (15ml) sugar
1 tbsp (15ml) dark soy sauce
1 tsp (5ml) light soy sauce
2 tsp (10ml) Chinese black rice
   vinegar or cider vinegar
2 tsp (10ml) sesame oil
salt

If required, peel the shrimp, and if you are using large, uncooked ones, cut them down the back and remove the fine digestive cord. Wash the shrimp and pat them dry with paper towels.

Mix the cornstarch with 2 tsp (10ml) of water. Finely chop the green onions, ginger and garlic and combine them with the cornstarch mixture, rice wine, sugar, soy sauces and vinegar in a wok or a large skillet. Season with 1 tsp (5ml) of salt, then bring to a simmer and add the shrimp. Braise the shrimp slowly over a low heat for 5 minutes. Serve at once.

Crab with Black Bean Sauce

This recipe can be made only with fresh crabs in the shell, since the shell has to protect the delicate crabmeat during the stir-frying process. If you can't get crab in the shell, use shrimp instead. I have added some ground pork, a Chinese trick that helps to stretch the crab, which can be expensive. (Of course you can always use just crab if you are feeling extravagant.)

SERVES 4–6

3 lb (1.5kg) freshly cooked crab, in the shell

2 tbsp (30ml) peanut oil

3 tbsp (45ml) black beans, rinsed and coarsely chopped

1½ tbsp (22ml) finely chopped garlic

1 tbsp (15ml) finely chopped fresh ginger

3 tbsp (45ml) finely chopped green onions

8 oz (225g) ground pork

2 tbsp (30ml) light soy sauce

1 tbsp (15ml) dark soy sauce

2 tbsp (30ml) Shaoxing rice wine or dry sherry

2 cups (450ml) Chicken Stock (page 75)

2 eggs, beaten

2 tsp (10ml) sesame oil

Remove the tail-flap, stomach sac and feathery gills from the crab. Using a heavy knife or cleaver, cut the crab, shell included, into large pieces.

Heat a wok or a large skillet over high heat until it is hot. Add the oil, and when it is very hot and slightly smoking, add the black beans, garlic, ginger and green onions and stir-fry for 20 seconds. Add the pork and stir-fry for 1 minute. Add the soy sauces, rice wine, chicken stock and the crab pieces and stir-fry over high heat for about 10 minutes.

Combine the eggs with the sesame oil and add this to the crab mixture, stirring slowly. There should be light strands of egg trailing over the crab. Turn it onto a large, warm serving platter and serve.

It is perfectly good manners to eat the crab with your fingers, but I suggest that you have a large bowl of water decorated with lemon slices on the table so that your guests can rinse their fingers.

Crab Casserole in a Clay Pot

Here is an interesting and innovative technique employed by Chinese chefs. The clay pot is traditionally used for the long simmering and braising of foods; nowadays, however, it is as often used to infuse intense flavors over high heat in a short length of time, as in this recipe. The classic Cantonese dish is given a new twist: the fresh crab is stir-fried with aromatic seasonings and then quickly finished over high heat in the covered clay pot. The pungent black beans permeate the rich crabmeat, enhancing it and adding to its subtle flavors. This delicious casserole is quite easy to prepare and turns an ordinary dinner into a special occasion.

SERVES 4

1½ lb (675g) fresh, whole crab
2 tbsp (30ml) peanut or
   vegetable oil
5 garlic cloves, crushed
2 slices of fresh ginger
3 green onions, cut into pieces
3 tbsp (45ml) black beans,
   rinsed and coarsely chopped
2 fresh red chilies, seeded and
   shredded
3 tbsp (45ml) Shaoxing rice
   wine or dry sherry
2 tbsp (30ml) light soy sauce
½ cup (120ml) Chicken Stock
   (page 75)

If you are using a whole crab, cut the body into quarters and lightly crack the claws and legs.

Heat a wok or a large skillet until it is hot and add the oil. Add the garlic, ginger and green onions and stir-fry for a few seconds to flavor the oil. Then add the black beans, chilies and crab. Stir-fry for 2 minutes, then add the rice wine, soy sauce and chicken stock.

Turn the contents of the wok into a clay pot or ovenproof casserole dish and cook over high heat for 5 minutes, or until the crab shell turns bright red. Serve immediately.

Crab in Egg Custard

There are many delicious and meaty varieties of crab that are harvested off the coast of eastern China. A favorite way to prepare them is to steam them whole, then crack them at the table and dip them in vinegar and sugar. In this Shanghai-inspired dish, cooked crab is mixed with a light egg custard and then steamed. The result is a sort of savory velvet- or satin-textured custard. I recommend using only the freshest cooked crabmeat for this dish.

SERVES 4

8 oz (225g) freshly cooked
   white crabmeat

FOR THE CUSTARD

4 eggs
1¼ cups (300ml) Chicken Stock
   (page 75)
2 tsp (10ml) finely chopped
   fresh ginger
3½ tbsp (50ml) finely chopped
   green onions, white part only
1½ tbsp (22ml) Shaoxing rice
   wine or dry sherry
salt and white pepper

FOR THE GARNISH

2 tsp (10ml) dark soy sauce
2 tbsp (30ml) green onions,
   finely chopped
1 tbsp (15ml) peanut or
   vegetable oil

Mix the custard ingredients in a bowl, season with 1 tsp (5ml) each of salt and white pepper, and add the cooked crabmeat. Mix well to blend all the ingredients together. Put the mixture into a deep, heatproof dish.

Next, set up a steamer, or put a rack into a wok or deep saucepan, and fill it with 2 in (5cm) of water. Bring the water to a boil over high heat. Carefully lower the dish with the crab mixture into the steamer or onto the rack. Turn the heat to low and cover the wok or saucepan tightly. Steam gently for about 18–20 minutes, or until the custard has set.

Remove the custard from the steamer, pour the soy sauce over the top and sprinkle with the green onions. Meanwhile, heat the oil in a small saucepan until it begins to smoke, then pour this over the custard and serve at once.

Steamed Crab with Vinegar and Ginger Sauce

One of the greatly anticipated events in Shanghai during late autumn is the arrival of fresh river crabs. The crabs are heavy with roe and the flesh is sweet and delicate. They are cooked by the simplest method possible, gently steamed with medicinal herbs to balance the richness of the crab, and are served with a vinegar and ginger dipping sauce. Here is my version of this delicious and easy crab dish. However, it must be made with freshest crab in the shell you can find. I make this dish when I want a special main course treat.

SERVES 4–6

3 lb (1.5kg) freshly cooked crab, in the shell
4 tbsp (60ml) Shaoxing rice wine or dry sherry
2 tbsp (30ml) finely shredded fresh ginger
3 green onions, finely shredded
FOR THE DIPPING SAUCE
2 tbsp (30ml) light soy sauce
3 tbsp (45ml) red or black rice vinegar
2 tsp (10ml) sugar
2 tbsp (30ml) finely shredded fresh ginger

Remove the tail-flap, stomach sac and feathery gills from the crab. Using a heavy knife or cleaver, cut the crab, shell included, into large pieces. Combine the pieces with the rice wine, ginger and green onions and allow to marinate for about 30 minutes.

Next, set up a steamer, or put a rack into a wok or deep saucepan, and fill it with 2 in (5cm) of water. Bring the water to a boil over high heat. Put the crab pieces with their marinade on an ovenproof plate and carefully lower it into the steamer or onto the rack. Turn the heat to low and cover the wok or saucepan tightly. Steam gently for 15 minutes.

Meanwhile, prepare the dipping sauce by combining all the sauce ingredients in a small bowl and mixing well. Set aside.

Remove the crab pieces from the steamer and drain, discarding the marinade ingredients. Turn the crab onto a large, warm serving platter and serve at once with the dipping sauce on the side.

It is perfectly good manners to eat the crab with your fingers, but I suggest that you have a large bowl of water decorated with lemon slices on the table so that your guests can rinse their fingers.

Stir-fried Scallops with Pig's Kidneys

This regional dish was a favorite in our family. My mother varied the traditional recipe a little by adding oyster sauce, thus changing the dish into a Cantonese version. Be assured that scallops and kidneys go very well together, even though they may seem an unlikely combination. If the kidneys are properly prepared, their texture is quite similar to that of scallops, and their two quite different flavors blend deliciously together. The richness of this dish means that it is best for special occasions.

SERVES 4

1 lb (450g) pig's kidneys
1 tsp (5ml) baking soda
1 tsp (5ml) Chinese white rice
   vinegar or cider vinegar
salt and white pepper
8 oz (225g) scallops
2 tbsp (30ml) peanut or
   vegetable oil
2 tsp (10ml) finely chopped
   fresh ginger
2 tbsp (30ml) finely chopped
   green onions
2 tbsp (30ml) Shaoxing rice
   wine or dry sherry
1 tbsp (15ml) light soy sauce
2 tsp (10ml) dark soy sauce
1 tsp (5ml) sugar
1 tsp (5ml) cornstarch,
   blended with 2 tsp (10ml)
   of stock or water
2 tsp (10ml) sesame oil

Using a sharp knife, remove the thin outer membrane from the kidneys. Then, with a sharp cleaver or knife, split each kidney in half lengthwise by cutting horizontally. Now cut away the small knobs of fat and any tough membrane surrounding them. Score the top surface of the kidneys in a crisscross pattern, then cut the halved kidneys into thin slices. Toss the kidney slices in the baking soda and let them sit for about 20 minutes.

Then rinse the kidneys thoroughly with cold water and toss them in the vinegar and ½ tsp (2ml) of salt. Put them into a colander and let them drain for 30 minutes.

Cut the scallops into thick slices horizontally and put them into a small bowl. Blot the kidney slices dry with paper towels.

Heat a wok or a large skillet over high heat until it is hot. Add 1 tbsp (15ml) of the oil, and when it is very hot and slightly smoking, add the scallops. Stir-fry them for about 30 seconds, then add the ginger and green onions. Stir-fry for another 30 seconds and then remove them, with the juices.

Wipe the wok or skillet clean. Immediately reheat it over a high heat until it is hot. Add the remaining tablespoon of oil, and when it is very hot and slightly smoking, add the kidneys and stir-fry for 1 minute. Add the rice wine, light and dark soy sauces, sugar, white pepper to taste and another ½ tsp (2ml) of salt and stir-fry for 1 minute, then return the scallops to the wok. Add the cornstarch mixture and stir for a minute or so. Finally, stir in the sesame oil. Turn onto a warm serving platter and serve straightaway.

Sichuan-style Scallops

Scallops are a favorite with the Chinese. We love them in two forms, fresh and dried. Stir-frying works especially well with scallops, because if they are overcooked they become tough. Just five minutes of stir-frying, as here, is quite sufficient to cook them thoroughly without robbing them of their sweet flavor. They are particularly tasty when prepared with this spicy Sichuan sauce.

SERVES 4

1½ tbsp (22ml) peanut or
   vegetable oil
1 tbsp (15ml) finely chopped
   fresh ginger
1 tbsp (15ml) finely chopped
   garlic
2 tbsp (30ml) finely chopped
   green onions
1 lb (450g) scallops

FOR THE SAUCE

1 tbsp (15ml) Shaoxing rice
   wine or dry sherry
2 tsp (10ml) light soy sauce
2 tsp (10ml) dark soy sauce
2 tbsp (30ml) chili bean sauce
2 tsp (10ml) tomato paste
1 tsp (5ml) sugar
salt and white pepper
2 tsp (10ml) sesame oil

Heat a wok or a large skillet over high heat until it is hot. Add the oil, and when it is very hot and slightly smoking, add the ginger, garlic and green onions and stir-fry for just 10 seconds. Immediately add the scallops and stir-fry them for 1 minute. Then add all the sauce ingredients except the sesame oil and season with ½ tsp (2ml) each of salt and white pepper. Continue to stir-fry for 4 minutes, until the scallops are firm and thoroughly coated with the sauce. Now add the sesame oil and stir-fry for another minute. Serve at once.

Stir-fried Squid with Vegetables

Squid cooked the Chinese way is both tender and tasty. The secret is to use very hot water for blanching and then a minimum amount of cooking time — just enough for the squid to firm up slightly. Cooking it too long will make it tough, like chewing on rubber bands! Unlike most seafood, frozen squid can be quite good, and when properly cooked it is often impossible to tell from fresh. This simple recipe can also be prepared with shrimp if you find squid difficult to obtain.

SERVES 4

1 lb (450g) squid, fresh or frozen and thawed

4 oz (100g) red or green bell pepper (about 1)

1½ tbsp (22ml) peanut or vegetable oil

2 tbsp (30ml) finely chopped garlic

1 tbsp (15ml) finely chopped fresh ginger

4 oz (100g) snow peas, trimmed

⅓ cup (85ml) Chicken Stock (page 75)

1 tbsp (15ml) Shaoxing rice wine or dry sherry

3 tbsp (45ml) oyster sauce

1 tbsp (15ml) light soy sauce

2 tsp (10ml) dark soy sauce

2 tsp (10ml) cornstarch, blended with 2 tsp (10ml) water

2 tsp (10ml) sesame oil

salt

The edible parts of the squid are the tentacles and the body. If it has not already been cleaned by your fishmonger, you can do it yourself by pulling the head and tentacles away from the body. Using a small, sharp knife, split the body in half. Remove the transparent bony section. Wash the halves thoroughly under cold running water, then pull off and discard the skin. Cut the tentacles from the head, cutting just above the eye. (You may also have to remove the polyp or beak from the base of the ring of tentacles.)

Cut the squid meat into 1½ in (4cm) strips. Blanch the strips and the tentacles in a large saucepan of boiling water for just 10 seconds. The squid will firm up slightly and turn an opaque white color. Remove and drain in a colander.

Cut the bell pepper into 1½ in (4cm) strips. Heat a wok or a large skillet over high heat until it is hot. Add the oil, and when it is very hot and slightly smoking, add the garlic and ginger and stir-fry for 15 seconds. Then add the bell pepper strips and snow peas and stir-fry for 1 minute. Finally, add the rest of the ingredients, except the squid, season with 2 tsp (10ml) of salt and bring the mixture to a boil. Give it a quick stir, then add the squid and mix well. Cook for just 30 seconds more. Serve at once.

Deep-Fried Oysters

Oysters are a staple item in southern China. The variety found in the South China Sea is quite large, and they are usually cut up, dipped in batter and deep-fried. The Chinese never eat oysters raw, believing them to be unhealthy when uncooked. This dish is based on a recipe given to me by a friend who is a chef in the fishing village of Lau Fau Shan, in the New Territories in Hong Kong. I have added a Western touch to it by using breadcrumbs on top of the batter. This dish makes an excellent cocktail snack.

SERVES 4

1 lb (450g) oysters, shelled
1 egg
2 tbsp (30ml) cornstarch
1 tbsp (15ml) water
2 tsp (10ml) baking powder
salt and white pepper
2 tsp (10ml) sesame oil
⅓ cup (85ml) toasted
   breadcrumbs
2⅓ cups (600ml) peanut or
   vegetable oil

TO SERVE

Salt and Pepper Dip (page 37)
lemon wedges

Drain the oysters in a colander and pat them dry with paper towels. Prepare a batter by mixing the egg, cornstarch, water, baking powder, 1 tsp (5ml) of salt, ½ tsp (2ml) of white pepper and the sesame oil in a small bowl. Let the mixture sit for about 20 minutes.

Place the breadcrumbs on a plate. Dip the oysters, a few at a time, first into the batter and then into the breadcrumbs. Put them on a plate.

Heat a wok or a large skillet over high heat until it is hot. Add the oil, and when it is very hot and slightly smoking, turn the heat down to medium. Deep-fry the coated oysters until they are golden brown. (This should take just a few minutes.) Drain them on paper towels and serve with lemon wedges and the Salt and Pepper Dip.

Steamed Fresh Oysters

The Chinese in Hong Kong enjoy fresh oysters steamed; it brings out their subtle taste and wonderful texture. Although they are sometimes steamed with zesty black beans, I enjoy them simply with ginger and green onions. This is a Hong Kong variation on a traditional recipe and is quite delicious. You may substitute clams or mussels if you like, but the cooking time will be shorter. Watch the oysters carefully to prevent overcooking. This is very simple to make, and I think it makes a dramatic opening for a special dinner party.

SERVES 4

16 large fresh oysters

FOR THE SAUCE

2 tsp (10ml) finely chopped garlic

1 tbsp (15ml) finely chopped fresh ginger

1 tsp (5ml) chili bean sauce

1 tbsp (15ml) Shaoxing rice wine or dry sherry

1 tbsp (15ml) light soy sauce

2 tsp (10ml) dark soy sauce

2 fresh red chilies, seeded and chopped

3 tbsp (45ml) finely shredded green onions

3 tbsp (45ml) peanut or vegetable oil

FOR THE GARNISH

cilantro sprigs

Scrub the oysters clean. Divide them in half and place them on 2 separate heatproof plates; you will need to steam them in 2 batches.

Next, set up a steamer, or put a rack into a wok or deep saucepan, and fill it with 2 in (5cm) of water. Bring the water to a boil over high heat. Put one of the plates with the oysters into the steamer or onto the rack. Turn the heat to low and cover the wok or saucepan tightly. Steam gently for 5 minutes, or until the oysters begin to open.

Meanwhile, combine all the sauce ingredients except the oil in a heatproof bowl. Heat a wok or a skillet over high heat until it is hot. Add the oil, and when it is very hot and slightly smoking, pour it over the sauce ingredients.

Remove the oysters from the steamer. Give the sauce a good stir. Remove the top shell of each oyster and add a bit of the sauce to each one. Garnish with cilantro sprigs and serve. While you are serving the first batch, repeat the cooking procedure with the other batch.

VEGETABLES

Vegetables suit the Chinese way
of cooking — the techniques of
stir-frying, blanching, deep-frying
and even braising all preserve the
flavors and textures of vegetables,
allowing their natural character to
come through.

Spiced Chinese Leaves

Unlike the more familiar green and red cabbage, Chinese cabbage (Chinese leaves), also known as Peking cabbage, has a sweet flavor that is delicate, rather like lettuce. Cooking is needed to make it palatable, and because it is so light it calls for a robust sauce. I like to serve it with this spicy sauce. For a variation you might substitute curry powder for the chili.

SERVES 2–4

1⅔ lb (750g) Chinese leaves
1 tbsp (15ml) peanut or
   vegetable oil
1 tbsp (15ml) finely chopped
   fresh ginger
1½ tbsp (22ml) finely chopped
   garlic
2 dried red chilies, split in half
1½ tbsp (22ml) Shaoxing rice
   wine or dry sherry
1 tbsp (15ml) dark soy sauce
1 tsp (5ml) light soy sauce
2 tsp (10ml) chili bean sauce
2 tsp (10ml) sugar
4 tbsp (60ml) Chicken Stock
   (page 75) or water
black pepper
1 tbsp (15ml) sesame oil

Separate the Chinese leaves and wash them well. Cut them into 1 in (2.5cm) strips.

Heat a wok or a large skillet over high heat until it is hot. Add the oil, and when it is very hot and slightly smoking, add the ginger, garlic and chilies. Stir-fry for a few seconds. Now add the Chinese leaves, stir-fry a few seconds, then add the rest of the ingredients, apart from the sesame oil, and season with ½ tsp (2ml) of black pepper. Turn the heat down and simmer for 8 minutes, until the leaves are tender. At this point you can, if you wish, remove the dried chilies. Just before serving, add the sesame oil and stir well. Serve at once.

Stir-fried Chinese Greens

Chinese greens are also known by their Cantonese name, bok choy. There are several varieties, including Chinese flowering cabbage, a favorite of mine. They were a staple food in my childhood, as they were inexpensive, nutritious and readily available. Even today I look forward to this simple stir-fried dish. Sometimes the greens are merely blanched, but I think they are delicious stir-fried with oil and garlic or with a little soy sauce and stock. They make a delicious dish to serve with meat and fish and are excellent in vegetarian menus. This is my mother's recipe.

SERVES 4

1 tbsp (15ml) peanut or
    vegetable oil
4 garlic cloves, peeled and
    crushed
salt
1½ lb (675g) Chinese greens,
    such as Chinese flowering
    cabbage or bok choy
2 tbsp (30ml) Chicken Stock
    (page 75) or water

Heat a wok or a large skillet over high heat until it is hot. Add the oil, and when it is very hot and slightly smoking, add the garlic and 2 tsp (10ml) of salt. Stir-fry the mixture for 15 seconds, or until the garlic is lightly browned. Then quickly add the Chinese greens. Stir-fry for 3–4 minutes, until the greens have wilted a little. Then add the chicken stock or water and continue to stir-fry for a few more minutes, until the greens are done but are still slightly crisp.

Stir-fried Snow Peas with Water Chestnuts

It is worth trying to get the fresh water chestnuts for this straightforward recipe.

SERVES 2–4

8 oz (225g) water chestnuts,
   fresh or canned
1 tbsp (15ml) peanut oil
3 tbsp (45ml) finely chopped
   green onions
8 oz (225g) mangetout, trimmed
1 tbsp (15ml) light soy sauce
2 tbsp (30ml) water
1 tsp (5ml) sugar
salt and black pepper
2 tsp (10ml) sesame oil

If you are using fresh water chestnuts, peel them and slice thinly. If you are using canned water chestnuts, drain them well and rinse in cold water, then slice thinly.

Heat a wok or a large skillet until it is hot. Add the oil, and when it is very hot, add the green onions. Stir-fry for 10 seconds, then add the snow peas and the fresh water chestnuts and stir-fry for 1 minute; coat the vegetables thoroughly with the oil. Then add the rest of the ingredients, apart from the sesame oil, season with 1 tsp (5ml) of salt and ½ tsp (2ml) of black pepper and continue to stir-fry for another 3 minutes. If you are using canned water chestnuts add these now, and cook for a further 2 minutes or until the vegetables are cooked. Stir in the sesame oil and serve at once.

Spicy Stir-fried Mushrooms

The mild, subtle flavor of button mushrooms makes them perfect for Chinese spices.

SERVES 4

1 garlic clove
2 tsp (10ml) fresh ginger
2 green onions
1 tbsp (15ml) peanut oil
1 lb (450g) small whole button
   mushrooms
2 tsp (10ml) chili bean sauce
1 tbsp (15ml) Shaoxing rice
   wine or dry sherry
2 tsp (10ml) dark soy sauce
1 tbsp (15ml) Chicken Stock
   (page 75) or water
2 tsp (10ml) sugar
salt and black pepper
2 tsp (10ml) sesame oil

Finely chop the garlic, ginger and green onions. Heat a wok or a large skillet over high heat until it is hot. Add the oil, and when it is very hot and slightly smoking, add the garlic, ginger, and green onions and stir-fry for about 20 seconds. Then add the mushrooms and stir-fry them for about 30 seconds. Quickly add the rest of the ingredients, apart from the sesame oil, and season with 1 tsp (5ml) of salt and ½ tsp (2ml) of black pepper. Continue to stir-fry for about 5 minutes, or until the mushrooms are cooked through and have absorbed all the spices and seasonings. Just before serving, add the sesame oil and give the mixture a couple of quick stirs. Turn onto a warm serving dish and serve at once.

Stir-fried Spinach with Garlic

Spinach has often been regarded with disdain in the West, probably because it is usually served overcooked. This is a time-honored and delicious southern Chinese recipe. The spinach is quickly stir-fried and then seasoned. It is very simple to prepare and may be served hot or cold.

SERVES 4

1½ lb (675g) fresh spinach
1 tbsp (15ml) peanut or
    vegetable oil
4 garlic cloves, peeled and
    crushed
salt
1 tsp (5ml) sugar

Wash the spinach thoroughly. Remove all the stems, leaving just the leaves. Heat a wok or a large skillet over high heat until it is hot. Add the oil, and when it is very hot and slightly smoking, add the garlic and salt and stir-fry for 25 seconds. Add the spinach leaves and stir-fry for about 2 minutes to coat them thoroughly with the oil, garlic and 1 tsp (5ml) of salt. When the spinach has wilted to about one-third of its original volume, add the sugar and continue to stir-fry for another 4 minutes. Transfer the spinach to a plate and pour off any excess liquid. Serve hot or cold.

Stir-fried Broccoli with Hoisin Sauce

I find that the sweet flavor of broccoli blends perfectly with the rich taste of hoisin sauce. This sauce gives a good color and pleasant fragrance to the broccoli, but remember that a little goes a long way. This dish is quick and easy to make. Served hot, it makes a perfect vegetable accompaniment to any meal. You can easily substitute carrots or zucchinis in place of the broccoli.

SERVES 4

1 lb (450g) fresh broccoli
1½ tbsp (22ml) peanut or
   vegetable oil
1 tbsp (15ml) finely chopped
   garlic
salt and black pepper
3 tbsp (45ml) hoisin sauce
2 tbsp (30ml) Shaoxing rice
   wine or dry sherry
3 tbsp (45ml) water

Separate the broccoli heads into florets and peel and slice the stems. Blanch all the broccoli pieces in a large saucepan of boiling, salted water for several minutes. Then drain them and plunge them into cold water. Drain again thoroughly in a colander.

Heat a wok or a large skillet over high heat until it is hot. Add the oil, and when it is very hot and slightly smoking, add the garlic, broccoli pieces, 2 tsp (10ml) of salt and 1 tsp (5ml) of black pepper. Stir-fry them for about 1 minute, and then add the hoisin sauce, rice wine and water. Continue to stir-fry on moderately high heat for about 5 minutes, or until the broccoli pieces are thoroughly cooked. Serve at once.

Hot and Sour Cucumber Salad

Cucumbers are an inexpensive and popular vegetable in China, and are nearly always served cooked. In summertime in northern China, however, they are served cold as a starter. They are especially tasty and refreshing when combined with a spicy and sour flavor. This easy-to-make recipe is perfect as a salad or for summer eating.

SERVES 4

1 lb (450g) cucumber
1 tsp (5ml) salt
1 tbsp (15ml) peanut or
   vegetable oil
3 garlic cloves, thinly sliced
1 tsp (5ml) Chili Oil (page 23)
2 tbsp (30ml) white rice wine
   vinegar
salt and white pepper

Peel the cucumber, halve it and remove the seeds with a teaspoon. Then cut it into 1 in (2.5cm) cubes, sprinkle with the salt and put into a colander to drain for 20 minutes. Rinse the cucumber under cold running water and blot dry with paper towels.

Heat a wok or a large skillet over high heat until it is hot. Add the oil, and when it is very hot and slightly smoking, turn the heat to low, add the garlic slices and stir-fry for 1 minute, or until they are brown. Remove them from the wok and drain on paper towels.

In a large bowl, combine the chili oil, vinegar, 1 tsp (5ml) of salt and white pepper to taste. Add the cucumber cubes and garlic and toss well. Allow to sit for 5 minutes. Drain well before serving.

Braised Cauliflower with Oyster Sauce

Cauliflower is a versatile vegetable that is both delicious and easy to prepare. It has a distinctive but rather mild taste that goes very well with oyster sauce, which provides it with color. It needs a longer cooking time than some vegetables, so stir-frying alone is usually not enough to make it palatable. I find it delicious when it is braised in oyster sauce.

SERVES 4

1½ lb (675g) cauliflower
1 tbsp (15ml) peanut or
   vegetable oil
4 garlic cloves, crushed
2 tbsp (30ml) finely shredded
   fresh ginger
1 tsp (5ml) light soy sauce
1 tsp (5ml) dark soy sauce
3½ tbsp (50ml) oyster sauce
2 cups (450ml) Chicken Stock
   (page 75) or water
2 tsp (10ml) sesame oil
FOR THE GARNISH
2 tbsp (30ml) finely chopped
   green onions

Cut the cauliflower into small florets about 1½ in (4cm) wide.
   Heat a wok or a large skillet over high heat until it is hot. Add the oil, and when it is very hot and slightly smoking, add the garlic and ginger. Stir-fry for about 20 seconds to flavor the oil. Quickly add the cauliflower florets and stir-fry them for a few seconds. Next, add the soy sauces, the oyster sauce and the stock or water. Turn the heat down and simmer for 8 minutes, or until the cauliflower is tender.
   Stir in the sesame oil, then turn onto a warm serving platter and sprinkle with the green onions. Serve at once.

Pan-fried Stuffed Cucumbers

The stuffing in this recipe uses seasoned ground pork, but you can use ground beef if you prefer. Thick cucumber slices are stuffed and then shallow-fried; this seals in the flavors of the stuffing. Then the cucumbers are simmered to create the sauce. I think you will agree that cucumbers have never tasted so good!

SERVES 4

1½ lb (675g) cucumbers

2 tbsp (30ml) cornstarch

3 tbsp (45ml) peanut oil

FOR THE STUFFING MIXTURE

8 oz (225g) ground fatty pork

1 egg white

1½ tbsp (22ml) finely chopped
   green onions

1 tbsp (15ml) finely chopped
   fresh ginger

2 tsp (10ml) Shaoxing rice wine
   or dry sherry

2 tsp (10ml) light soy sauce

2 tsp (10ml) sugar

1 tsp (5ml) sesame oil

salt and black pepper

FOR THE SAUCE

1¼ cups (300ml) Chicken Stock
   (page 75)

2 tbsp (30ml) Shaoxing rice
   wine or dry sherry

1 tbsp (15ml) light soy sauce

1 tbsp (15ml) oyster sauce

2 tsp (10ml) sugar

1 tsp (5ml) cornstarch, mixed
   with 2 tsp (10ml) water

FOR THE GARNISH

2 tsp (10ml) sesame oil

2 tbsp (30ml) finely chopped
   cilantro

Cut the cucumbers into 1 in (2.5cm) slices without peeling them. Remove the seeds and pulp from the center of each cucumber slice using a small, sharp knife. Hollow the cucumber so that you have at least a ¼ in (5mm) shell. Lightly dust the hollow interior of the cucumber rings with cornstarch.

Mix all the stuffing ingredients together in a large bowl and season with 1 tsp (5ml) each of salt and black pepper. Then stuff each cucumber ring with this mixture.

Heat a wok or a large skillet and add the oil. When it is moderately hot, add the stuffed cucumber rings and cook them slowly until they are slightly browned. Turn them over and brown the other side, adding more oil if necessary. You may have to do this in several batches. When the cucumber rings are brown, remove them from the oil and put them on a plate. When you have fried all the cucumber rings, wipe the wok or skillet clean.

Mix the sauce ingredients and put them into the reheated wok or skillet. Bring to a simmer, then add the stuffed cucumber rings. Cover the wok with a lid and simmer slowly for about 7 minutes, or until the cucumbers are completely cooked. Transfer them to a serving platter, lifting them out of the sauce with a slotted spoon.

Reduce the sauce by a third over high heat. Then add the sesame oil and cilantro. Pour the sauce over the stuffed cucumbers and serve at once.

Stir-fried Curry Celery

Celery is an undervalued vegetable and deserves more respect. It is delicious in its own crunchy, mild and unassuming way. And its distinctive taste makes it an ideal foil for spicy flavors. Here it is combined with curry in a simple, easy-to-make dish. You will see that this humble vegetable has a real role to play.

SERVES 4

1 lb (450g) celery
1 tbsp (15ml) peanut or
    vegetable oil
2 tbsp (30ml) coarsely chopped
    garlic
2 tsp (10ml) finely chopped
    fresh ginger
1 tbsp (15ml) Shaoxing rice
    wine or dry sherry
2 tsp (10ml) Madras curry
    powder
1 tsp (5ml) light soy sauce
2 tsp (10ml) sugar
salt and black pepper
3 tbsp (45ml) water

FOR THE GARNISH

2 tbsp (30ml) finely chopped
    green onions
1 tbsp (15ml) finely chopped
    cilantro

Trim the base of the celery and all the top leaves. Separate the stalks. With a small, sharp knife, string a few of the tough stalks. Chop the stalks into 1 in (2.5cm) sections.

Heat a wok or a large skillet over high heat until it is hot. Add the oil, and when it is very hot and slightly smoking, add the garlic and ginger and stir-fry for 10 seconds. Add the celery and continue to stir-fry for 1 minute. Add the rice wine or sherry, curry powder, soy sauce, sugar, ½ tsp (2ml) of salt and a little black pepper and continue to stir-fry for another minute. Then add the water and continue to cook over high heat for 3–4 minutes, until just tender.

Sprinkle the mixture with the green onions and cilantro, mix well, transfer to a platter and serve straightaway.

Deep-fried Green Beans

This tasty dish (made with ground pork) originated in western China, as its seasonings indicate. The traditional recipe calls for Chinese asparagus or long beans, but I have found runner beans equally suitable. The beans are deep-fried to transform their texture, but they should remain green and not be overcooked. Deep-frying merely gives them a soft instead of a crunchy texture. After deep-frying, the beans are stir-fried in an array of spices to create a delectable dish. They should be slightly oily, but if they are too oily for your taste you can blot them with paper towels before stir-frying them. For best results, serve them as soon as they are cooked.

SERVES 4

2⅓ cups (600ml) peanut or vegetable oil

1 lb (450g) runner beans, trimmed and sliced if long, otherwise left whole

1½ tbsp (22ml) finely chopped garlic

1½ tbsp (22ml) finely chopped fresh ginger

3 tbsp (45ml) finely chopped green onions, white part only

1½ tbsp (22ml) chili bean sauce

1 tbsp (15ml) whole yellow bean sauce

2 tbsp (30ml) Shaoxing rice wine or dry sherry

1 tbsp (15ml) dark soy sauce

2 tsp (10ml) sugar

1 tbsp (15ml) water

2 tsp (10ml) chili oil

Heat a wok or a large skillet over high heat until it is hot. Add the oil, and when it is very hot and slightly smoking, deep-fry half the beans until they are slightly wrinkled, which should take about 3–4 minutes. Remove the beans and drain them. Deep-fry the second batch in the same way.

Transfer about 1 tbsp (15ml) of the oil in which you have cooked the beans to a clean wok or skillet. Heat the wok or skillet, add the garlic, ginger and green onions, and stir-fry for about 30 seconds. Then add the rest of the ingredients. Stir-fry the mixture for 30 seconds, then add the cooked, drained beans. Mix well, until all the beans are thoroughly coated with the spicy mixture. Serve as soon as the beans have heated through.

Crispy "Seaweed"

This is one of the most popular dishes among frequent Chinese restaurant diners in this country. I am not sure who was the first to bring this unique eastern-northern Chinese dish to England; suffice it to say, however, that not "seaweed" but cabbage is now being used. The special type of seaweed that is indeed used in China is unfortunately not yet available in the UK or the West. The adaptability of Chinese cuisine is once again demonstrated in this dish: if the original ingredients are not available, technique and ingenuity will overcome the deficiency. This dish is delicious and easy to make, and, speaking of adaptability, the recipe can also be tried with spinach leaves.

SERVES 4

2½ lb (1.25kg) bok choy

3⅔ cups (900ml) peanut or
  vegetable oil

2 tsp (10ml) sugar

salt

2 oz (50g) pine nuts, lightly
  roasted

Separate the stalks from the bok choy and cut the green leaves from the white stalks. (Save the stalks, as you can stir-fry them with garlic or use them for soup.) Wash the green leaves in several changes of cold water, then drain them thoroughly in a colander and spin them dry in a salad spinner. Take the leaves, roll them tightly and finely shred them. Lay them on a baking sheet and put them into a preheated oven at 250°F (120°C) for 10 minutes to dry slightly. They should not be completely dried, otherwise they will burn when fried. Remove from the oven and allow to cool. All this can be done the day before.

Heat a wok over high heat until it is hot, then add the oil. When it is hot and slightly smoking, deep-fry the greens in 2 or 3 batches. In about 30 seconds, when they have turned deep green, remove them quickly, drain well on paper towels and allow to cool.

Toss the crispy greens in the sugar and 1 tsp (5ml) of salt, then sprinkle with the pine nuts and serve.

Stir-fried Bean Sprouts

Mung beans provide most of the bean sprouts consumed in China. The soy bean is also sprouted, but its sprouts are not as tender as those of the mung bean. Because mung beans are grown everywhere in China except the coldest and driest areas, their sprouts are a common item in the daily diet. In the West, sprouts were not cultivated until very recently, but they have been a staple in Asian cuisine for centuries. They are a nutritious food, containing many vitamins and minerals, but their popularity derives mainly from their sweet, nutty-flavored crunchiness and their congeniality with other foods. This last feature is why they are so commonly used in stir-fries.

SERVES 4

1 lb (450g) fresh bean sprouts
1 tbsp (15ml) peanut oil
3 green onions, finely shredded
2 tbsp (30ml) thinly sliced
    garlic
salt and black pepper
2 tsp (10ml) light soy sauce
1 tsp (5ml) Chinese white rice
    vinegar
1 tsp (5ml) sesame oil

Pick over the bean sprouts, removing any yellow or dark, soft sprouts. Rinse them several times and drain them well in a colander.

Heat a wok or a large skillet over high heat until it is hot. Add the oil, and when it is very hot and slightly smoking, quickly add the green onions, garlic, 1 tsp (5ml) of salt and black pepper to taste and stir-fry for 30 seconds. Add the bean sprouts and stir-fry for 2 minutes, then add the light soy sauce and stir to mix well. Add the white rice vinegar and give the mixture several good stirs. Finally, add the sesame oil, give the mixture another good stir, transfer to a platter and serve at once.

Salt and Pepper Beancurd

This is a vegetarian version of the popular salt and pepper dish that one can find in southern China, usually made with shrimp or spareribs. It is a tasty way to enjoy beancurd and is easy to make. The beancurd is deep-fried first, then stir-fried with salt, aromatics and chilies. I think it makes a delicious starter for any meal.

SERVES 4

1 lb (450g) beancurd
2 tsp (10ml) roasted and ground
   Sichuan peppercorns
   (page 29)
1 tsp (5ml) sugar
salt and black pepper
1¼ cups (300ml) peanut oil
2 tbsp (30ml) finely chopped
   garlic
2 tsp (10ml) finely chopped
   fresh ginger
3 fresh red or green chilies,
   coarsely chopped
FOR THE GARNISH
3 tbsp (45ml) finely chopped
   green onions

Drain the beancurd and rinse it in cold water. Blot it dry with paper towels, then cut it into ½ in (1cm) cubes and drain it on more paper towels. In a small bowl, combine the Sichuan peppercorns and sugar with 2 tsp (10ml) of salt and 1 tsp (5ml) of black pepper.

Heat a wok or a large skillet over high heat until it is hot. Add the oil, and when it is very hot and slightly smoking, add the beancurd cubes and deep-fry them until they are lightly brown on all sides. Remove with a slotted spoon and drain on paper towels.

Pour off most of the oil, leaving about 1 tbsp (15ml) in the wok. Reheat the oil, and when it is hot, add the garlic, ginger and chilies and stir-fry for 20 seconds.

Return the beancurd to the wok and continue to stir-fry for 1 minute, then add the salt and pepper mixture and continue to stir-fry for another 2 minutes.

Turn the mixture onto a platter, garnish with the green onions and serve at once.

Stir-fried Ginger Broccoli

Broccoli is a colorful and extraordinarily nutritious vegetable. The type known in the West is different from the Chinese variety. The Western variety is often considered to combine the best features of cauliflower and asparagus, and its distinctive flavor is milder than the Chinese type. It goes well with many seasonings, but ginger is one of its most congenial companions. After stir-frying this dish, I let it cool and serve it at room temperature, so it is particularly suitable for summertime.

SERVES 4

1 lb (450g) fresh broccoli
1½ tbsp (22ml) peanut or
   vegetable oil
2 tbsp (30ml) finely shredded
   fresh ginger
salt and black pepper
4–5 tbsp (60–75ml) water
2 tsp (10ml) sesame oil

Separate the broccoli heads into small florets and peel and slice the stems. Blanch all the broccoli pieces in a large saucepan of boiling salted water for several minutes, then plunge them into cold water. Drain thoroughly.

Heat a wok or a large skillet until it is hot. Add the oil, and when it is very hot and slightly smoking, add the ginger shreds, 1 tsp (5ml) of salt and ½ tsp (2ml) of pepper. Stir-fry for a few seconds, then add the blanched broccoli and a few tablespoons of water. Stir-fry at a moderate to high heat for 4 minutes, until the broccoli is thoroughly heated through. Add the sesame oil and continue to stir-fry for 30 seconds.

Chinese Leaves in Soy Sauce

This simple dish is one of my favorite ways of preparing Chinese leaves. The blanching preserves the sweetness, while the hot oil imparts a rich, nutty flavor to the vegetable. It is quick and easy to make. You can also use white cabbage or any other leafy green vegetable for this dish.

SERVES 2

1 lb (450g) Chinese leaves
1 tbsp (15ml) peanut or
   vegetable oil
1 tbsp (15ml) light soy sauce
2 tsp (10ml) dark soy sauce
3 tbsp (45ml) green onions,
   finely chopped

Cut the Chinese leaves into 1½ in (4cm) strips and blanch them in a saucepan of boiling, salted water for about 5 minutes. Drain thoroughly, then put the blanched leaves on a platter and sprinkle the soy sauces and green onions over them.

Heat the oil in a wok or a skillet until it is almost smoking, then pour the hot oil over the leaves. Serve at once. For a spicy taste, try using Chili Oil (page 23) instead of peanut oil.

Stir-fried Cucumbers with Hot Spices

I am always surprised to see people eating cucumbers raw! We Chinese almost never eat them like this. If they are not pickled then they must be cooked. We prefer them when they are in season, young, tender and bursting with juice. This is a simple stir-fried cucumber dish from western China. Once the ingredients are assembled, it is very quick to cook. The chili and garlic contrast well with the cool, crisp cucumber. Once you get into the habit of cooking cucumbers, you will be delighted by their transformation into a true vegetable.

SERVES 4

1½ lb (675g) cucumbers
  (about 1½)
salt and black pepper
1 tbsp (15ml) peanut or
  vegetable oil
1½ tbsp (22ml) finely chopped
  garlic
2 tbsp (30ml) black beans,
  rinsed and coarsely chopped
1 tbsp (15ml) finely chopped
  fresh ginger
2 tbsp (30ml) finely chopped
  green onions
1 tbsp (15ml) chili bean sauce
2 tsp (10ml) sugar
½ cup (120ml) water
2 tsp (10ml) sesame oil

Peel the cucumbers, slice them in half lengthwise and, using a teaspoon, remove the seeds. Then cut the cucumber halves into 1 in (2.5cm) cubes. Sprinkle them with 2 tsp (10ml) of salt and mix well, then put into a colander and leave for about 20 minutes to drain. This rids the cucumber of any excess liquid. When the cucumber cubes have drained, rinse them in water and blot them dry with paper towels.

Heat a wok or a large skillet over high heat until it is hot. Add the oil, and when it is very hot and slightly smoking, add the garlic, black beans, ginger and green onions and stir-fry for about 30 seconds. Add the cucumbers, chili bean sauce, sugar, 1 tsp (5ml) of salt and ½ tsp (2ml) of black pepper and stir for another 30 seconds, until they are well coated with the spices and flavorings, then add the water and continue to stir-fry over high heat for 3–4 minutes, until most of the water has evaporated and the cucumbers are cooked through. At this point, add the sesame oil and bring to the table immediately.

Stir-fried Watercress with Chili

Watercress for the Chinese is a vegetable and not simply a garnish. It has its own value and integrity. This recipe is a quick and easy vegetarian dish my mother often made. Watercress was abundant, as it grew by the rice fields as well as along the banks of rivers and lakes; it was inexpensive, and cooked in literally seconds, and all these virtues made it most acceptable in my mother's repertoire. Watercress has its own mild bite, and she would combine it with garlic and chilies to make a tasty and pungent treat. It is a refreshing contribution to any dinner table.

SERVES 4, AS A SIDE DISH

2 lb (900g) watercress

1½ tbsp (22ml) peanut or vegetable oil

2 tbsp (30ml) coarsely chopped garlic

1 tbsp (15ml) chopped red or green chilies

salt and black pepper

2 tbsp (30ml) light soy sauce

2 tsp (10ml) sugar

2 tsp (10ml) sesame oil

Wash the watercress thoroughly and remove any tough stems. Spin dry in a salad spinner or drain well in a colander, and dry thoroughly in a clean tea towel.

Heat a wok or a large skillet over high heat until it is hot. Add the oil, and when it is very hot and slightly smoking, add the garlic, chilies, 1 tsp (5ml) of salt and ½ tsp (2ml) of black pepper and stir-fry for 10 seconds. Then add the watercress and continue to stir-fry for 3 minutes over high heat, until wilted. Now add the soy sauce and sugar and stir well. Finally, drizzle in the sesame oil, mix well and serve.

Braised Spicy Eggplants

Eggplants are one of my favorite vegetables. I love their color, taste and texture. Their subtle flavor is receptive to a good zesty sauce, such as this one from western China. It's worth trying to get the small, long, thin Chinese eggplants for their sweet taste. However, this recipe also works perfectly well with the large Western variety. The Chinese prefer to leave the skin on because it holds the eggplant together throughout the cooking and because the skins are tender, tasty and nutritious, but you may prefer to skin them.

Two techniques are employed here: a quick stir-frying to blend the seasonings, and braising, which cooks the eggplants and makes a sauce.

SERVES 4

1 lb (450g) eggplants
salt
1½ tbsp (22ml) peanut or
  vegetable oil
2 tbsp (30ml) finely chopped
  garlic
1½ tbsp (22ml) finely chopped
  fresh ginger
3 tbsp (45ml) finely chopped
  green onions, white part only
2 tbsp (30ml) dark soy sauce
1 tbsp (15ml) chili bean sauce
1 tbsp (15ml) whole yellow bean
  sauce
1 tbsp (15ml) sugar
1 tbsp (15ml) Chinese black
  vinegar or cider vinegar
2 tsp (10ml) roasted and ground
  Sichuan peppercorns
  (page 29)
1¼ cups (300ml) Chicken Stock
  (page 75) or water
FOR THE GARNISH
chopped green onions

Roll-cut the Chinese eggplants (see page 40), if you are using them. If you are using the regular large variety, trim them and cut them into 1 in (2.5cm) cubes. Sprinkle with 2 tsp (10ml) of salt and leave in a sieve to drain for 20 minutes. Then rinse them under cold running water and pat dry with paper towels.

Heat a wok or a large skillet over high heat until it is hot. Add the oil, and when it is very hot and slightly smoking, add the garlic, ginger and green onions and stir-fry them for 30 seconds. Add the eggplants and continue to stir-fry for 1 minute, then add the rest of the ingredients. Turn the heat down and cook uncovered for 10–15 minutes, until the eggplants are tender, stirring occasionally.

Return the heat to high and continue to stir until the liquid has been reduced and has thickened slightly. Turn the mixture onto a serving dish and garnish with the chopped green onions.

Braised Beijing (Peking) Cabbage in Cream Sauce

Vegetarian dishes are common throughout China. Historic and religious influences and rituals have played a part, but the availability of so many different vegetables, especially soy beans, has had a practical influence. Chinese cabbage, also known as Beijing (Peking) cabbage (and commonly as Chinese leaves), for example, was enjoyed pickled as well as fresh. One of the best versions is this traditional dish. The cabbage was first stir-fried, then slowly braised in chicken stock, with the stock reduced, thickened and enriched with chicken fat. I omit the latter step here, which makes the dish purely vegetarian if you also use water, thickened with a little cornstarch, to make the cream sauce rather than chicken stock. A humble dish, but one worthy of the Imperial banquet hall.

SERVES 4

1 lb (450g) Chinese leaves
1½ tbsp (22ml) peanut or
  vegetable oil
3 garlic cloves, peeled and
  finely sliced
2 cups (450ml) Chicken Stock
  (page 75) or water
salt and white pepper
2 tsp (10ml) cornstarch, mixed
  with 1 tbsp (15ml) water

Cut the Chinese leaves into 2-in (5cm) thick strips.

Heat a wok or a large skillet over high heat until it is hot. Add the oil, and when it is very hot and slightly smoking, add the garlic and stir-fry for 15 seconds. Add the Chinese leaves and stir-fry for 2 minutes, then add the stock or water, 2 tsp (10ml) of salt and 1 tsp (5ml) of white pepper. Turn the heat to low, cover and cook for 10 minutes, or until the Chinese leaves are very tender. Remove the leaves with a slotted spoon.

Reduce the liquid in the wok by half, add the cornstarch mixture and continue to reduce by half again until the sauce is thick. Arrange the leaves on a platter, pour over the sauce and serve at once.

Braised Beancurd with Mushrooms

Beancurd, which is also known as doufu or, in Japanese, tofu (see page 17), is a versatile and nutritious food. It is derived from the soy bean, which is exceedingly rich in protein. Beancurd on its own is rather bland, but this is easily remedied by recipes such as this one, in which it is deep-fried, which alters its texture, then braised, which makes it tasty. The result is a delicious and unusual vegetable dish. An additional bonus is that it reheats well.

SERVES 4

1 lb (450g) fresh beancurd
2 oz (50g) green onions
2 cups (450ml) peanut
  or vegetable oil, plus
  1 tbsp (15ml)
1½ tbsp (22ml) finely chopped
  garlic
2 tsp (10ml) finely chopped
  fresh ginger
4 oz (100g) small whole button
  mushrooms, washed
2 tsp (10ml) chili bean sauce
1½ tbsp (22ml) Shaoxing rice
  wine or dry sherry
1 tbsp (15ml) dark soy sauce
2 tbsp (30ml) Chicken Stock
  (page 75) or water
2 tsp (10ml) roasted and ground
  Sichuan peppercorns
  (page 29)
salt and black pepper

Cut the beancurd into 1 in (2.5cm) cubes. Trim the green onions and cut them into 1 in (2.5cm) segments.

Heat the larger quantity of oil in a deep-fat fryer or a large wok until it almost smokes, and deep-fry the beancurd cubes in 2 batches. When each batch of beancurd is lightly browned, remove and drain well on paper towels. Let the cooking oil cool and discard it.

Heat a wok or a large skillet over high heat until it is hot. Add the 1 tbsp (15ml) of oil, and when it is very hot and slightly smoking, add the garlic and green onions. Stir-fry for a few seconds and then add the mushrooms. Stir-fry for 30 seconds, then add all the other ingredients. Season with 1 tsp (5ml) of salt and ½ tsp (2ml) of black pepper, reduce the heat to very low and add the beancurd cubes. Cover the wok and slowly simmer the mixture for 8 minutes.

Firecracker Corn

Years ago in Sichuan I had the most delightful but unusual dish: corn stir-fried with chilies. I must admit I was rather surprised. It was a most unexpected experience, but it turned into a culinary revelation. This is such a simple, quick and satisfying recipe.

SERVES 4

1 lb (450g) fresh corn on the
   cob (about 2 ears), or 10 oz
   (275g) canned corn
1 tbsp (15ml) peanut or
   vegetable oil
2 small, mild red chilies, seeded
   and finely chopped
salt and black pepper
1 tsp (5ml) sugar
2 tsp (10ml) Shaoxing rice wine
   or dry sherry
1 tsp (5ml) sesame oil

If the corn is fresh, cut the kernels off the cob. Blanch frozen corn for 10 seconds in boiling water and drain. If you are using canned corn, simply drain it.

Heat a wok or a large skillet over high heat until it is hot. Add the oil, and when it is very hot and slightly smoking, add the corn, chilies, ½ tsp (2ml) of salt and black pepper to taste, and stir-fry for 1 minute. Then add the sugar and the rice wine and continue to stir-fry for 2 minutes. Finally, stir in the sesame oil and serve at once.

Buddhist Casserole

This is my adaptation of a famous Buddhist dish. The original recipe calls for many obscure dried Chinese vegetables, but my version uses vegetables that are readily available. I like to add a little cilantro, which Buddhists do not eat. A deeply satisfying dish, this casserole is suitable for both summer and winter. I prefer to cook it in a Chinese clay pot, but you can also use a good, small cast-iron pot. Take care not to overcook the vegetables. The casserole may be made in advance and reheated very slowly. It is delicious with rice, noodles or fresh bread.

SERVES 4

8 oz (225g) fresh beancurd

4 oz (100g) broccoli

4 oz (100g) Chinese leaves or white cabbage

4 oz (100g) small zucchinis

4 oz (100g) red bell pepper (about 1), sliced

4 oz (100g) snow peas, washed and trimmed

2 cups (450ml) peanut or vegetable oil

2⅓ cups (600ml) Chicken Stock (page 75) or water

2 tbsp (30ml) light soy sauce

3 tbsp (45ml) hoisin sauce

2 tbsp (30ml) whole yellow bean sauce

1 tbsp (15ml) finely chopped fresh coriander

salt and black pepper

1 tbsp (15ml) sesame oil

Cut the beancurd into 1 in (2.5cm) cubes and drain them on paper towels. Next, prepare all the vegetables. Separate the broccoli heads and break them into small florets. Peel and slice the broccoli stems. Cut the Chinese leaves or cabbage into 1 in (2.5cm) hunks. Slice the zucchinis into rounds ¼ in (5mm) thick, or roll-cut them (see page 40). Thinly slice the bell pepper. Leave the snow peas whole, but trim the ends.

Heat a wok over high heat until it is very hot and add the oil. Alternatively, heat the oil in a deep-fat fryer. When the oil is very hot and slightly smoking, deep-fry the beancurd cubes in 2 batches. Drain each cooked batch on paper towels.

Put the chicken stock or water, soy sauce, hoisin sauce and whole yellow bean sauce into a large, cast-iron enamel pot or Chinese clay pot and bring it to a boil. Next, add the broccoli and stir in the Chinese leaves or cabbage. Boil for 2 minutes. Add the zucchinis and bell pepper and cook for another 2 minutes. Finally, add the snow peas and the beancurd cubes. Cook for 1 minute more, then stir in the cilantro, 1 tsp (5ml) of salt and ½ tsp (2ml) of black pepper. Finally, stir in the sesame oil and the dish is ready to serve.

To reheat, bring to a simmer on very low heat until all the vegetables are hot.

Lettuce with Oyster Sauce

Here is lettuce prepared in a very familiar Chinese way — blanched and served with oyster sauce. Lettuce prepared like this retains a crispy texture, and its delicate flavor is unimpaired by cooking. The combination makes a simple, quickly prepared, tasty vegetable dish.

SERVES 2–4

1½ lb (675g) iceberg or romaine
    lettuce
salt
3 tbsp (45ml) oyster sauce
1 tbsp (15ml) peanut or
    vegetable oil

Separate the lettuce leaves and blanch them in a saucepan of boiling salted water for about 30 seconds, or until they have wilted slightly. Remove them and drain well. Mix the oyster sauce with the oil. Arrange the lettuce leaves on a warmed serving dish, pour the oyster sauce and oil mixture over them, and serve immediately.

Braised Beancurd Casserole Family Style

Beancurd is ideal for braising, as it readily absorbs flavors and colors, and Chinese beancurd seems to me the best in the world, smooth and satiny in texture and invariably perfectly prepared.

Here is a particularly tasty and easy-to-prepare recipe that reheats extremely well. One of the ingredients, hoisin sauce, adds color and a slightly sweet flavor to the beancurd. Dishes like this are often called "red-cooked."

SERVES 4

1 lb (450g) beancurd
8 green onions
2 cups (450ml) peanut
   or vegetable oil, plus
   1½ tbsp (22ml)
2 tbsp (30ml) coarsely chopped
   garlic
2 tbsp (30ml) Shaoxing rice
   wine or dry sherry
3 tbsp (45ml) hoisin sauce
1 tbsp (15ml) light soy sauce
2 tsp (10ml) dark soy sauce
1 tsp (5ml) sugar
1 cup (250ml) Chicken Stock
   (page 75)
1 tbsp (15ml) sesame oil

Cut the beancurd into 1 in (2.5cm) cubes and drain on paper towels. Trim the green onions and cut them into segments roughly 1 in (2.5cm) in size.

Heat the 2 cups (450ml) of oil in a deep-fat fryer or a large wok until it almost smokes, and deep-fry the beancurd cubes in 2 batches. When each batch is lightly browned, remove and drain well on paper towels. Let the cooking oil cool, then discard it.

Wipe the wok clean and reheat it over high heat until it is hot. Add the remaining 1½ tbsp (22ml) of oil, and when it is very hot and slightly smoking, add the garlic and green onions. Stir-fry for a few seconds, then add the drained beancurd. Stir-fry for 30 seconds, then add all the other ingredients apart from the sesame oil. Reduce the heat to low and slowly simmer the mixture for 8 minutes, then turn the heat to high and cook until most of the liquid has evaporated. Stir in the sesame oil and serve at once.

Eggplant with Sesame Sauce

This simple eggplant dish is easy to make and is delicious as a starter or as part of a meal. I found it often in the street markets of Beijing (Peking) and Chengdu. Try to obtain the smaller, more delicately flavored Chinese eggplants, if you can. I deviate from the traditional Chinese method of steaming the eggplants and prefer roasting. The roasting is in fact a steaming process that leaves the eggplants sweet, tender and moist, and increases their receptivity to the classic sesame sauce. As a tasty starter, it is served cold, and it may be made hours in advance; the sauce, however, should not be mixed with the cooked eggplants until you are ready to serve the dish.

SERVES 4

1½ lb (675g) Chinese eggplants or regular eggplants

FOR THE SAUCE

2 tbsp (30ml) sesame paste or peanut butter

½ tsp (2ml) roasted and ground Sichuan peppercorns (page 29)

2 tbsp (30ml) sesame oil

2 tsp (10ml) chili oil

2 tsp (10ml) sugar

1 tbsp (15ml) finely chopped garlic

2 tsp (10ml) chili bean sauce

2 tbsp (30ml) finely chopped cilantro

salt

Preheat the oven to 400°F (200°C). Put the eggplants into a roasting pan, and bake them for about 35 minutes if they are the Chinese variety, or 50 minutes if they are the larger variety. They should be charred outside and tender inside. Allow them to cool thoroughly and peel them. Set them aside until you are ready to use them.

When you are ready to serve the dish, mix all the sauce ingredients together, season with 1½ tsp (7ml) of salt, add the cooked eggplants and mix well. Serve at once, at room temperature.

Stir-fried Pickled Ginger with Beancurd

This recipe is derived from a Hong Kong treat. The beancurd is pan-fried, which gives it a golden crust, and then stir-fried with Pickled Young Ginger (page 58).

SERVES 4

1 lb (450g) firm beancurd
½ cup (120ml) peanut oil
1 x quantity Pickled Young
  Ginger (page 58)
2 tbsp (30ml) finely chopped
  green onions
2 tbsp (30ml) Shaoxing rice
  wine or dry sherry
1 tbsp (15ml) light soy sauce
1 tbsp (15ml) dark soy sauce
2 tsp (10ml) sugar
salt and black pepper
1 tsp (5ml) sesame oil

Cut the pickled ginger into thin slices and set aside.

Drain and quarter the beancurd, then cut it into squares. Heat a wok or a large skillet until it is hot and add the oil. Gently pan-fry the beancurd until it is golden brown, then drain on paper towels and set aside.

Drain away all but 1 tbsp (15ml) of oil and reheat the wok. When it is hot, add the pickled ginger and stir-fry for 30 seconds. Then add the rest of the ingredients apart from the sesame oil, season with ½ tsp (2ml) of salt and a little black pepper and continue to stir-fry for another minute. Return the beancurd to the wok and stir-fry for a further minute, then finally add the sesame oil and give the mixture a last stir. Transfer to a platter and serve at once.

Spinach with Fermented Beancurd

The fermented beancurd seasoning provides a zesty dimension here. It makes a fine accompaniment to any meat dish and is perfect with rice.

SERVES 4

2¼ lb (1kg) fresh Chinese water
  spinach or ordinary spinach
2 tbsp (30ml) peanut oil
4 garlic cloves, peeled and
  thinly sliced
3 tbsp (45ml) chili-fermented
  beancurd or plain fermented
  beancurd
2 tbsp (30ml) Shaoxing rice
  wine or dry sherry
3 tbsp (45ml) water

If using Chinese water spinach, wash it thoroughly and drain. Cut off 2 in (5cm) from the bottom of the stem, which tends to be tough. Cut the rest of the spinach into 3 in (7.5cm) segments. If you are using ordinary spinach, wash it thoroughly and remove all the stems, leaving just the leaves.

Heat a wok or a large skillet over high heat until it is hot. Add the oil, and when it is very hot and slightly smoking, add the garlic and stir-fry for 15 seconds. Then add the fermented beancurd and crush it with a spatula, breaking it into small pieces. Add the spinach and stir-fry for 3 minutes. Pour in the rice wine or sherry and water and cook for another 3 minutes. Put onto a serving platter and serve at once.

Country-style Eggplant

This dish is quite delicious because of its use of spices and seasonings: it is hot, sour, salty and sweet at the same time. It sounds (and tastes) very Sichuan, and indeed it is. You can find this dish in countless homes in the countryside throughout China. Pork is used to stretch this comfort dish, which is easy to make and reheats quite well. The name eggplant no doubt is derived from the ivory-colored variety that in fact does look like a large egg. Eggplants, which originated in northern India and migrated to China hundreds of years ago, come in various sizes, shapes and colors: red, yellow, white, striped and purple-black. I find the smaller Chinese varieties are generally the tastiest.

SERVES 4

1 lb (450g) eggplants
salt and black pepper
2 cups (450ml) peanut or
   vegetable oil
1 lb (450g) ground pork
2 tbsp (30ml) finely chopped
   garlic
2 tbsp (30ml) finely chopped
   fresh ginger
3 tbsp (45ml) finely chopped
   green onions
2 tbsp (30ml) dark soy sauce
3 tbsp (45ml) Shaoxing rice
   wine or dry sherry
3 tbsp (45ml) Chinese black
   vinegar
2 tbsp (30ml) sugar
1 tbsp (15ml) roasted and
   ground Sichuan peppercorns
   (page 29)
1 tbsp (15ml) chili bean sauce
½ cup (120ml) Chicken Stock
   (page 75)
2 tsp (10ml) sesame oil

Roll-cut the Chinese eggplants, if using (see page 40), or, if you are using the regular large variety, trim and cut them into 1 in (2.5cm) cubes. Sprinkle with 2 tsp (10ml) of salt and leave them in a sieve to drain for 20 minutes. Then rinse them under cold running water and pat them dry with paper towel.

Heat a wok or a large skillet over high heat until it is hot. Add the oil, and when it is very hot and slightly smoking, deep-fry the eggplants in 2 batches. Reserving 1 tbsp (15ml) of the oil, drain them well in a colander and then on paper towels.

Wipe the wok clean and reheat. When it is hot, return the reserved 1 tbsp (15ml) of oil to the wok. Add the pork and stir-fry for 3 minutes, then add the garlic, ginger and green onions and stir-fry for 2 minutes more. Add the rest of the ingredients apart from the sesame oil, season with ½ tsp (2ml) of black pepper and bring the mixture to a boil. Return the eggplants to the wok and continue to cook over high heat until they are tender and most of the liquid has evaporated. Stir in the sesame oil and either serve at once or leave to cool and serve at room temperature.

Beijing (Peking) Pan-fried Beancurd

This is a delightful beancurd dish from Beijing (Peking). The beancurd is coated with a batter, pan-fried slowly, then braised over low heat until all the savory liquid is absorbed, as if into a sponge. Beancurd's versatility makes it adaptable to any seasoning. If you are a vegetarian, simply use wine or water instead of stock. This goes well with noodles or rice and can be served as a vegetable accompaniment to any number of meat or fish dishes.

SERVES 4

1 lb (450g) firm beancurd
cornstarch, for dusting
1 egg, beaten
1¼ cups (300ml) peanut or
  vegetable oil
2 tbsp (30ml) coarsely chopped
  garlic
2 tbsp (30ml) finely chopped
  fresh ginger
3 tbsp (45ml) finely chopped
  green onion
3 tbsp (45ml) Shaoxing rice
  wine or dry sherry
2 tbsp (30ml) whole yellow
  bean sauce
1 tbsp (15ml) chili bean sauce
2 tsp (10ml) sugar
1¼ cups (300ml) Chicken Stock
  (page 75)
2 tsp (10ml) sesame oil
salt

Gently cut the block of beancurd crosswise into ½ in (1cm) slices and drain them on paper towels for 10 minutes. Dust the beancurd slices with cornstarch, then dip into the beaten egg and coat well.

Heat a wok until it is hot, then add the oil. When it is hot and slightly smoking, add the beancurd slices and pan-fry for 4–5 minutes, until they are golden. Then turn over and pan-fry the other side. Drain them well on paper towels. Discard all the oil except for 1½ tbsp (22ml).

Reheat the wok over high heat until it is hot. When the oil is hot and slightly smoking, add the garlic and ginger and stir-fry for 1 minute. Then add the green onions and stir-fry for 30 seconds. Return the beancurd to the wok, add the rest of the ingredients, season with 1 tsp (5ml) of salt and cook for 5 minutes over low heat, until the beancurd has absorbed all the liquid. Transfer to a serving platter and serve at once.

Cold Sweet and Sour Chinese Leaves

In northern China, with its short growing season and long, cold winters, fresh vegetables are available for only a few months of the year. In the absence of modern refrigeration, other means of preserving foods are necessary. Some of the most common methods are pickling in brine, in salt and wine; in a mixture of sugar and salt; or by inducing fermentation.

In this recipe from the north, Chinese leaves undergo what is essentially a sweet and sour pickling process. They can be eaten at once or stored for later use. Dishes like this are served at room temperature at the beginning of a meal, and their sweet and sour flavors are designed to stimulate the palate and whet the appetite.

SERVES 4-6

1½ lb (675g) Chinese leaves

⅓ cup (85ml) peanut or vegetable oil

1 tbsp (15ml) sesame oil

5 dried red chilies

2 tbsp (30ml) roasted Sichuan peppercorns (page 29)

½ cup (120ml) sugar

⅔ cup (150ml) Chinese white rice vinegar or cider vinegar

salt

1½ tbsp (22ml) finely chopped fresh ginger

3 tbsp (45ml) finely chopped garlic

3 tbsp (45ml) coarsely chopped fresh red chilies

Cut the Chinese leaves into 2 in (5cm) strips and blanch them in hot water for a few seconds, until they wilt. Drain them and put them to one side in a glass bowl. Heat the two oils in a saucepan or wok until they are hot. Add the dried chilies and the roasted peppercorns. When the chilies and peppercorns turn dark, turn the heat off. Pour the flavored oil through a strainer and then over the leaves or cabbage strips. Wrap the chilies and peppercorns in cheesecloth and tie into a bag like a bouquet garni, so that it can be removed later. Place it among the vegetable strips.

Now add the sugar and vinegar to the leaves and mix well. Add 2 tbsp (30ml) of salt and the ginger, garlic and fresh chilies and make sure all the ingredients are well combined. Let the mixture sit at room temperature for several hours. It is now ready to be refrigerated overnight and then served. This dish will keep for up to 1 week in the fridge. Before you serve it, drain off all the marinade and remove the chili-peppercorn bouquet garni.

Cold Bell Peppers with Black Beans

Peppers, both mild and hot, are enjoyed throughout China. This dish is inspired by a Sichuan recipe that uses fresh, mild, whole chilies. Here bell peppers are combined with zesty and spicy aromatics from Sichuan province. The black beans add a pungent aroma, as well as a delectable touch to this vegetarian dish. It is easy to prepare and tastes even better if you let it sit for 2 hours before serving. Use it as a main dish in summer, served at room temperature, or as a vegetable accompaniment.

SERVES 4

6 oz (175g) red bell peppers
6 oz (175g) yellow bell peppers
6 oz (175g) green bell peppers
1½ tbsp (22ml) peanut or
  vegetable oil
3 tbsp (45ml) finely chopped
  shallots
2 tbsp (30ml) black beans,
  rinsed and coarsely chopped
1½ tbsp (22ml) finely chopped
  garlic
1 tbsp (15ml) finely chopped
  fresh ginger
2 tbsp (30ml) Shaoxing rice
  wine or dry sherry
1 tbsp (15ml) chili bean sauce
1 tbsp (15ml) light soy sauce
2 tbsp (30ml) dark soy sauce
2 tsp (10ml) sugar
⅔ cup (150ml) Chicken Stock
  (page 75) or water
2 tsp (10ml) sesame oil

Cut the bell peppers into 1 in (2.5cm) squares. Heat a wok or large skillet over high heat until it is hot, then add the oil. When the oil is hot and slightly smoking, add the shallots, black beans, garlic and ginger and stir-fry for 1 minute. Then add all the bell peppers and stir-fry for 1 minute. Finally, add the rice wine, chili bean sauce, soy sauces, sugar and chicken stock. Continue to cook over high heat for 5 minutes, or until the peppers are soft and most of the liquid has evaporated. Add the sesame oil and mix well. Turn onto a platter and leave to cool. Serve at room temperature.

Cold Marinated Bean Sprouts

This is a nutritious salad, easy to make and perfect either as an appetizer or as a salad course with barbecued meat or fish. Always use the freshest bean sprouts you can find. I prefer to trim the sprouts at both ends. Although this is a bit laborious, it is well worth the effort as it makes the finished dish look more elegant. This dish may be prepared up to 4 hours in advance, and may be served cold or at room temperature. It is perfect for warm summer days.

SERVES 4

1 lb (450g) fresh bean sprouts
2 fresh red or green chilies
3 tbsp (45ml) Chinese white rice vinegar or cider vinegar
2 tbsp (30ml) light soy sauce
2 tbsp (30ml) finely chopped cilantro
2 tsp (10ml) finely chopped garlic

Trim and discard both ends of the bean sprouts and put the trimmed sprouts into a glass bowl. Split the chilies in half and carefully remove and discard the seeds. Shred the chilies as finely as possible, then add, together with all the other ingredients, to the trimmed bean sprouts. Mix well. Let the mixture marinate for at least 2–3 hours, turning the bean sprouts in the marinade from time to time. When you are ready to serve the salad, drain the bean sprouts and discard the marinade.

Pickled Cucumber Salad

In private homes in Taiwan or Beijing, I have often been served a modest dish of pickled cucumber, which it is said helps to stimulate the appetite. It certainly works for me. The dish should be made the night before it is to be served. It is simple to prepare and makes a nice opener for a summer meal. Try to find pickling cucumbers, but if you can't, then ordinary cucumbers are a suitable substitute.

SERVES 4

12 oz (350g) pickling
   cucumbers
salt
3 tbsp (45ml) sugar
2 tbsp (30ml) white rice vinegar
3 tbsp (45ml) sesame oil

FOR THE GARNISH

2 fresh red chilies, seeded and
   thinly sliced

Trim the cucumbers, slice them thinly, and put them into a large bowl. Add 1½ tbsp (22ml) of salt and the sugar and toss with the cucumbers, then cover with plastic wrap and refrigerate overnight.

Just before serving, squeeze out all the excess liquid from the cucumbers. Add the vinegar and sesame oil and toss well. Garnish with the sliced chilies and serve.

Spicy Spinach Salad

Summer in Sichuan province, with its hot, humid weather that goes on and on, always reminds me of my childhood summers in Chicago. Those who could ran for relief to the lakes and rivers, or at least sought out some shade. As in Chicago, so in Sichuan: in such weather, people eat light meals, especially salads such as this one. It is a delicious alternative to a lettuce salad and, being light and lively, makes a perfect accompaniment to barbecued foods during the hot summer months.

SERVES 4

1½ lb (675g) fresh spinach

2 tsp (10ml) finely chopped fresh ginger

3 tbsp (45ml) finely chopped green onions, white part only

2 tbsp (30ml) light soy sauce

2 tsp (10ml) sugar

2 tsp (10ml) sesame oil

1 tbsp (15ml) white rice vinegar

1 tsp (5ml) chili oil

Wash the spinach thoroughly. Remove all the stems, leaving just the leaves. In a small bowl, combine the rest of the ingredients to make a sauce. Mix well and set aside.

Blanch the spinach in a large saucepan of boiling salted water for just 10 seconds, so that it is barely wilted. Remove and drain immediately. Add the sauce to the salad and toss well to coat the spinach leaves thoroughly.

Transfer the spinach to a plate and pour off any excess liquid. Serve warm or cold.

Refreshing Watercress Salad with Sesame Dressing

In my mother's kitchen when I was growing up, watercress quickly stir-fried with an array of spices and condiments was a familiar and much-favored aromatic treat.

SERVES 4

1 lb (450g) watercress
2 tsp (10ml) toasted sesame seeds

FOR THE DRESSING

1 tbsp (15ml) light soy sauce
1 tsp (5ml) sugar
2 tsp (10ml) Chinese white rice
   vinegar or cider vinegar
2 tsp (10ml) peanut oil
2 tsp (10ml) sesame oil
salt and black pepper

Wash the watercress thoroughly and remove any tough stems. Spin dry in a salad spinner or drain well in a colander and dry thoroughly in a clean tea towel.

Put all the dressing ingredients into a small bowl along with ½ tsp (2ml) of salt and a little black pepper and mix thoroughly. Combine the watercress and dressing, sprinkle the toasted sesame seeds on the top just before serving and serve at once.

Cold Sesame Broccoli

This dish makes a good garnish for meats and a wonderful vegetable dish for summer picnics. The cold crunchiness of the broccoli goes well with the texture of the sesame seeds. For a tangy alternative, you could substitute finely chopped fresh ginger for the sesame seeds (using roughly the same amounts).

SERVES 4-6

1–1⅔ lb (450–750g) broccoli
1 tbsp (15ml) sesame seeds
1 tbsp (15ml) peanut or
   vegetable oil
2 tsp (10ml) sesame oil
2 tsp (10ml) finely chopped
   garlic
1½ tbsp (22ml) light soy sauce
2 tbsp (30ml) finely chopped
   green onions

Cut off the broccoli heads and break them into small florets. Peel and slice the broccoli stems. Blanch all the broccoli pieces in a large saucepan of boiling salted water for 4–5 minutes, then plunge them into cold water. Next, drain the broccoli dry in a colander or a salad spinner and put it into a clean bowl.

Roast the sesame seeds in a preheated oven set to 375°F (190°C), or under a broiler, until they are brown. In a small, glass bowl combine the roasted sesame seeds with the rest of the ingredients and mix them together well. Pour the mixture into the bowl of broccoli and toss. If you are using this dish the next day, tightly cover the bowl with plastic wrap and keep it in the fridge until it is needed.

Deep-fried Milk

One of the most interesting dishes I have encountered in Hong Kong is this dish of so-called Deep-fried Milk, which has become quite popular in Chinese restaurants in the West. The cooking process allows the milk to be digested by people who ordinarily cannot take milk. Milk custard is lightly battered and deep-fried, and the result is a crispy exterior with a creamy custard-like interior, a combination of textures that appeals to the Chinese taste.

How milk got into Hong Kong cuisine is an intriguing question. I suspect it is a northern dish that perhaps made its way into southern cooking. The dish I had in Hong Kong contained ham, and the contrast between the slightly salty ham and the sugar was striking. There, Deep-fried Milk is served with spareribs or simply dipped in sugar, as in this vegetarian version. Either way, I think you will discover, as I have, that this wonderful dish is indeed delicious.

SERVES 4

1⅓ cups (350ml) milk
¾ cup (175ml) evaporated milk
salt and white pepper
6 tbsp (90ml) cornstarch
2 cups (450ml) peanut
    or vegetable oil, plus
    1 tbsp (15ml) for oiling
    the pan

FOR THE BATTER
½ cup (120ml) all-purpose flour
4 tbsp (60ml) cornstarch
2 tsp (10ml) baking powder
¾ cup (175ml) water
sugar, for dipping

In a medium-sized bowl, combine the two types of milk with 2 tsp (10ml) of salt, 1 tsp (5ml) of pepper and the cornstarch.

Beat the mixture until it is smooth and pour into a saucepan. Simmer the mixture over low heat for about 10 minutes, or until the mixture has thickened. Oil a 6-in (15cm) square baking pan , then pour in the cooked mixture and allow it to cool thoroughly. Cover with plastic wrap and refrigerate. This can be done the night before.

In a medium-sized bowl, mix the batter ingredients and allow to sit at room temperature for 30 minutes. Cut the milk curd into 2 in (5cm) cubes.

Heat a wok or a large skillet over high heat until it is hot. Add the oil, and when it is very hot and slightly smoking, dip several of the milk curd cubes into the batter with chopsticks or a slotted spoon and deep-fry them for 3 minutes, or until they are golden and crispy. Drain them on paper towels and repeat the process until you have fried all the milk cubes.

Serve the fried milk with a small dish of sugar for dipping.

RICE, NOODLES & DOUGH

This trinity of foods has been the lifeblood of Chinese society for many hundreds of years. I love the way it takes only a few ingredients to turn something bland and dependable into a spectacular and exciting dish.

Perfect Steamed Rice

Steaming rice the Chinese way is the most simple, direct and efficient technique. I prefer to use long-grain white rice, which is drier and fluffier when cooked. Don't use pre-cooked or "easy-cook" rice for Chinese cookery, as both of these types of rice have insufficient flavor and lack the texture and starchy taste that is fundamental to Chinese rice cooking.

The secret of preparing rice without it being sticky is to cook it first in an uncovered saucepan at high heat until most of the water has evaporated. Then the heat should be turned very low, the pan covered and the rice cooked slowly in the remaining steam. As a child I was always instructed never to peek into the rice pot during this stage, otherwise precious steam would escape and the rice would not be cooked properly, bringing bad luck.

Here is a good trick to remember: if you make sure you cover the rice with about 1 in (2.5cm) of water, it should always cook properly without sticking. Many packet recipes for rice use too much water and result in a gluey mess. Follow my method and you will have perfect steamed rice, the easy Chinese way.

For the most authentic Chinese cooking, the required rice is simple long-grain rice, of which there are many varieties, all very good. A few rules worth repeating in regard to long-grain rice:

• The water should be at a level 1 in (2.5cm) above the surface of the rice; too much water means gummy rice. Recipes on commercial packages generally recommend too much water.
• Never uncover the pan once the simmering process has begun; time the process and wait.
• Follow the directions below and you are on your way to perfect rice.

SERVES 4

1⅔ cups (400ml) long-grain white rice
2⅓ cups (600ml) water

Put the rice into a large bowl and wash it in several changes of water until the water becomes clear. Drain the rice and put it into a heavy saucepan with 2⅓ cups (600ml) of water and bring it to a boil. Continue boiling until most of the surface liquid has evaporated — about 15 minutes. The surface of the rice should have small indentations, like a pitted crater. At this point, cover the saucepan with a lid, turn the heat as low as possible and let the rice cook undisturbed for 15 minutes. Let it rest on the turned-off heat for 5 minutes before serving.

Fried Rice - the basic recipe

In China fried rice is eaten as a "filler" at the end of a dinner party. It is not eaten with other dishes in place of steamed rice, although many Westerners do so. Here are a few important points to remember when making authentic fried rice:

- The cooked rice should be thoroughly cool, preferably cold. Once cooled, much of the moisture in the rice evaporates, allowing the oil to coat the dry grains and keep them from sticking. Store the cooked rice in the fridge until you are ready to use it.
- Never put any soy sauce into fried rice. It not only colors the rice unnaturally but also makes it too salty. Any moisture will make the rice gummy. Fried rice should be quite dry.
- Always be sure the oil is hot enough to avoid saturating the rice. Saturated rice is greasy and heavy. The finished fried rice should have a wonderful smoky taste and flavor.

If you follow these simple guidelines, you will be rewarded with perfect fried rice as it should be.

SERVES 4

2 oz (50g) cooked ham
4 oz (100g) fresh or frozen peas
2 eggs, beaten
2 tsp (10ml) sesame oil
2 tbsp (30ml) peanut or
  vegetable oil
1⅔ cups (400ml) long-grain
  white rice, cooked according
  to the method on page 288
salt and black pepper
3 tbsp (45ml) finely chopped
  green onions, white part only
4 oz (100g) fresh bean sprouts
FOR THE GARNISH
2 tbsp (30ml) finely chopped
  green onions

Cut the ham into fine dice. If you are using fresh peas, blanch them in a saucepan of boiling water for about 5 minutes and drain them in a colander. If you are using frozen peas, simply thaw them. Combine the eggs and sesame oil in a small bowl and set aside.

Heat a wok or a large skillet over high heat until it is hot. Add the peanut oil, and when it is very hot and slightly smoking, add the cooked rice and stir-fry it for 3 minutes until it is heated through. Add the ham, peas, 2 tsp (10ml) of salt and ½ tsp (2ml) of black pepper and stir-fry for 5 minutes over a high heat. Next, add the egg mixture and stir-fry for another minute. Then add the green onions and bean sprouts and continue to stir-fry for 2 minutes, or until the eggs have set. Turn the mixture onto a plate and garnish it with the green onions. Serve at once, or let it cool and serve as a cold rice salad.

Rice Congee

Rice congee is what many Chinese eat for breakfast; it is simply a boiled rice porridge. In various areas of China, fried bread dough, fermented beancurd, pickles, preserved salt or spicy mustard greens may be added to the congee. In the south, meat, chicken, roast duck, peanuts or fermented eggs are added. Interestingly enough, the word congee is a Hindi word and this perhaps indicates the origin of the dish.

The technique used in making congee is to boil the rice and then simmer it slowly. The starch is released gradually, thickening the porridge without the rice grains disintegrating. I find short-grain rice best for making congee, but you can use long grain. In this recipe the rice needs no washing, as all the starch is needed to thicken the porridge.

SERVES 4

8 oz (225g) Chinese sausages (or any flavoring of your choice, such as Sichuan preserved vegetables, or diced cooked chicken or duck, or leftover meats, fish, etc.)

6 cups (1.5L) water

⅔ cup (150ml) short-grain white rice, unwashed

salt

3 tbsp (45ml) finely chopped green onions

2 tbsp (30ml) finely chopped cilantro

Cut the Chinese sausages, or whatever flavoring you are using, into fine dice and set aside.

Bring the water to a boil in a large saucepan and add the rice and 2 tsp (10ml) of salt. Let the mixture come back to a boil and give it several good stirs. Then turn the heat down to low and cover the saucepan. Let the mixture simmer for about 1 hour, stirring occasionally. Then add the Chinese sausages or your chosen flavoring and simmer for a further 5 minutes with the saucepan uncovered. Just before serving, add the green onions and cilantro. Serve it at once.

If you like, congee can be made in advance. In this case reheat it slowly and simply add some more water if the porridge is too thick.

Sichuan-style Congee

Congee is a soothing, savory rice porridge or gruel. It is very versatile because you can add seasonings or leftovers to make a quick meal or even a special celebration dish. Over 1,000 years ago Chinese Buddhists put together a speciality they called "seven treasure five taste congee," to be eaten on the eighth day of the twelfth full moon of the year. Unfortunately, I have not been able to come upon that recipe in my research. However, this recipe is a more than adequate substitute!

Congee freezes well and a good batch can be made in advance. It is truly comfort food at its best.

SERVES 4

11¼ cups (2.8L) water
4 oz (100g) long-grain white rice
salt
4 oz (100g) Sichuan preserved vegetables, rinsed and chopped
3 tbsp (45ml) finely chopped green onions
3 tbsp (45ml) finely chopped cilantro

Bring the water to a boil in a large saucepan and add the rice and 1 tsp (5ml) of salt. Bring back to a boil and give it several good stirs. Then turn the heat down to low and partially cover the saucepan. Let the rice simmer for about 1 hour, stirring occasionally. The result will be a rather thick rice porridge, as most of the water will be absorbed in the cooking process.

Add the preserved vegetables and simmer for a further 5 minutes with the saucepan uncovered. Just before serving, add the green onions and cilantro. If you would prefer the congee thinner, simply add more water. Serve at once.

If you like, the rice porridge can be made in advance. When you are ready to serve, add the preserved vegetables and reheat slowly, adding more water if you feel that the porridge is too thick.

Steamed Rainbow Rice

This dish is the inspiration of the talented young Chinese chef Tam, who directs the kitchen at the widely acclaimed China House of the Oriental Hotel in Bangkok. His technique is to stir-fry the delectable mixture, which is then wrapped in lotus leaves and briefly steamed.

Here I have modified the exotic effect by omitting the lotus leaves and simply steaming the ensemble, but with the same admirable results. The stir-frying step initiates the cooking process but retains all of the colors and flavors of the ingredients. Then the steaming process gives the rice a moist texture but without overcooking the vegetables. Of course, if you have any lotus leaves about the house, feel free to use them!

SERVES 4

1⅔ cups (400ml) long-grain white rice, cooked according to the method on page 288
2 oz (50g) Chinese dried mushrooms
2 oz (50g) red bell pepper (about ½)
2 oz (50g) carrots
4 oz (100g) zucchinis
2 oz (50g) fresh or frozen peas
1½ tbsp (22ml) peanut or vegetable oil
2 tbsp (30ml) finely chopped shallots
3 tbsp (45ml) finely chopped green onions
1 tbsp (15ml) light soy sauce
salt and black pepper
2 tsp (10ml) sesame oil

Allow the cooked rice to cool thoroughly by spreading it on a baking sheet. When it is cool, refrigerate. When the rice is cold, proceed with the rest of the recipe.

Soak the dried mushrooms in warm water for 20 minutes, until they are soft. Squeeze the excess liquid from the mushrooms and remove and discard their stems. Cut the caps into small dice.

Cut the red bell pepper, carrots and zucchinis into small evenly-sized dice. If you are using frozen peas, make sure they are thoroughly thawed.

Heat a wok or a large skillet over high heat until it is hot. Add the oil, and when it is very hot and slightly smoking, add the shallots and green onions and stir-fry for about 30 seconds. Then add all the rice and vegetables and stir-fry for about 4 minutes. Add the soy sauce, 1 tsp (5ml) of salt and ½ tsp (2ml) of black pepper, give the mixture a few stirs and add the sesame oil. Remove the wok from the heat and place the mixture in a heatproof dish.

Set up a steamer, or put a rack into a wok or deep saucepan, and fill it with 2 in (5cm) of water. Bring the water to a boil over high heat. Put the dish of rice and vegetables into the steamer or onto the rack. Cover tightly and gently steam for 10 minutes. Then remove from the steamer and serve at once.

Rainbow Rice

Rice is so basic that it is usually taken for granted. This recipe gives a touch of glamour to the prosaic staple. It is a popular rice dish in the south. At first glance the recipe may seem similar to Fried Rice (page 289), but it is really quite different, since the rice and the other ingredients all have to be cooked separately, and then combined. It is a substantial dish, beautifully colored and ideal for a special dinner.

SERVES 4

1⅔ cups (400ml) long-grain white rice, cooked according to the method on page 288
2 oz (50g) Chinese dried mushrooms
2 oz (50g) red bell pepper (about ½)
2 oz (50g) carrots
4 oz (100g) Chinese sausages or cooked ham
2 oz (50g) fresh or frozen peas
2 tbsp (30ml) peanut or vegetable oil
3 tbsp (45ml) finely chopped green onions
1 tbsp (15ml) light soy sauce
2 tsp (10ml) sesame oil

Prepare the rice as instructed on page 288. Soak the dried mushrooms in warm water for about 20 minutes, until they are soft. Meanwhile, cut the red bell pepper, carrots and sausages or ham into small dice. Squeeze the excess liquid from the mushrooms and remove and discard their stems. Cut the caps into small dice. If you are using frozen peas, make sure they are thoroughly thawed.

Heat a wok or a large skillet. Add the oil and green onions and stir-fry for about 30 seconds. Then add all the vegetables and the sausages or ham. Stir-fry the mixture for about 2 minutes, then add the soy sauce, 1 tsp (5ml) of salt and ½ tsp (2ml) of black pepper. Give the mixture a few stirs and then add the sesame oil. Remove the wok from the heat and let the mixture cool.

When the rice is almost ready, pour the cooked mixture over it to cover the rice. Let the rice and the stir-fried mixture cook for a further 5 minutes. Then stir to mix well. Turn onto a serving platter and serve at once.

Chicken, Sausage and Rice Casserole

I have many pleasant memories of this dish. Even though I grew up in America, I often went to school with a typically Chinese lunch. Very early in the morning, my mother would steam chicken and sausage with rice and put it into a flask to keep it warm. I would often exchange bits of my hot lunch for portions of my classmates' sandwiches! This dish is easy to make and is a simple but fully satisfying meal in itself. It is easy to reheat.

It is well worth the effort to obtain authentic Chinese sausages from a Chinese grocer or supermarket. Although this dish will work with ordinary pork sausages, the end result just isn't quite the same.

SERVES 4

14 oz (400g) glutinous rice
1½ lb (675g) boneless, skinless
   chicken thighs
1 oz (25g) Chinese dried
   mushrooms
6 oz (175g) Chinese sausages or
   pork sausages
3⅔ cups (900ml) Chicken
   Stock (page 75) or water
1½ tbsp (22ml) finely chopped
   fresh ginger
3 tbsp (45ml) finely chopped
   green onions

FOR THE MARINADE

1 tbsp (15ml) Shaoxing rice
   wine or dry sherry
2 tbsp (30ml) light soy sauce
2 tsp (10ml) dark soy sauce
2 tsp (10ml) sugar
1 tsp (5ml) sesame oil
salt and black pepper

Soak the glutinous rice in cold water for at least 8 hours.

Cut the chicken into 2 in (5cm) pieces. Put them into a bowl with the marinade ingredients, add 1 tsp (5ml) each of salt and black pepper and let the mixture sit for at least 20 minutes.

Soak the mushrooms in warm water for 20 minutes. Then drain them and squeeze out the excess liquid. Remove and discard the stems and coarsely chop the caps. Slice the Chinese sausages thinly on a slight diagonal into 2-in (5cm) long pieces.

Bring the chicken stock to a boil in a large saucepan. Drain the rice and add it to the saucepan, then turn the heat to low. Cover and leave to cook for 2 minutes.

Now add the chicken with its marinade, the mushrooms, sausages, ginger and green onions. Stir well and continue to cook for about 25 minutes, until the rice, chicken and sausages are cooked. Serve at once.

Shanghai Vegetable Rice

This is a popular native Shanghai dish that combines so-called Shanghai bok choy with rice. This variety of bok choy is harvested young, when it is tender and its flavor is most intense. It is delicious with the blander rice and mushrooms. Some chefs cook the vegetables and rice together, others partially cook the rice first and then combine it with the vegetables. I prefer this second technique — I think it produces a tastier dish. Real home-cooked comfort food.

SERVES 4

1⅔ cups (400ml) long-grain white rice

2 oz (50g) Chinese dried mushrooms

12 oz (350g) Shanghai bok choy or ordinary bok choy

1½ tbsp (22ml) peanut or vegetable oil

3 tbsp (45ml) finely chopped green onions

2 tbsp (30ml) finely chopped garlic

2 tsp (10ml) sesame oil

salt and black pepper

2¼ cups (570ml) water

Put the rice into a large bowl and wash it in several changes of water until the water becomes clear.

Soak the mushrooms in warm water for 20 minutes, then drain them and squeeze out the excess liquid. Remove and discard the stems and coarsely chop the caps. Wash and coarsely chop the bok choy.

Heat a wok or a large skillet over high heat until it is hot. Add the oil, and when it is very hot and slightly smoking, add the green onions and garlic and stir-fry for 10 seconds. Add the mushrooms, bok choy, sesame oil, 2 tsp (10ml) of salt and ½ tsp (2ml) of black pepper and continue to stir-fry for 2 minutes, or until the bok choy has slightly wilted. Remove from the heat and set aside.

Drain the rice, then put it into a heavy saucepan with the water and bring it to a boil. Continue boiling until most of the surface liquid has evaporated. This should take about 15 minutes. The surface of the rice should have small indentations, like a pitted crater. At this point, add the entire contents of the wok, liquid and all, and stir to mix well. Cover the saucepan with a very tight-fitting lid, then turn the heat as low as possible and let the rice and vegetables cook undisturbed for 25 minutes. The rice will be slightly overcooked and mushy, which is how it should be. Turn onto a serving platter and serve at once.

Fried Rice with Pineapple

Fried rice is often served at meals that include many dishes. Generally, it is meant as a filler, just in case anyone is still hungry. But fried rice lends itself to many variations. This is a popular and unusual rice dish in Hong Kong, one that I suspect is of Thai origin. Thai cooks commonly hollow out a pineapple and fill it with fried rice or some other tasty stuffing, and it is often presented this way in Hong Kong restaurants. Southeast Asian influences in Hong Kong have always been strong, especially since the influx into Hong Kong in the mid-1970s of southeastern Asian immigrants escaping the turmoils of war and persecution. Although many who arrived were ethnic Chinese, they brought with them the flavors of their former country.

Because many of the countries of southeast Asia are also eager to sell their food products to an affluent Hong Kong, there is a vast variety of fruits available there, and this recipe demonstrates one use to which fruit is put. The result is a refreshing and piquant finish to any meal. It is a colorful dish that can be served at room temperature, great for a buffet or a simple family meal.

SERVES 4

1⅔ cups (400ml) long-grain
   white rice, cooked according
   to the method on page 288
2 tbsp (30ml) peanut or
   vegetable oil
8 oz (225g) ground pork
1 tsp (5ml) light soy sauce
2 tbsp (30ml) finely chopped
   fresh ginger
2 tbsp (30ml) finely chopped
   green onions
salt and white pepper
1 pineapple, peeled, cored and
   cut into 2 in (5cm) cubes

Allow the cooked rice to cool thoroughly by spreading it on a baking sheet. When it is cool, refrigerate. When the rice is cold, proceed with the rest of the recipe.

Heat a wok or a large skillet until it is hot and add the oil. Stir-fry the pork for 2 minutes, then add the soy sauce, ginger, green onions, ½ tsp (2ml) of salt and a little white pepper and stir-fry for another minute. Add the rice, stirring to mix well, and continue to stir-fry for 2–3 minutes, until the rice is hot. Finally, add the pineapple and continue to stir-fry for another 3 minutes, or until the fruit is heated through. Serve at once.

Chicken Fried Rice

The best chicken fried rice I have ever had was from a street food stall in China. Instead of tough, overcooked chicken, with the fried rice as an afterthought, the dish was cooked fresh from scratch. The cooking time was literally minutes and the result was delicious. I have re-created a version that comes very close to the original. It is quick and easy and makes a meal in itself. The rice to be fried is cooked beforehand.

SERVES 4

1⅔ cups (400ml) long-grain white rice, cooked according to the method on page 288

4 oz (100g) fresh or frozen peas

3 tbsp (45ml) peanut or vegetable oil

3 tbsp (45ml) finely chopped shallots

2 tbsp (30ml) finely chopped garlic

1 tbsp (15ml) finely chopped fresh ginger

3 tbsp (45ml) finely chopped green onions, white part only

8 oz (225g) boneless, skinless chicken thighs, coarsely chopped

salt and black pepper

4 eggs, beaten

2 tsp (10ml) sesame oil

1 tbsp (15ml) chili bean sauce or paste

2 tsp (10ml) shrimp paste or sauce

3 tbsp (45ml) finely chopped green tops of green onions

Allow the cooked rice to cool thoroughly by spreading it on a baking sheet. When it is cool, refrigerate. When the rice is cold, proceed with the rest of the recipe.

Cook the fresh peas in a saucepan of boiling water for about 5 minutes, then drain them in a colander. If they are frozen, simply thaw them.

Heat a wok or a large skillet over high heat until it is hot. Add 1½ tbsp (22ml) of the oil, and when it is very hot and slightly smoking, add the shallots, garlic, ginger and white part of the green onions and stir-fry for 1 minute. Then add the chicken, 2 tsp (10ml) of salt and ½ tsp (2ml) of black pepper and continue to stir-fry for 3 minutes. Remove from the heat and put the contents of the wok into a bowl. Wipe the wok clean.

Combine the eggs, sesame oil and a pinch of salt in a small bowl and set aside. Reheat the wok or skillet over a high heat until it is hot. Add the remaining 1½ tbsp (22ml) of oil, and when it is very hot and slightly smoking, turn the heat to moderate and add the eggs. Stir-fry the eggs for 2 minutes, then add the cooked rice and stir-fry it for 3 minutes, mixing well. Add the peas, cooked chicken, chili bean sauce and shrimp paste and continue to stir-fry for 5 minutes over high heat. Add the green tops of the green onions and stir-fry for a further 2 minutes, then turn the mixture onto a plate and serve at once.

Egg Fried Rice

The secret of perfect egg fried rice is cold, cooked rice and a very hot wok. It is simple, quick and easy to make.

SERVES 4

1⅔ cups (400ml) long-grain white rice, cooked according to the method on page 288
2 large eggs, beaten
2 tsp (10ml) sesame oil
salt and black pepper
2 tbsp (30ml) peanut or vegetable oil
2 tbsp (30ml) finely chopped green onions

Allow the cooked rice to cool thoroughly by spreading it on a baking sheet. When it is cool, refrigerate. When the rice is cold, proceed with the rest of the recipe.

Combine the eggs, sesame oil and ½ tsp (2ml) of salt in a small bowl and set aside.

Heat a wok or a large skillet over high heat until it is hot. Add the oil, and when it is very hot and slightly smoking, add the cooked rice and stir-fry it for 3 minutes, or until it is thoroughly warmed through.

Drizzle in the egg mixture and continue to stir-fry for 2–3 minutes, or until the eggs have set and the mixture is dry.

Now add ½ tsp (2ml) of salt and ¼ tsp (1ml) of black pepper and continue to stir-fry for 2 minutes. Toss in the green onions, stir several times, turn onto a platter and serve at once.

Fried Rice with Beef

Dependable but bland rice is easily enlivened with a small amount of beef.

SERVES 4

1⅔ cups (400ml) long-grain white rice, cooked according to the method on page 288
8 oz (225g) ground beef
2 tsp (10ml) light soy sauce
1 tsp (5ml) dark soy sauce
1 tbsp (15ml) fresh ginger
3 tbsp (45ml) green onions
2 tbsp (30ml) peanut oil
salt and black pepper
2 tsp (10ml) sesame oil

Allow the cooked rice to cool thoroughly by spreading it on a baking sheet. When it is cool, refrigerate. When the rice is cold, proceed with the rest of the recipe.

Mix the beef with the soy sauces. Finely chop the ginger and green onions. Heat a wok or a large skillet over high heat until it is hot. Add the oil, and when it is very hot and slightly smoking, add the beef and stir-fry for 2 minutes. Then add the ginger, green onions, 1 tsp (5ml) of salt and ½ tsp (2ml) of black pepper and stir-fry for 2 minutes. Add the rice, mix well and continue to stir-fry for another 5 minutes, until the rice is heated through and well mixed. Stir in the sesame oil and serve at once.

Fragrant Fried Ginger and Green Onion Rice

Fresh ginger has been a major part of my culinary life — I may say forever, inasmuch as it always graced my mother's kitchen. Along with soy sauce, green onions and garlic, ginger forms the four basic spices of southern Chinese cuisine. And for good reason: its zesty bite can transform even the most mundane and bland food, rice for example, into something special.

Here is a simple rice dish that I often make to accompany other foods. The ginger is slowly stir-fried so that it caramelizes slightly and sends off a toast-like fragrance.

SERVES 4

1⅔ cups (400ml) long-grain white rice, cook according to the method on page 288

2 tbsp (30ml) peanut or vegetable oil

3 tbsp (45ml) finely chopped fresh ginger

4 oz (100g) green onions, coarsely chopped

salt and black pepper

2 tbsp (30ml) finely chopped cilantro

Cook the rice at least 2 hours ahead or the night before. Allow it to cool thoroughly and put it into the fridge.

Heat a wok or a large skillet over high heat until it is hot. Add the oil, and when it is hot, add the ginger, turn down the heat and slowly stir-fry until the ginger has browned.

Add the green onions, 2 tsp (10ml) of salt and ½ tsp (2ml) of black pepper and stir-fry for 2 minutes. Then add the rice and continue to stir-fry for 5 minutes, or until it is heated through. Finally, add the cilantro. Give the mixture several good stirs, then turn onto a platter and serve at once.

Chiu Chow Fried Rice

The Chiu Chow peasant cooking of southern China that is so popular in Hong Kong is characterized by the use of shrimp paste. It is not difficult to see why shrimp paste is so widely used by the Chiu Chow people, as they are seafaring people from the Swatow port district of Guangdong province. They have been dubbed "the Sicilians of China." Their food is bold and hearty — as this recipe readily illustrates. Shrimp paste is akin to anchovy paste in Western cookery. Its acquired taste is quite addictive.

SERVES 4

1⅔ cups (400ml) long-grain white rice, cooked according to the method on page 288

4 oz (100g) fresh or frozen peas

1½ tbsp (22ml) peanut or vegetable oil

8 oz (225g) raw shrimp, peeled and coarsely chopped

3 tbsp (45ml) finely shredded fresh ginger

salt and black pepper

2 eggs, beaten

2 tsp (10ml) sesame oil

2 tsp (10ml) shrimp paste or sauce

FOR THE GARNISH

3 tbsp (45ml) finely chopped green tops of green onions

Allow the cooked rice to cool thoroughly by spreading it on a baking sheet. When it is cool, refrigerate. When the rice is cold, proceed with the rest of the recipe.

If you are using fresh peas, blanch them for 2 minutes in boiling water and refresh them in cold water. If you are using frozen peas, simply thaw them.

Heat a wok or a large skillet until it is hot and add the oil. When it is hot, add the shrimp, ginger, 2 tsp (10ml) of salt and ½ tsp (2ml) of black pepper and stir-fry for about 3 minutes. Then stir in the rice and stir-fry for 3 minutes, until it is heated through. Add the eggs and stir-fry for 2 minutes, until the mixture is slightly dry, then stir in the sesame oil and shrimp paste and stir-fry for another 2 minutes, mixing well. Serve at once, garnished with the green tops of green onions.

Savory Glutinous Rice Stuffing

This is such a truly delicious rice stuffing that it can even be eaten on its own. Glutinous rice is very absorbent and holds up well under long cooking, so is ideal for use in stuffing. I have even used it for roast turkey. You can make this a day in advance, but remember that you will need to soak the rice.

SERVES 4

12 oz (350g) glutinous rice, soaked for at least 4 hours or overnight

2 oz (50g) Chinese dried black mushrooms

1 lb (450g) ground fatty pork

2 tbsp (30ml) peanut or vegetable oil

4 Chinese pork sausages, coarsely chopped

4 oz (100g) Parma ham or lean smoked bacon, coarsely diced

3 oz (75g) Barbecued Roast Pork (page 104) or cooked ham, coarsely chopped

3 tbsp (45ml) finely chopped green onions

2 tbsp (30ml) Shaoxing rice wine or dry sherry

1 tbsp (15ml) light soy sauce

2 cups (450ml) Chicken Stock (page 75)

salt and black pepper

FOR THE MARINADE

1 tbsp (15ml) light soy sauce

1½ tbsp (22ml) Shaoxing rice wine or dry sherry

1 tbsp (15ml) finely chopped green onions

2 tsp (10ml) finely chopped fresh ginger

Drain the glutinous rice in a colander. Soak the mushrooms in warm water for 20 minutes. When soft, squeeze dry, cut off the tough stems and chop coarsely.

Combine the pork with the marinade ingredients and set aside for 20 minutes.

Heat a wok or a large skillet until it is hot, then add the oil. When it is smoking, add the pork and stir-fry for 5 minutes. Add the mushrooms, sausages, ham, barbecued pork and green onions and stir-fry for 10 minutes. Then add the drained rice, rice wine, soy sauce and stock and mix well. Season with salt and pepper, cover the wok and simmer for 15 minutes, or until the rice has absorbed all the liquid and is completely cooked. Allow to cool thoroughly before using as a stuffing.

Fried Rice "Yang Chow" Style

I grew up with this eastern Chinese fried rice dish, which seems to mark the end of any Chinese banquet. Usually everyone was so full by then, some lucky guest at each table always got a dish full of this delectable rice to take home.

SERVES 4

8 oz (225g) uncooked shrimp

4 oz (100g) fresh or frozen peas

2 eggs, beaten

2 tsp (10ml) sesame oil

2 tbsp (30ml) peanut or
   vegetable oil

2 tbsp (30ml) finely chopped
   garlic

1²⁄₃ cups (400ml) long-grain
   white rice, cooked according
   to the method on page 288

salt and black pepper

3 tbsp (45ml) finely chopped
   green onions, white part only

4 oz (100g) iceberg lettuce,
   finely shredded

FOR THE GARNISH

2 tbsp (30ml) finely chopped
   green onions

If required, peel the shrimp and cut into fine dice. If you are using fresh peas, cook them in a saucepan of boiling water for about 5 minutes and drain them in a colander. If you are using frozen peas, simply thaw them. Combine the eggs and sesame oil in a small bowl and set aside.

Heat a wok or a large skillet over high heat until it is hot. Add the peanut oil, and when it is very hot and slightly smoking, add the garlic and shrimp and stir-fry for a few seconds until lightly browned. Add the cooked rice and stir-fry for 3 minutes, until it is heated through. Then add the peas, 2 tsp (10ml) of salt and a little black pepper and continue to stir-fry the mixture for 5 minutes over high heat.

Next, add the egg mixture and stir-fry for another minute. Then add the green onions and lettuce and stir-fry for 2 minutes, or until the eggs have set. Turn the mixture onto a plate and garnish with the green onions. Serve at once.

Rice Cake

Rice cakes were probably invented by a thrifty Chinese cook centuries ago in order to make use of that thin layer of rice that sometimes gets stuck at the bottom of the pot. This crispy leftover has evolved into an accompaniment to many dishes. Its taste and crunchy texture go deliciously with Sizzling Rice Shrimp (page 222), for example. My mother often used to serve rice cakes with hot chicken broth for a sizzling rice soup. We also ate them as a snack with just a touch of oil and salt. After trying them you will never discard your leftover rice crust again.

Do not use "easy-cook" rice for this dish because it does not have enough starch to form a crust; use long-grain white rice. Basically, the method is the same as for steamed rice but the cooking time is longer.

MAKES ONE 9-IN (23CM) RICE CAKE

8 oz (225g) long-grain white rice
2⅓ cups (600ml) water
2 tsp (10ml) peanut or
   vegetable oil

Wash the rice and put it, with the water, into a 9–9½ in (23-24cm) wide, heavy saucepan. Bring the water to a boil over high heat. Then turn the heat down as low as possible, cover and let the rice cook for about 45 minutes. The rice should form a heavy crust on the bottom. Remove all the loose rice, leaving the crust in the pan. This loose rice can be used for making Fried Rice (page 289).

Drizzle the oil evenly over the top of the crust and let it cook over a very low heat for 5 minutes. The crust should lift off easily at this point. If it is still sticking, add another teaspoon of oil and continue to cook until the whole thing comes loose. Put the crust on a plate and set aside. Do not cover it, or moisture will form and make the cake moldy or soggy.

Let the rice cake dry out, and it is then ready to be deep-fried and put into hot chicken stock to make a soup or used for Sizzling Rice Shrimp (page 222). To eat as a simple snack in front of the TV, watching football, for example, simply break it into chunks and eat it hot with a sprinkling of salt.

Deep-fried Glutinous Rice Cakes

In China, almost any edible ingredient can be turned into a quick meal. What is offered as a snack varies with the region, according to preference and availability, but wherever you wander in China you are sure to find something tasty if you want a quick bite to keep you going, whether you are shopping, working or just strolling along.

While exploring the fascinating markets of the remote village of Yi Liang Gou Jie, I happened upon an elderly woman selling these glutinous rice cakes. She wrapped the cakes in bamboo leaves and boiled them. When a customer ordered one, she unwrapped the cake and dropped it into hot oil. It quickly puffed up and turned golden brown and crispy. She scooped it out, drained it and sprinkled it with sugar, presenting the patron with a simple but substantial and delicious treat.

Glutinous rice is sweet and has a sticky texture that makes it easy to mold into any shape. In this recipe, I have slightly altered the method by cooking the rice in a saucepan first and then pressing it all into a cake pan, bamboo leaves not always being available! The final results are the same. This is not only a delicious snack but can also serve as a rather unusual dessert.

SERVES 6–8, AS A SNACK OR DESSERT

1 lb (450g) glutinous sweet rice
2 cups (450ml) water
2 cups (450ml) peanut or
  vegetable oil, plus
  1 tbsp (15ml)
sugar, for dipping

In a large bowl, combine the rice with enough cold water to cover it by at least 2 in (5cm). Soak for 8 hours or overnight. Drain well.

In a medium-sized saucepan, combine the rice and water. Bring the mixture to a boil, then reduce the heat, cover the saucepan and cook for 40 minutes.

Using paper towels, rub the 1 tbsp (15ml) of oil over all sides of an 8-in (20cm) square cake pan. Press the rice into the greased tin, cover it with foil, and press down on all sides until the rice is compressed as much as possible. Allow to cool thoroughly.

Turn the rice out onto a board. It should fall out in one piece. Cut it into 3 x 1½ in (7.5 x 4cm) pieces and allow to dry thoroughly.

Heat a wok or a large skillet until it is hot. Add the oil, and when it is hot, drop in the rice squares, a few at a time, and deep-fry until they are golden and crispy. Drain the squares thoroughly on paper towels. Serve warm, with a dish of sugar so that diners may serve themselves as much as they wish.

Chiu Chow Noodles in Sesame Sauce

I love the aroma of these delicious noodles, which are usually served at the end of a banquet. Even though I am usually quite full by then, I can never refuse them. You can use ordinary dried egg noodles if you are unable to get the dried E-fu noodles, which come in round cakes and are a Chiu Chow speciality.

SERVES 4

8 oz (225g) dried E-fu noodles (about 6 cakes) or dried egg noodles
2 tbsp (30ml) sesame oil
FOR THE SESAME SAUCE
4 tbsp (60ml) sesame paste or peanut butter
1 tbsp (15ml) dark soy sauce
2 tbsp (30ml) light soy sauce
2 tsp (10ml) sugar
1 cup (225ml) Chicken Stock (page 75)
salt and white pepper

Blanch the noodles in a large saucepan of boiling salted water for 2 minutes, or until they are barely soft. Drain the noodles well, toss immediately with the sesame oil and arrange on a serving platter.

Mix all the sauce ingredients in a small saucepan, season with ½ tsp (2ml) of salt and a touch of white pepper and bring to a simmer. Allow the sauce to cool slightly and toss with the noodles. Serve at once.

Sichuan Garden's Dan-dan Noodles

Sichuan Garden is a popular restaurant in Hong Kong; the chefs were trained by master chefs from Sichuan. Although many of the dishes remain authentic and delicious, there is a subtle Hong Kong touch. For example, unlike the traditional dan-dan noodles, at Sichuan Garden they are lighter and less oily, which is the way they are prepared by many of the best restaurants in Hong Kong. Moreover, instead of using the thicker, traditional noodles of western China, Sichuan Garden uses the thin, dried egg noodles so characteristic of southern Chinese cooking. Here one gets the full bite of chilies, garlic and other seasonings without the heaviness. The noodles are usually served after a meal, making a tasty finale. When I first sampled these noodles, I liked them immediately.

This dish can be a delicious part of any meal or a simple luncheon dish in itself.

SERVES 4

1 tbsp (15ml) peanut or
   vegetable oil
4 oz (100g) Sichuan preserved
   cabbage, rinsed and finely
   chopped
1 tbsp (15ml) finely chopped
   garlic
2 tsp (10ml) finely chopped
   fresh ginger
2 tbsp (30ml) Shaoxing rice
   wine or dry sherry
2 tbsp (30ml) chili bean sauce
1 tbsp (15ml) Chinese sesame
   paste or peanut butter
1 tbsp (15ml) dark soy sauce
1 tbsp (15ml) sugar
2 cups (450ml) Chicken Stock
   (page 75)
8 oz (225g) Chinese fresh flat
   or thin wheat noodles, or thin
   Chinese dried egg noodles

Heat a wok or a large skillet over high heat and add the oil. Add the preserved cabbage, garlic and ginger and stir-fry for 1 minute. Add the rice wine, chili bean sauce, sesame paste, soy sauce, sugar and chicken stock. Reduce the heat and simmer for 3 minutes over low heat.

Cook the noodles in a large saucepan of boiling water for 2 minutes if they are fresh or 5 minutes if they are dried. Drain them well in a colander. Divide the noodles between individual bowls and ladle the sauce over them. Serve at once.

Chicken on Crispy Noodles

This noodle dish is a great favorite of many dim sum diners in Hong Kong and Canton. In fact, I love it so much that I tend to order it whenever I can. Thin, crispy fresh egg noodles are browned on both sides, then served with a shredded chicken sauce, making a wonderful finale to any dim sum meal.

SERVES 4

8 oz (225g) boneless, skinless chicken breasts, finely shredded

1 egg white

2 tsp (10ml) cornstarch

salt and white pepper

8 oz (225g) thin Chinese fresh egg noodles

1¼ cups (300ml) peanut or vegetable oil or water, plus 2–3 tbsp (30–45ml) oil

FOR THE SAUCE

6 oz (175g) fresh bean sprouts

2 tbsp (30ml) Shaoxing rice wine or dry sherry

2 tbsp (30ml) oyster sauce

1 tbsp (15ml) light soy sauce

1¼ cups (300ml) Chicken Stock (page 75)

salt and black pepper

1 tbsp (15ml) cornstarch, mixed with 1½ tbsp (22ml) water

FOR THE GARNISH

coarsley chopped green onions

Combine the chicken, egg white, cornstarch, 1 tsp (5ml) of salt and ½ tsp (2ml) of white pepper in a small bowl. Mix well and leave in the fridge for at least 20 minutes.

Blanch the noodles for 2 minutes in a large saucepan of salted boiling water. Drain them well.

Heat a skillet until it is hot and add 1½ tbsp (22ml) of oil. Spread the noodles evenly over the surface, then turn the heat to low and allow them to slowly browned. This should take about 5 minutes. When the noodles are browned, gently flip them over and brown the other side, adding more oil if needed. When both sides are browned, remove the noodles to a platter and keep warm.

Heat a wok until it is very hot and then add the larger quantity of oil (if using water, see below). When the oil is very hot, remove the wok from the heat and immediately add the chicken shreds, stirring vigorously to keep them from sticking together. After about 2 minutes, when the chicken has turned white, quickly drain it in a stainless steel colander set over a bowl. Discard the oil.

If you choose to use water instead of oil, bring it to a boil in a saucepan. Remove the saucepan from the heat and immediately add the chicken pieces, stirring vigorously to keep them from sticking together. After about 2 minutes, when the chicken has turned white, quickly drain it in a stainless steel colander set over a bowl. Discard the water.

Clean the wok and reheat it over high heat. Add the bean sprouts, rice wine, oyster sauce, soy sauce, chicken stock, 1 tsp (5ml) of salt and ½ tsp (2ml) of black pepper. Bring to a boil and stir in the cornstarch mixture. Bring it to a simmer again, then return the chicken to the sauce and give the mixture a few stirs. Pour the sauce over the noodles, garnish with the green onions and serve at once.

Chow Mein

Chow Mein literally means "stir-fried noodles," and this dish is as popular outside China as it is in southern China. It is a quick and delicious way to prepare egg noodles. Almost any ingredient you like, such as fish, meat, poultry or vegetables, can be added to it. It is a popular lunch dish, either served at the end of a meal or eaten by itself. It also makes a tasty noodle salad when served cold.

SERVES 4

8 oz (225g) Chinese fresh or dried egg noodles

2 tsp (10ml) sesame oil, plus 1 tbsp (15ml) for tossing noodles

4 oz (100g) boneless, skinless chicken breasts

2½ tbsp (22ml) peanut or vegetable oil

1 tbsp (15ml) finely chopped garlic

2 oz (50g) snow peas, trimmed

2 oz (50g) Parma ham or cooked ham, finely shredded

2 tsp (10ml) dark soy sauce

2 tsp (10ml) light soy sauce

½ tsp (2ml) sugar

3 tbsp (45ml) finely chopped green onions

1 tbsp (15ml) Shaoxing rice wine or dry sherry

salt and white pepper

FOR THE MARINADE

2 tsp (10ml) light soy sauce

2 tsp (10ml) Shaoxing rice wine or dry sherry

1 tsp (5ml) sesame oil

salt and black pepper

Cook the fresh or dried noodles for 3–5 minutes in a saucepan of boiling water. Cool them in cold water, drain them thoroughly, then toss them in 1 tbsp (15ml) of sesame oil and put them aside until you are ready to use them. They can be kept in this state, if tightly covered with plastic wrap, for up to 2 hours in the fridge.

Using a cleaver or a sharp knife, slice the chicken breasts into fine shreds 2 in (5cm) long. Combine the chicken shreds with the marinade ingredients in a small bowl. Mix well and season with ½ tsp (2ml) of salt and ½ tsp (2ml) of black pepper; leave the chicken to marinate for 10 minutes.

Heat a wok or a large skillet over high heat until it is hot. Add 1 tbsp (15ml) of the peanut oil, and when it is very hot and slightly smoking, add the chicken shreds. Stir-fry for about 2 minutes, then transfer the chicken to a plate. Wipe the wok or skillet clean.

Reheat the wok until it is very hot, then add the remaining 1½ tbsp (22ml) of oil. When the oil is slightly smoking, add the garlic. Stir-fry for 10 seconds, then add the snow peas and shredded ham. Stir-fry for about 1 minute, then add the noodles, dark and light soy sauces, sugar, green onions, rice wine, 1 tsp (5ml) of salt and ½ tsp (2ml) of white pepper. Continue to stir-fry for about 2 minutes, then return the chicken and any juices to the noodle mixture. Continue to stir-fry for about 3–4 minutes, or until the chicken is cooked. Add the remaining 2 tsp (10ml) of sesame oil to the wok and give the mixture a final stir. Turn it onto a warm platter and serve at once.

Cold Spicy Noodles

These savory noodles are perfect for summertime, and I enjoy making them because much of the work can be done ahead of time. Most people enjoy the nutty fragrance of the sesame paste in this recipe, but if you can't get it you can use peanut butter instead. Cold Spicy Noodles can be served with a mixed grill of meats and vegetables.

SERVES 4

1 lb (450g) Chinese fresh or dried
    egg noodles
2 tbsp (30ml) sesame oil
FOR THE SAUCE
3 tbsp (45ml) sesame paste or
    peanut butter
1 tbsp (15ml) chili bean sauce
1½ tbsp (22ml) finely chopped
    garlic
2 tsp (10ml) Chili Oil (page 23)
2 tbsp (30ml) Chinese white
    vinegar or cider vinegar
2 tbsp (30ml) light soy sauce
2 tsp (10ml) dark soy sauce
2 tsp (10ml) sugar
2 tsp (10ml) roasted and ground
    Sichuan peppercorns
    (page 29)
3 tbsp (45ml) finely chopped
    green onions
1 tbsp (15ml) peanut or
    vegetable oil
1½ tbsp (22ml) sesame oil
salt and black pepper
FOR THE GARNISH
2 tbsp (30ml) finely chopped
    green onions

Cook the fresh or dried noodles for 3–5 minutes in a saucepan of boiling water. Cool them in cold water, drain them thoroughly, then toss them in the sesame oil and put them aside until you are ready to use them. They can be kept in this state, if tightly covered with plastic wrap, for up to 2 hours in the fridge. Arrange them on a platter or in a large bowl.

Mix the sauce ingredients together, along with 1 tsp (5ml) each of salt and black pepper, in a bowl or in an electric blender. This can be done in advance and then refrigerated, as the sauce is meant to be cold. Pour the sauce over the noodles and toss well. Garnish with the green onions and serve.

If you wish to make this dish ahead of time, keep the sauce and noodles separate, tossing them at the last moment.

Stir-fried Rice Noodles with Beef Chili Bean Sauce

People in southern China habitually eat late meals. With a mild climate for much of the year, and restaurants open all night, they live a very Mediterranean type of life. Being in Canton reminds me of my stays in Naples, where at 11pm you can satisfy your urge for a quick pasta dish. This popular noodle dish is one of my favorites.

SERVES 4

8 oz (225g) Chinese dried thin
   or wide rice noodles
1 lb (450g) beef fillet
3 tbsp (45ml) peanut or
   vegetable oil
2 garlic cloves
2 tsp (10ml) fresh ginger
3 fresh red chilies, seeded and
   shredded
2 tbsp (30ml) chili bean sauce
2 tsp (10ml) dark soy sauce
4 tbsp (60ml) Chicken Stock
   (page 75)
2 tsp (10ml) sugar
2 tsp (10ml) Shaoxing rice wine
   or dry sherry
2 tsp (10ml) sesame oil
FOR THE MARINADE
1 egg white
2 tsp (10ml) light soy sauce
2 tsp (10ml) Shaoxing rice wine
   or dry sherry
1 tsp (5ml) sesame oil
1 tsp (5ml) cornstarch
salt and black pepper
FOR THE GARNISH
3 tbsp (45ml) finely chopped
   green onions

Soak the noodles in a bowl of warm water for 20 minutes, or until they are soft and pliable. Drain and set aside.

Place the beef fillet in the freezer for about 20 minutes, or until it is firm to the touch. Then cut it into slices against the grain. Put it into a bowl with the marinade ingredients, add ½ tsp (2ml) of salt and some black pepper to taste and refrigerate for 20 minutes.

Heat a wok or a large skillet until it is hot and add the oil. Add the beef and stir-fry for 1 minute, then immediately drain in a colander set over a bowl.

Coarsley chop the garlic and finely chop the ginger. Reheat the wok and return 1 tbsp (15ml) of the drained oil. Add the garlic, ginger, chilies, chili bean sauce and dark soy sauce and stir-fry for 30 seconds. Add the drained rice noodles and the stock, mix well, and stir-fry for 2 minutes. Return the drained meat to the wok and stir-fry for 2 more minutes, then add the sugar, rice wine, and sesame oil and give the mixture a final stir. Ladle onto a platter, garnish with the green onions and serve.

Hot Bean Thread Noodles

Bean thread, transparent or cellophane noodles are delightfully light. They are very fine, white and almost transparent and can be easily obtained from Chinese grocers and some supermarkets. They are quite easy to prepare and go well with almost any kind of sauce. Unlike other types of noodle, they can be very successfully reheated. The spicy sauce in this recipe gives the noodles body and character, and I think it makes an excellent dish for lunch or a light supper. It is also delicious with plain rice.

SERVES 4

4 oz (100g) bean thread
   (transparent) noodles
1 tbsp (15ml) peanut or
   vegetable oil
3 tbsp (45ml) finely chopped
   green onions
2 tbsp (30ml) finely chopped
   garlic
450g (1lb) minced beef
FOR THE SAUCE
2 cups (450ml) Chicken Stock
   (page 75)
2 tbsp (30ml) chili bean sauce
1 tbsp (15ml) whole yellow
   bean sauce
2 tbsp (30ml) light soy sauce
2 tsp (10ml) dark soy sauce
salt and black pepper
2 tsp (10ml) sesame oil
FOR THE GARNISH
2 tsp (10ml) coarsely chopped
   green tops of green onions

Soak the noodles in a large bowl of warm water for 15 minutes. When they are soft, drain them and discard the water. Cut them into 3 in (7.5cm) lengths using scissors or a knife.

Heat a wok or a large skillet over high heat until it is hot. Add the oil, and when it is very hot and slightly smoking, add the green onions and garlic and stir-fry quickly for just 15 seconds. Add the meat and stir-fry it for 8 minutes, or until it is cooked.

Then add all the sauce ingredients, except the sesame oil, season with ½ tsp (2ml) each of salt and black pepper and cook over a gentle heat for about 5 minutes. Now add the drained noodles and the sesame oil and cook for a further 5 minutes, or until most of the liquid has evaporated. Ladle the noodles into individual bowls or a large serving bowl and serve at once, garnished with the green tops of green onions.

Spicy Sichuan Noodles

This is a typical Sichuan dish. Although it is spicy and pungent with aromatics, it is nevertheless quite popular throughout China, especially in the north.

SERVES 4

8 oz (225g) ground fatty pork

1 lb (450g) Chinese fresh or dried
   egg noodles

1 tbsp (15ml) sesame oil

2 tbsp (30ml) peanut or
   vegetable oil

2 tbsp (30ml) finely chopped
   garlic

2 tbsp (30ml) finely chopped
   fresh ginger

5 tbsp (75ml) finely chopped
   green onions

2 tbsp (30ml) sesame paste or
   peanut butter

2 tbsp (30ml) dark soy sauce

2 tsp (10ml) light soy sauce

2 tsp (10ml) chili bean sauce

2 tbsp (30ml) Chili Oil (page 23)

1 cup (250ml) Chicken Stock
   (page 75)

salt and black pepper

FOR THE MARINADE

1 tbsp (15ml) dark soy sauce

2 tsp (10ml) Shaoxing rice wine or
   dry sherry

salt and black pepper

FOR THE GARNISH

2 tsp (10ml) roasted and ground
   Sichuan peppercorns
   (page 29)

Combine the pork with the marinade ingredients in a bowl, add 1 tsp (5ml) of salt and ½ tsp (2ml) of black pepper and mix well. Leave to marinate for 10 minutes.

Cook the fresh or dried noodles for 3–5 minutes in a saucepan of boiling water. Cool them in cold water, drain them thoroughly, then toss them in the sesame oil and put them aside until you are ready to use them. They can be kept in this state, if tightly covered with plastic wrap, for up to 2 hours in the fridge.

Heat a wok or a large skillet over high heat until it is hot. Add the oil, and when it is very hot and slightly smoking, add the garlic, ginger and green onions. Stir-fry for 30 seconds, then add the pork and continue to stir-fry until the meat loses its pink color. Add the rest of the ingredients except the garnish, season with 1 tsp (5ml) each of salt and black pepper and cook for 2 minutes.

Now add the noodles, mixing well. Turn onto a serving platter, garnish with the peppercorns and serve at once.

Braised Noodles with Crabmeat

One of the most appealing aspects of walking through the streets of Hong Kong, Taipei or Beijing (Peking) is seeing the countless noodle stalls ladling out delicious, inexpensive dishes that can be eaten quickly. These dishes have to be easy to make, as many of the clients are in a great hurry, but it is "fast food" that is nutritious as well as satisfying. The versatility of noodle dishes is such that once everything is prepared, it takes literally seconds to put together a tasty meal.

SERVES 4

8 oz (225g) dried wheat noodles

2 oz (50g) Chinese black
   mushrooms

1½ tbsp (22ml) peanut or
   vegetable oil

1 tbsp (15ml) finely shredded
   fresh ginger

4 oz (100g) Chinese yellow or
   green chives, cut into 2 in
   (5cm) pieces

12 oz (350g) fresh crabmeat

FOR THE SAUCE

1 tbsp (15ml) light soy sauce

2 tsp (10ml) dark soy sauce

1 tbsp (15ml) Shaoxing rice
   wine or dry sherry

2 tbsp (30ml) oyster sauce

1 tsp (5ml) sesame oil

1 tsp (5ml) sugar

1 cup (250ml) Chicken Stock
   (page 75)

FOR THE GARNISH

coarsely chopped green onions

Soak the mushrooms in warm water for 20 minutes, then drain them and squeeze out the excess liquid. Remove and discard the stems and finely shred the caps into thin strips.

Blanch the noodles in a large saucepan of boiling water for 5 minutes, or until they are soft. Drain well and set aside.

Heat a wok or a large skillet over high heat until it is hot. Add the oil, and when it is very hot and slightly smoking, add the ginger and chives and stir-fry for 30 seconds. Then add the mushrooms and the sauce ingredients and cook over high heat for 1 minute. Add the noodles and cook in the sauce for about 2 minutes, or until the sauce is absorbed into the noodles. Add the crabmeat and mix well. Ladle the noodles into a large bowl or individual bowls, garnish with green onions and serve at once.

Bean Sauce Noodles

Noodles are so popular in northern China that they are even eaten for breakfast, usually in soup. They are a common snack for the millions of patrons of the food stalls throughout the capital city of Beijing (Peking). This recipe is an adaptation of a common noodle dish, of which there are hundreds of variations. Once you have mastered this recipe you can add your own touches, just as the Chinese do.

SERVES 4

1 lb (450g) Chinese fresh or
  dried egg noodles
1½ tbsp (22ml) sesame oil

FOR THE SAUCE

1½ tbsp (22ml) peanut or
  vegetable oil
1½ tbsp (22ml) finely chopped
  garlic
1 tbsp (15ml) finely chopped
  fresh ginger
3 tbsp (45ml) finely chopped
  green onions
1 lb (450g) ground pork
3 tbsp (45ml) whole yellow
  bean sauce
1 tbsp (15ml) chili bean sauce
1½ tbsp (22ml) Shaoxing rice
  wine or dry sherry
2 tbsp (30ml) dark soy sauce
2 tsp (10ml) Chili Oil (page 23)
2 tsp (10ml) sugar
1¼ cups (300ml) Chicken Stock
  (page 75) or water
salt and black pepper

FOR THE GARNISH

3 tbsp (45ml) coarsely chopped
  green onions

Cook the fresh or dried noodles for 3–5 minutes in a saucepan of boiling water. Cool them in cold water, drain them thoroughly, then toss them in the sesame oil and put them aside until you are ready to use them. They can be kept in this state, if tightly covered with plastic wrap, for up to 2 hours in the fridge.

Heat a wok or a large skillet over high heat until it is hot. Add the oil, and when it is very hot and slightly smoking, add the garlic, ginger and green onions. Stir-fry for 15 seconds, then add the pork. Stir well to break it up and continue to stir-fry for about 2 minutes or more, until the pork loses its pink color. Then add the rest of the sauce ingredients, stirring all the time, and season with 2 tsp (10ml) of salt and ½ tsp (2ml) of black pepper. Bring the mixture to a boil, turn the heat down to low and simmer for 5 minutes. Plunge the noodles into boiling water for 30 seconds, or until they are just heated through, then drain them well in a colander or sieve. Quickly tip them into a large bowl and pour the hot sauce over the top. Sprinkle over the green onions, mix everything together well and serve at once.

Singapore Noodles

Curry is not original to Chinese cuisine. It was introduced to China centuries ago, but has now been incorporated into dishes such as this delightful noodle recipe.

SERVES 4–6

8 oz (225g) thin Chinese rice noodles or dried egg noodles

2 oz (50g) Chinese dried black mushrooms

6 oz (175g) frozen garden peas or petit pois

6 water chestnuts, fresh or canned

4 eggs, beaten

1 tbsp (15ml) sesame oil

salt and white pepper

1½ garlic cloves

1 tbsp (15ml) fresh ginger

3 tbsp (45ml) peanut oil

6 fresh red or green chilies

4 oz (100g) Barbecued Roast Pork (page 104) or cooked ham, finely shredded

3 green onions, finely shredded

4 oz (100g) small cooked shrimp, shelled

FOR THE CURRY SAUCE

2 tbsp (30ml) light soy sauce

3 tbsp (45ml) Madras curry paste or powder

2 tbsp (30ml) Shaoxing rice wine or dry sherry

1 tbsp (15ml) sugar

1 cup (250ml) coconut milk

¾ cup (175ml) Chicken Stock (page 75)

salt and black pepper

FOR THE GARNISH

cilantro leaves

Soak the rice noodles in a bowl of warm water for 25 minutes. Then drain them in a colander or sieve. If you are using dried egg noodles, cook them for 3–5 minutes in boiling water, then plunge them into cold water, drain them thoroughly and toss them in a little peanut oil. Set them aside until you are ready to use them.

Soak the mushrooms in warm water for 20 minutes, then drain them and squeeze out the excess liquid. Remove and discard the stems and finely shred the caps.

Put the peas into a small bowl and leave them to thaw. If you are using fresh water chestnuts, peel them. If you are using canned water chestnuts, rinse them well in cold water. Combine the eggs with the sesame oil, 1 tsp (5ml) of salt and ½ tsp (2ml) of white pepper and set aside.

Finely chop the garlic and ginger and seed and finely shred the red or green chilies. Heat a wok or a large skillet over high heat until it is hot. Add the oil, and when it is very hot and slightly smoking, add the garlic, ginger and chilies and stir-fry for 30 seconds. Add the water chestnuts, mushrooms, pork or ham and green onions and stir-fry for 1 minute. Then add the noodles, shrimp and peas and continue to stir-fry for 2 minutes.

Now add all the sauce ingredients, season with 1 tsp (5ml) each of salt and black pepper and continue to cook over high heat for another 5 minutes, or until most of the liquid has evaporated. Add the egg mixture and stir-fry constantly until the egg has set.

Turn the noodles onto a large platter, garnish with the cilantro leaves and serve at once.

Steamed Buns

Steamed buns are popular throughout China. Their texture is soft and light, fluffy yet firm. In the north and west they are served with Crispy Sichuan Duck (page 176) or Tea-smoked Duck (page 183). Steamed buns reheat well; and they can also be frozen and, once thawed, resteamed. They make a satisfying alternative to rice.

MAKES ABOUT 18

¾ cup (175ml) warm water
1 x ¼ oz (7g) packet of active
   dry yeast
1 tbsp (15ml) sugar
2 tbsp (30ml) peanut or
   vegetable oil
3 cups (750ml) all-purpose flour
parchment paper or wax paper,
   for cooking

Combine the warm water and yeast and allow to sit in a warm place for 2 minutes. The mixture should become slightly foamy. Add the sugar and the oil. Now combine the yeast mixture with the flour in a large bowl or alternatively, in a food processor, and mix until you have a smooth dough. Meanwhile, cut out 18 x 2½ in (6cm) squares of wax paper.

Take the dough out of the bowl and knead it for a few minutes on a floured board. If it is still sticky, dust lightly with a few tablespoons of flour. Then form it into a roll about 18 in (45cm) long and about 2 in (5cm) wide. Take a sharp knife and cut the roll into equal segments. There should be about 18 pieces. Take a segment of dough and work it in the palm of your hand until it forms a smooth ball. Put the ball on a wax paper square. Do the same with the rest of the pieces of dough, and put them, together with their paper bases, on ovenproof plates. Cover the buns with a large sheet of parchment paper or wax paper and then with a damp tea towel and let them rest for about 30 minutes in a warm place. After this period the buns should have doubled in size.

Next, set up a steamer, or put a rack into a wok or deep saucepan, and fill it with 2 in (5cm) of water. Bring the water to a boil over high heat, then carefully lower the plate of buns into the steamer or onto the rack (you may need to do this in batches). Turn the heat to low and cover the wok or saucepan tightly. Steam over high heat for 15 minutes.

The steamed buns are now ready to be served with Crispy Sichuan Duck (page 176), Beijing (Peking) Duck (page 182) or Tea-smoked Duck (page 183). Alternatively, you can let them cool, then pack them into a plastic bag and freeze them. Be sure to thaw them completely before reheating. The best way to reheat them is to cover them with plastic wrap and warm them in a microwave oven.

Chinese Pancakes

These pancakes are the classic accompaniment to Beijing (Peking) Duck (page 182) and Mu Shu Pork (page 114). The unusual method of rolling "double" pancakes is designed to ensure thinner, moister pancakes with less risk of overcooking them. Since they can be frozen, it is possible to make them weeks ahead.

MAKES ABOUT 18

2¼ cups (560 ml) all-purpose flour
1 cup (250ml) very hot water
2 tbsp (30ml) sesame oil

Put the flour into a large bowl. Stir in the hot water gradually, mixing all the while with chopsticks or a fork until the water is fully incorporated. Add more water if the mixture seems dry. Then remove the mixture from the bowl and knead it with your hands for about 8 minutes until smooth. Put the dough back into the bowl, cover it with a damp tea towel and let it rest.

After about 30 minutes, take the dough out of the bowl and knead it again for about 5 minutes, dusting with a little flour if it is sticky. Once the dough is smooth, form it into a roll about 18 in (45cm) long and about 1 in (2.5cm) in diameter. Take a knife and cut the roll into equal segments. There should be about 18. Roll each segment into a ball.

Take 2 of the dough balls. Dip one side of one ball into the sesame oil and place the oiled side on top of the other ball. Take a rolling pin, and roll the two simultaneously into a circle about 6 in (15cm) in diameter.

Heat a skillet or a wok over very low heat. Put the double pancake into the wok or skillet and cook it until it has dried on one side. Flip it over and cook the other side. Remove from the skillet, peel the 2 pancakes apart and set them aside. Repeat this process until all the dough balls have been cooked. (There should be about 18 pancakes in all.)

Steam the pancakes to reheat them, or alternatively, you could wrap them tightly in a double sheet of foil and put them into a saucepan containing 1 in (2.5cm) of boiling water. Cover the saucepan, turn the heat down very low and simmer until they are reheated. Don't be tempted to reheat them in the oven, as this will dry them out too much.

If you want to freeze the cooked pancakes, wrap them tightly in plastic wrap first. When using pancakes that have been frozen, let them thaw in the fridge first before reheating them by steaming.

Beijing (Peking) Onion Cakes

This is a wonderful snack that you find in restaurants in Beijing (Peking). You can make these either with two flat Chinese Pancakes (see opposite), or roll them up — both ways are equally delicious.

MAKES ABOUT 18 ROLLED OR 9 FLAT

1 quantity Chinese Pancakes (opposite)
2 eggs, beaten
9 green onions, finely chopped
salt and black pepper
3⅔ cups (900ml) peanut or vegetable oil

If you are making flat onion cakes, take 2 pancakes and brush the inside with beaten egg. Sprinkle with green onions, salt and pepper and press them together to seal them.

If you are rolling them, take 1 pancake and brush the inside with beaten egg. Sprinkle with green onions, salt and pepper and roll the pancake into a cylinder.

Heat a wok until it is hot. Add the oil, and when it is hot, hold the cakes, either flat or rolled, with tongs and deep-fry until crispy. Drain on paper towels.

Continue until you have deep-fried all the cakes. Cut them into bite-sized pieces and serve immediately.

DESSERTS

Although desserts are not a major part of Chinese cuisine, I do believe that the flavors of China lend themselves well to sweet treats.

Sweet Almond Soup

I remember my mother grinding almonds into a purée with water, then adding sugar and heating the mixture until it was a rich, thick, milky, fragrant, warm "soup." We would have it as a snack with cookies during the day or as a dessert. Such sweet soups are a traditional Cantonese favorite. Sometimes they are made with black sesame seeds or red beans. Almonds are usually ground by hand in a stone mortar — blenders and food processors for some reason make them bitter, at least to my taste. But, unless you like to grind things by hand, let me suggest commercially made almond paste — marzipan. It tastes very similar to what my mother used to make and it certainly saves time. The result is a warm, sweetly delicious dessert that evokes the fragrance of Hong Kong.

SERVES 4

3 oz (75g) marzipan
1¼ cups (300ml) milk
2¼ cups (570ml) water

Combine the marzipan, milk and water in a medium-sized saucepan and simmer for 15 minutes. Serve at once.

Cold Honeydew Melon and Coconut Soup

I have a suspicion that this dessert, now popular throughout China, had its origins in Hong Kong, where the soup is usually followed by rich pastries. Without a doubt this soup gives a sweet and refreshing coda to any Chinese meal. I use tapioca here rather than sago, which is a starch obtained from the stem of the southeast Asian sago palm. It comes in varying sizes and consists almost entirely of starch. It is used in soups and puddings in Hong Kong to make them more digestible. Tapioca is prepared from the tuberous roots of the tropical cassava or manioc shrub and is a good substitute for sago, which is less available here. It is used to thicken the soup. The melons should be very ripe and full of flavor. I think you will find this soup a perfect ending to any meal, especially during warm weather.

SERVES 4–6

1 oz (25g) small pearl tapioca
4 tbsp (60ml) water
2 cups (450ml) coconut milk, fresh or canned
6 tbsp (90ml) sugar
⅔ cup (150ml) cold milk
1 or 2 ripe honeydew melons, about 3 lb (1.5kg)

FOR THE GARNISH

fresh mint leaves

Combine the tapioca and water in a small bowl and leave for 45 minutes. Drain the tapioca and set aside.

In a medium-sized saucepan, combine the coconut milk, sugar and tapioca and simmer for 10 minutes, or until the mixture begins to thicken. Add the milk and allow it to cool thoroughly, then cover with plastic wrap and refrigerate.

Cut the melons into quarters, then remove the seeds and cut off the rind. Cut the melons into large pieces and purée in a blender or food processor until you have a thick liquid. Pour into a medium-sized bowl, cover with plastic wrap and refrigerate.

When you are ready to serve the soup, combine the two mixtures as follows: take a soup tureen and place the coconut and tapioca mixture on one side. Then add the honeydew purée on the other side, forming a yin/yang pattern. Garnish with the mint leaves, bring to the table and stir a few times before serving.

Warm Banana Compote in Plum Wine with Candied Ginger

This dessert is typical of the experimentation we are now seeing by Chinese chefs within China, as they expand their horizons on the culinary front.

SERVES 4–6

1 vanilla pod, split in half, or
    1 tsp (5ml) vanilla extract
2 tsp (10ml) sugar
1¼ cups (300ml) Japanese
    sweet plum wine or port wine
6 ripe bananas
2 tsp (10ml) unsalted butter, cut
    into small pieces (optional)
2 tbsp (30ml) finely chopped
    candied ginger
1 tbsp (15ml) lemon juice

Scrape out the inside of each half of the vanilla pod, if using, and put into a bowl with the sugar. Set it aside. Put the plum wine into a wok or a large skillet and add the vanilla pods. Bring to a simmer until reduced by one-third. Peel the bananas and cut them in half lengthwise. Add them to the reduced plum wine with the sugar and vanilla seed mixture (or the vanilla extract) and simmer for 5 minutes, until warmed through. Whisk in the butter, if using, and add the candied ginger and lemon juice. Serve at once.

Double-steamed Bird's Nest with Coconut

If you want an unforgettable Chinese culinary experience for a very special dinner party, you should consider this version of a popular dessert. A bird's nest, inside a hollowed-out coconut shell and, if possible, set within a coconut-shaped tureen, will certainly make an impression. The silky, soft texture of the bird's nest in the sweet, fragrant coconut milk is indeed a grand finale to your meal. Bird's nest can be found in Chinese grocers.

SERVES 4–6

50g (2oz) loosely packed dried
   bird's nest
2⅓ cups (600ml) fresh or
   canned coconut milk
2 oz (50g) sugar
⅔ cup (150ml) water

Soak the bird's nest overnight in warm water. Next day, drain and rinse under cold running water. Blanch the bird's nest in boiling water for 15 minutes, then drain thoroughly and set aside.

Put the bird's nest into a saucepan with the coconut milk, sugar and water and simmer for 25 minutes. Ladle the mixture into individual bowls or a soup tureen and serve at once.

Egg Custard

I love egg custard served on its own in a cup or as a filling for little pastry tartlets.

SERVES 4–6

2 cups (450ml) water
½ cup (120ml) sugar
6 eggs, beaten
¼ tsp (1ml) vanilla or almond
   extract
2 tbsp (30ml) crystallized
   ginger or fresh orange zest,
   finely chopped

Combine the water and sugar in a large saucepan and bring to a boil. Continue to boil the mixture until the sugar has entirely dissolved, then set aside and let the mixture cool completely.

In a large bowl, combine the eggs, vanilla or almond extract and ginger or orange zest. Mix them thoroughly and add the cooled sugar-water mixture. Pour into a heatproof shallow bowl. Cut a round piece of wax paper or parchment paper to cover the top of the bowl. (This will prevent the top of the custard from drying out.)

Set up a steamer, or put a rack into a wok or saucepan. Add 2 in (5cm) of water and bring to a simmer, then lower the bowl of custard carefully into the steamer or onto the rack and cover the wok or saucepan tightly. Gently steam for about 20 minutes, or until the custard has set. Remove the cooked custard and allow it to cool slightly before serving. Alternatively, let it cool completely, wrap it in plastic wrap and put it into the fridge until you are ready to serve.

Honeydew Pudding

Traditionally, Chinese dinners and banquets have no dessert course. Instead, fresh fruits may be offered, sometimes presented dramatically, with the fruits elaborately carved and with dry ice sending off smoke-like vapors. The Chinese think of the fruits as, at best, a cooling, refreshing contrast to the seasoned, hot foods that have comprised the dinner. However, dessert courses are now making their appearance on a regular basis in Chinese restaurants. Still linked to tradition, they tend to make use of fruit, as this recipe shows. Sweet honeydew melons with a rich, creamy pudding provide a cooling, sweet close to any meal. This is easy to make, can be done hours ahead of time, and is thus perfect for entertaining.

SERVES 4

1 or 2 ripe honeydew melons,
    about 3 lb (1.5kg)
1 packet of unflavored gelatin
4 tbsp (60ml) cold water
4 egg yolks
½ cup (120g) sugar
a pinch of salt
¾ cup (175ml) milk
1 cup (250ml) heavy cream

Cut the honeydew melon into quarters, then remove the seeds and cut off the rind. Cut the melon into large pieces and purée in a blender or food processor until you have a thick liquid. Pour into a medium-sized bowl, cover with plastic wrap and refrigerate. You will need 14 oz (400g) of the melon purée for this recipe.

Combine the gelatin and water and set aside.

In a large bowl, beat the egg yolks, sugar and salt until they are a light yellow color. Bring the milk to a boil, then remove from the heat and gradually pour in a steady stream into the egg mixture, beating all the while. Return to the stove and cook, stirring constantly, until the mixture is thick. Remove from the heat, stir in the gelatin mixture and allow to cool.

When the mixture is cold, fold in 14 oz (400g) of the honeydew purée. Beat the cream until it is stiff and fold into the mixture. Turn the mixture into a mold or into individual dishes and chill for at least 2 hours before serving.

Almond Jelly with Fresh Oranges

This is my version of a classic Chinese dessert. In the original version, agar-agar (a type of seaweed) is used instead of gelatin, almond milk is used instead of almond extract and a sugar syrup is served with it instead of orange juice. The original version involves a long and laborious process requiring obscure ingredients. I think this recipe, although it departs from the original, is nevertheless a delicious and refreshing variation.

SERVES 4

1 tbsp (15ml) gelatin
1¼ cups (300ml) water
1¼ cups (300ml) milk
5 tbsp (75ml) sugar
1½ tsp (7ml) almond extract
2 oranges
1¼ cups (300ml) fresh orange
   juice

Put the gelatin into a small bowl. Add half the water to the bowl and bring the other half to a boil in a small saucepan. Pour the boiling water into the bowl and stir until the gelatin has completely dissolved. Combine the gelatin mixture with the milk, sugar and almond extract in a large bowl. Pour the mixture into a Pyrex dish or a square baking pan about 7 in (18cm) square and 1½ in (4cm) deep. Put it into the fridge for about 2 hours, or until it has completely set.

Peel the oranges and remove all the white pith. Separate them into segments by cutting down both sides between the flesh and the membrane. Save any juice and set aside.

When the almond jelly is ready, cut it into 1 in (2.5cm) cubes. Put some orange segments into individual bowls. Add some almond jelly cubes, and pour a little orange juice over each portion.

Cold Almond Pudding with Fresh Fruit

Puddings made with gelatin are a popular offering in many homes and restaurants in China. The light textural quality of gelatin makes a soothing finish to meals in which strong flavors such as garlic, ginger, chili, shrimp paste, oyster sauce and black beans are often used to enhance meats or vegetables. Here an almond inspiration is combined with fresh oranges to make a typical light dessert.

SERVES 4

2 tbsp (30ml) sugar
1 packet of unflavored gelatin
⅔ cup (150ml) evaporated milk
2 cups (450ml) coconut milk
1 tsp (5ml) almond extract
2 oranges, peeled

Mix the sugar and gelatin together in a large stainless steel bowl.

Combine the two milks in a medium-sized saucepan and bring them to a simmer. Add the almond extract and pour in a steady stream into the sugar and gelatin mixture, stirring all the while with a whisk. Pour the mixture back into the saucepan and continue to cook over low heat for 2 minutes, stirring constantly. Remove from the heat and strain the mixture if it is lumpy. When it is cool, pour it into a mold or into individual dishes, cover with plastic wrap, and refrigerate for 4 hours or until it has set.

Peel the oranges and remove all the white pith. Separate them into segments by cutting down both sides between the flesh and the membrane. Save any juice and set aside.

To unmold, dip the bottom of the mold briefly into warm water, being careful not to let any of the water inside. Hold the mold firmly against a serving plate and invert.

Garnish the pudding with the fresh orange segments and juice. Serve at once.

Fruit Compote

Lychees were so sought after by the Imperial court that, once picked, they were rushed to the court by special fast horse relays. Some of these special fruits are now available in cans. They are acceptable, but should be served without their overly sweet syrup. A mixed compote of fresh and canned fruits is a delicious and most appropriate dessert for any dinner party.

SERVES 4–6

2 apples
2 mangoes
6 oz (175g) cantaloupe melon
14 oz (400g) canned lychees,
    drained

Using a sharp knife, peel and core the apples and slice into thin wedges. Peel and stone the mangoes and slice the flesh into segments. Cut the melon in half, then scoop out and discard the pulp and seeds. Cut the melon flesh into 1 in (2.5cm) cubes. Put the apples, mangoes and melon into a large bowl. Add the lychees and mix the fruits gently together. Cover tightly with plastic wrap and refrigerate before serving.

Peaches in Honey Syrup

Any list of the classical fruits of China should begin with the peach, which figures prominently in folklore, traditional religion, literature and popular affection. New and exotic varieties were introduced into China from Central Asia during the Tang dynasty (AD 618–907). The dish can be served warm or cold and makes a simple, light, sweet dessert.

SERVES 4

2 large firm peaches
4 tbsp (60ml) Chinese rock
    sugar or granulated sugar
⅔ cup (150ml) water

Bring a saucepan of water to a boil and blanch the peaches in it for a few seconds. Remove them with a slotted spoon. With a sharp knife, peel off the skin and split each peach in half, discarding the stone.

Combine the sugar and water in a small saucepan and boil until the sugar dissolves. Add the peach halves and turn the heat down to a low simmer. Simmer for about 15 minutes, or until the peaches are tender. Gently remove them from the saucepan with a slotted spoon. Turn the heat to high and reduce the liquid to about half the amount — it should become a sweet syrup. If you are serving the dish hot, pour the liquid over the peaches and serve at once. If you are serving it cold, let the liquid cool, pour it over the peaches and refrigerate until you are ready to serve.

Steamed Pears

Pears are a northern Chinese fruit and are eaten fresh, cooked in soups, deep-fried and steamed, the last of which is especially delicious. The steaming process cooks the pears without drying them out. The Chinese traditionally serve this dish hot, but I find it equally good cold.

SERVES 4

4 firm pears
3 tbsp (45ml) Chinese rock
  sugar or granulated sugar
⅓ cup (85ml) water
2 pieces of Chinese cinnamon
  bark or cinnamon sticks

Peel the pears and cut them in half. Remove the core and seeds. Combine the sugar and water in a small saucepan and boil until the sugar has completely dissolved. Allow to cool slightly.

Put the pears, sugar-water and cinnamon together in a heatproof shallow bowl. Next, set up a steamer, or put a rack into a wok or deep saucepan, and fill it with 2 in (5cm) of water. Bring the water to a boil over high heat, then carefully lower the dish of pears into the steamer or onto the rack. Turn the heat to low and cover the wok or saucepan tightly. Steam gently for 15–25 minutes, until they are tender. (The cooking time will depend on the ripeness of the pears.)

When the pears are cooked, drain all the liquid, including the cinnamon stick or bark, into a small saucepan and reduce to a syrup by boiling fast. Remove and discard the cinnamon stick. Pour the syrup over the pears and serve at once.

Alternatively, you can let the mixture cool, then cover it with plastic wrap and refrigerate until you are ready to serve it.

Toffee Apples and Bananas

Although apples and bananas are most often associated with southern China, they are glazed with honey or sugar and eaten as snacks throughout the country. The dish requires some dexterity, which will come with experience. Make it for yourself a few times before you attempt it for guests.

SERVES 4

2 large firm apples
2 firm bananas
1¼ cups (300ml) peanut or
   vegetable oil
2 tsp (10ml) sesame oil
¾ cup (175g) sugar
2 tbsp (30ml) white sesame
   seeds

FOR THE BATTER
½ cup (120ml) all-purpose flour
4 tbsp (60ml) cornstarch
2 tsp (10ml) baking powder
¾ cup (175ml) water
1 tsp (5ml) sesame oil

In a medium-sized bowl, mix the batter ingredients and allow to sit at room temperature for 30 minutes.

Peel and core the apples and cut each one into 8 large thick wedges. Peel the bananas, split them in half lengthwise, and cut them into 1½ in (4cm) chunks.

Combine the peanut or vegetable oil and sesame oil in a deep-fat fryer or a wok and heat until moderately hot. Put the fruit into the bowl of batter mixture. Lift out several pieces at a time, using a slotted spoon, and drain off any excess batter. Deep-fry for about 2 minutes, until golden. Remove with a slotted spoon and drain on paper towels. Repeat the process until you have deep-fried all the fruit.

Just before serving, prepare a bowl of iced water filled with ice cubes. Reheat the oil to a moderate heat and deep-fry the fruit a second time, for about 2 minutes. Drain on paper towels. Put the sugar, sesame seeds and 2 tbsp (30ml) of the deep-frying oil into a saucepan. Heat the mixture until the sugar melts and begins to caramelize. (Watch the heat to prevent it burning.) When the caramel is light brown, add the fruit pieces a few at a time and stir gently to coat them, then take them out and put them into the iced water to harden the caramel. Remove them from the water and place on a serving platter. Serve at once.

Sweet Walnut Cream

My aunt made this lovely and easy dish often, although it was not necessarily served as a dessert. However, I think it makes a splendid ending to any Chinese meal.

SERVES 4

6 oz (175g) walnuts
2 cups (450ml) water
1 cup (250ml) evaporated milk
1 cup (250ml) sugar

Blanch the walnuts for 5 minutes in a small saucepan of boiling water, then drain and rinse well in warm water. Remove as much of the skin from the walnuts as possible. Allow the nuts to dry.

Preheat the oven to 350°F (180°C). Place the walnuts on a baking sheet and bake for 15 minutes, until they are light brown and crisp. Set aside to cool.

In a blender, combine the walnuts and water and blend until the walnuts are reduced to a fine purée, adding more water if necessary. Strain through a fine sieve.

Combine the walnut purée and milk in a medium-sized saucepan and simmer for 1 minute. Beat in the sugar and simmer for a further minute. Serve immediately.

Walnut Cookies

Although baking is not a common Chinese cooking method, cookies of all kinds are quite popular now in China. The most famous is the almond cookie in the south, but walnut cookies are equally delicious. They can be served alone or with fresh fruit. Although I prefer to make these using lard for a fuller flavor, butter is now quite common in Hong Kong and China, and will work well here.

MAKES ABOUT 12 BISCUITS

12 walnut halves
⅞ cup (210ml) all-purpose flour
2 tsp (10ml) baking powder
2 oz (50g) butter or lard
½ cup (120ml) sugar
2 eggs

Immerse the walnut pieces in a saucepan of boiling water for about 5 minutes. Remove them with a slotted spoon, pat dry with paper towels and set aside.

Preheat the oven to 400°F (200°C). Put the flour and baking powder into a large bowl and rub in the butter or lard until it is well mixed. Add the sugar and 1 egg and mix to form a thick paste. Divide the mixture into 12 balls and press them into flattish cookie shapes about 2 in (5cm) in diameter. Put them on a non-stick baking sheet or a plain oiled baking sheet. Press a piece of walnut onto each cookie. Using a pastry brush, glaze the tops with the remaining beaten egg.

Put the cookies into the oven and bake for 20 minutes. Remove when cooked and put them on a wire rack. Once cooled, the cookies can be stored in an airtight jar, where they will keep for about a week.

Index

Notes on the recipes

Eggs are large
Pepper is freshly ground
Wash all fresh produce before preparation
Spoon measurements are level
Conversions are approximate and have been rounded up or down. Follow one set of measurements only; do not mix imperial and metric

Conversion tables

WEIGHTS

Imperial	Metric
½ oz	15 g
1 oz	25 g
1½ oz	40 g
2 oz	50 g
3 oz	75 g
4 oz	100 g
5 oz	150 g
6 oz	175 g
7 oz	200 g
8 oz	225 g
9 oz	250 g
10 oz	275 g
12 oz	350 g
13 oz	375 g
14 oz	400 g
15 oz	425 g
1 lb	450 g
1¼ lb	550 g
1½ lb	675 g
2 lb	900 g
3 lb	1.5 kg
4 lb	1.75 kg
5 lb	2.25 kg

VOLUME

Imperial	Metric
5 tsp	25 ml
4 tbsp	60 ml
⅓ cup	85 ml
⅔ cup	150 ml
1¼ cups	300 ml
2 cups	450 ml
2⅓ cups	600 ml
2¾ cups	700 ml
3⅔ cups	900 ml
4 cups	1 L
5 cups	1.2 L
5 cups	1.25 L
6 cups	1.5 L
6½ cups	1.6 L
7 cups	1.75 L
7¼ cups	1.8 L
8 cups	2 L
8⅓ cups	2.1 L
9 cups	2.25 L
10⅔ cups	2.75 L
14 cups	3.4 L
15⅔ cups	3.9 L
1 gallon	4 L

MEASUREMENTS

Imperial	Metric
¼ inch	0.5 cm
½ inch	1 cm
1 inch	2.5 cm
2 inches	5 cm
3 inches	7.5 cm
4 inches	10 cm
6 inches	15 cm
7 inches	18 cm
8 inches	20 cm
9 inches	23 cm
10 inches	25 cm
12 inches	30 cm

OVEN TEMPERATURES

275°F	140°C
300°F	150°C
325°F	160°C
350°F	180°C
375°F	190°C
400°F	200°C
425°F	220°C
450°F	230°C
475°F	240°C

Acknowledgments

Every endeavor requires team work, and this book is no exception. I am grateful to Muna Reyal, who commissioned the book; Joe Cottington, for his editorial guidance; Jean Cazals, whose wonderful photographs have brought my recipes to life and Marie-Ange Lapierre, whose skilful cooking and sharp styling have brought them beauty and a modern look. I also thank James Empringham, Noel Murphy, Wei Tang, Rachel Jukes, Shirley Patton and Antony Heller for all their hard work on the book. I was so lucky to have Annie Lee, whose sharp eye as copyeditor made this a better book. Finally, heartfelt thanks to my literary agents, Carol Blake and Julian Friedmann, for their usual wise counsel. I am truly fortunate to have all these talented people helping me.

Also by Ken Hom

Ken Hom's Chinese Cookery
Simple Asian Cookery
Simple Thai Cookery
Simple Chinese Cookery
Ken Hom's Top 100 Stir-fry Recipes
Ken Hom's Foolproof Asian Cookery
My Favourite Chinese Recipes
Ken Hom's Foolproof Thai Cookery
Ken Hom's Quick Wok
Ken Hom's Foolproof Chinese Cookery
Ken Hom Cooks Thai
Easy Family Dishes: A Memoir with Recipes
Ken Hom Travels with a Hot Wok
Ken Hom Cooks Noodles & Rice

Ken Hom's Hot Wok
Ken Hom Cooks Chinese
Ken Hom's Vegetarian Cookery
Chinese Recipes
Ken Hom's Chinese Kitchen
Ken Hom's Illustrated Chinese Cookery
Cooking of China
Fragrant Harbour Taste
The Taste of China
Ken Hom's Quick & Easy Chinese Cookery
Ken Hom's Vegetable & Pasta Book
Ken Hom's East Meets West Cuisine
Ken Hom's Encyclopaedia of Chinese Cookery Techniques